STRENGTH

by

Herman Wong

PublishAmerica
Baltimore

Softcover 9781462656943
PUBLISHED BY PUBLISHAMERICA, LLLP
www.publishamerica.com
Baltimore

Printed in the United States of America

Dear Reader:

Thank you for your generous support, so that I could continue to use my full energy to complete "Strength" before May 2, 2012. I planned 126,193 words in 28 chapters, and destiny brought about what I expected.

One of the hardest times in my writing career was working for at least six months, work eight-hour sessions, seven days a week, to bring it to birth in the time allotted. To produce a book of the size that I desired has been quite a chore.

In this book, I discuss many different topics and have a lot to say about the power of strength. I hope the book will catch your full attention and, with a "great heart," I give you this special edition, as, without you, it could not possibly have happened.

Blessings to you in the year 2012

—Herman Wong

Contents

I feel the inner blissfulness of the positive energy that I create, which is inspired by the oneness of the Source. In fact, I do not claim to gain any position of success, or to know anything, as knowledge springs from the void of nothingness, and the honor all goes to the Source way.

Sending love, light and peace your way

——Herman Wong

British Columbia, Canada

— **W**here my Heart is, **W**here I feel a Sense of Belonging

"Your life will transform when you are consciously aware who you are, what you are and inevitably conscious to seek for the answer within."

—AUBUGALATAYULA

Strength

What is strength?

Strength is a power from within that enables a person to do things that are out of the ordinary and beyond explanation. Recently, I was diagnosed with lymphoma and anemia. With anemia I had no strength or energy, and the worst part was the shortness of breath. It was very difficult for me to continue my daily activities because my breathing was affected by every motion. I had to stop and rest before carrying on with my activities. Short walks and grocery shopping became very hard for me. In this book, I write about how I was healed and how I overcame these difficulties without abandoning what I like to do. My red blood cells have now returned to normal. However, I do not forget that I was also diagnosed with lymphoma. I thought my life was over when I found out I had lymphoma. Perhaps it was engraved in my belief system that people who are diagnosed with cancer cannot live long. It was as though a death warrant had been sent to me, and I was waiting to be called. In fact, I was absolutely wrong. I have gone through eight cycles of chemotherapy, but now I am free of cancer. It is due to my faith in God that I survived this terrifying disease. I wrote an article about my road to recovery from lymphoma and anemia. My strength allowed me to see the end before the treatment started, and now I am well and absolutely sound. I believe that we know a great deal about ourselves, and if we don't give up, everything will get better, not bitter.

Why did you write 'Strength'?

I believe we are unique and have different powers, strengths and feelings. Seven years ago, I started writing my very first book. I realized that I could not simply just write: I needed to tap into the power of God. The Spirit inspired me to choose a subject, and then I began to compose the book. I started writing, and I could not stop. If I was interrupted, all my feelings and senses were gone. It is difficult to reconnect with a particular feeling: it is different from retrieving data or recalling memories. Hence, when that moment comes, I must write it down. I connect my inner strength to God's spirit, which guides me to write what He desires me to compose. It is the power and the sense that draws from above, and it is not obtained from my five physical senses. It is a special power that I received from the God's Source that inspires me to write what I write.

You simply feel strength: you cannot explain what it is that makes you feel or why you feel it. You feel unrested and discontented because your inner emotions and feelings are alerting you so you can escape from the hazards and free yourself from harm.

So where does the strength come from? It comes from your Inner Source. Your inner Authentic Self is susceptible to such strong emotions that it can cause the inner and outer selves to become unbalanced. When this happens, it's a warning sign: you must do something and make some changes! This inner strength is powerful, and inspired by the God-Source who communicates with you. I believe that when something happens, it is for a reason and so can be explained, and the explanation is always that your strength from the Inner Source has saved you.

I wrote my book 'Strength' after a period in which I found myself tapping into the same things again and again. I received the message repeatedly that I was healed and blessed. I had recurring dreams telling me that I was free from cancer and that my mission was far from over and must continue to the end.

Still I wanted to search further and know more. I became obsessed with finding an answer. My mind and spirit craved the answer, and then, without my doing anything, the ultimate answer came to me. The answer was, "Write a book entitled 'Strength'. You are healed now, and you should write a new book. All you need will be provided as you write."

In what way are your explanations of strength due to your inner-power?

That's a bit of a puzzle. I find it difficult to explain in words how inner strength can be felt by an individual. In my opinion, inner power is hidden inside, and, in an emergency, it will emerge to assist a person automatically. For example, in a traffic accident, a woman's child was run over by a car. Because of this life-or-death situation, the woman was able to lift the car and to remove her child safely. It is the inner power that allowed her to do something that she would not normally be able to do. It is the energy of the inner power that is reserved inside you to aid you and save you from something that causes harm.

Strength is an inner energy you can implement in any situation you think fit, but you must believe in it and follow those feelings when they emerge. For example, I was doing my grocery shopping, when all of sudden I felt restless. A feeling tells me that something bad is about to happen, so I stopped what I had been doing and went home. I arrived home and the phone rang. It was my doctor (Dr. Eichhorst) calling to tell me that I needed a blood transfusion immediately. Indeed, this inner urge saved my life.

Doesn't that make it sound like strength is really something inside each one of us?

Yes. It is. It is absolutely the power from within every one of us. Though it is latent, it will emerge whenever we need it. Emergency situations are not the only time this power can help. Any situation where we find ourselves in despair can be helped through our inner strength. We can apply our inner strength to support what we do in our daily activities. Our inner strength supports and aids us when we feel negative emotions: our inner strength will aid us by lifting us up.

What is the most surprising pattern that you have found while examining your strengths?

During the course of my treatment for cancer, I realized that this disease did not signal the end of my life. My inner strength gave me support so I could complete the eight cycles of my treatment. Each cycle had a different level of pain that I had to endure. As the treatment progressed, it became easier, and the pain and fatigue lessened. Now, I have finished the treatment. I have realigned myself and regained my strength and can now concentrate on getting well. My body is free from cancer, but I still need to go through a clinic every three months. I believe I can do that. I am more powerful than before. I am getting stronger and better every day because I have something I need to complete before I return to the nothingness and to the Source. My strength allows me to write again and complete this book: 'Strength'.

How will people benefit from Strength?

Each person should apply their own strengths in different situations. We should not give up because we live in a world where there is both the positive and negative. However, once a person experiences a difficult situation, that person does not need to experience it again. It is better only to remember the good things and to focus on day-to-day life. In my book, 'Strength', I have discussed many strategies people can implement in their lives for their own benefit. You must remember that your perceptions and the things that you project outwardly become your reality. I want people to believe that everything under the sun is possible. They should not abandon anything. Instead, they should have inner strength and continue until the end. That way they will have no regrets. I believe that, once a person gets used to applying his own strength to each activity, he will not want to tear himself away from it.

Vision from the Source

I go to bed after finishing the last chapter of my manuscript. I am extremely tired and soon fall into a deep sleep, almost like a coma. I am walking along in a silent, tranquil place, where I have never set foot before. I actually do not know where I am or the purpose of being in a strange place, but it seems to be full of calmness and peace. Perhaps my mind, heart, and soul are feeling calm and peaceful at the moment, since I have completed what I needed to get done. I am still thinking about my manuscript, but I know that it is completed already, so I should not be too concerned about it. I only need to send it to the publisher, and that will be it. As soon as I have had this thought, I suddenly see my body transform into ashes, and from the ashes I transcend into a beam of light. Immediately, I am far away from planet Earth, in outer space of the unknown Universe. I see that the black space of this Universe is an empty void, but it exists with the sun, moon, and stars all in their proper places. I see the galaxy and planet Earth, and then I am at the edge of the Universe. I keep going until I reach the Divine planet where the Source dwells. I assume this is the fifth dimension where God meets humans, and to where masters ascend. The beings that dwell here are Angels and Archangels, sages, gurus, transcendent human beings, and reincarnated beings. I continue on, and then I stop in front of a fantastic, mysterious golden temple. The color of it is brilliant, and I have never thought of it before. It is totally beyond human imagination and comprehension. I enter the temple and notice that on both sides the posts are covered with gold and silver. Radiant light shines through the whole temple. In the center of the temple is a Divine throne. A voice says, "Come near to me, for I am expecting you. I knew you would be here."

"You are here at the right time and place. Come, and extend your hands to connect with me. I am not going to hurt you. I am your Lord God. I would like to speak with you. I know you need help and, perhaps, that is one of the reasons that bring you to my Kingdom. I am delighted to see you and glad that you have made it this far. Allow me to heal your physical body, which sometimes causes you pain. I know that physical health is your utmost concern. Allow me to touch your crown, sending you my golden light. Let it run through your mortal body and start healing your organs, cells, heart, arteries, and lungs. Allow it to extend outside your body and continue to shield you with radiant light, so that you are protected. No negative force can come near, so that when you return to Earth, you can complete your mission for me without worry or concern. I believe you should feel better now. Are you feeling better, now that I have bestowed my light upon you? It will always be with you, at any time you need it. You will always feel my presence, and you can speak to me in silence. I will be there, listening to your concern."

"Thank you, my Lord God, for your healing, and for blessing my mortal body and helping with every concern I meet. I appreciate you." As soon as I have said that, I realize I have returned to the third dimension on the planet Earth.

Then, the voice says, "I am the honor within you, and I will help you every step of the way. You should never underestimate yourself. You are a divine and unfailing source of your own support; comfort and optimism that portray everything are auspicious, beautiful and plentiful: you are a part of me without limitation and, in its essential nature, the truth never changes. This fountain of love pours over everything in your life. Be well, and continue to do good work on the Earth so that all of your fellow beings, in every pillar of the Earth, are benefited. Farewell now! I love you."

Foreword

Peace Begins Within

The truth is that peace has reached you, through alignment with the power of the Universal Source, the Mind of God.

I wrote this forward in the winter of 2002. I saw this stillness that was beyond my comprehension, when a dying person was so calm and peaceful and still even had a sense of humor towards the end of his journey on Earth. I knew the pain he suffered was unbearable, but he radiated that stillness beyond understanding. It was probably because of his faith, and that he knew pretty well that the grave was not his goal. He refused to accept the illness that caused it; he saw it rather as a natural occurrence towards the end of his life. It brought his earthly visit to its completion and brought about his decision now to be home free. The soul is infinite and trustworthy while it accompanies our trip and lessons on Earth.

When you track your accomplishments through your eagle eyes, you may notice that not one has been directly created by you. In fact, every action possesses one thing in general, that is, it has been guided by an invisible Source of the Spirit. However, when we realize material necessities are essential for survival on Earth, then the meaning, the audacity and the purpose of being here have changed to a different conclusion. The Source will not prevent events from happening in the physical realm. Unhappy events will change everything into a lemon yellow, because of our freedom of choice.

Our five physical senses have restricted us from doing all we desire. The Ego has played mind-games with you and let you think that you are in charge of everything. The truth is, you do not have control of your domain, and the real transformation takes place from nothingness.

After we have transformed into Being from the pure formless spirit, we continue the journey we have undertaken that leads us to our destination: Planet Earth. The events on Earth do not unfold to us by desire. Whatever we do, we experiment with them before everything comes to pass. As humans, we want to own something; we want to have value as a person. This is a part of the Ego component and its identification. So, the nature of the false self's control comes in. You learn that the more success you have, the more people will come to greet you. Folks say to you, "Well done, you have done a great job; we need you to keep on keeping on." You do not want to disappoint these folks who greeted you in your success. You are a tremendous success in your profession. Yet, you have gone through sweat, blood and tears before you reach your current status. More money flows to you. You make big money; you feel great. You feel you can conquer the world. This is the beginning of your shift to become part of the twisted egoistic world, which is full of ambition, greed, envy and challenges. You love to win: you want to win; you want to show these folks you can do better and become the best of the best. This shift to ambition requires you to embrace the Ego and ignore God. The false self has brought you many false hopes and ideas to encourage you to gain more money and possessions, in order that you continue to feel good. Because of the Ego's encouragement you want to show how important you are in front of others. The Ego corrects you: there is no other, only you.

As the time dragged by, you felt like you always needed to accomplish something and there was no end. You feel that you spent your entire life chasing after the symbols of fame, wealth and success. Moreover, you do not feel it filled the gap of your emptiness within. You had this kind of thinking for a while, but you thought it was not important, so, you did not pay attention to it until now. You hear the still, small voice speaking to you and offering to help. You choose to listen to this intuition and that leads you to the paths of peace and contentment.

The solution to your problems is that you need to make your mind quiet. When the mind is empty, and you have not thought of any earthly possessions, you choose detachment rather than attachment. You are willing to relinquish a part of your assets to the world, and free yourself from fears, worries and concerns. This permits the change to begin to take place that will transform your life. You feel peace with love. This transformation will take place inside you. The spirit is stuck in the clutter and gaps in your thoughts, in a sacred place called "the silence". From this secret, sacred space, you can gain insight, knowledge and wisdom from the Divine.

You have experienced at least three stages transforming to being, beginning with you as a sufferer, then you as a creator, then you surrendered to what is occurring, and finally you align with the Divine; all things happen to you effortlessly and easily. You can see things and events happen to you almost instantaneously, like a miracle. However, you must earnestly desire that you want to achieve your goal; otherwise, you will not use the power needed to make it happen. You need to make conscious alignment with your conscious wants by trigger your subconscious mind to connect with the Source-Mind. This helps you gather all the information and let the Universe show you how to make it work. Then, you convert that into relationships, health, possessions, and accomplishments to make your dream become known. You perceive all your wishes are manifested within before it occurs in the external world. So you know what to expect; you sure what that something is and always will be your desire before it occurs in the physical world.

The Earth is a remarkable living thing. Since its earliest form, every living original thing has been an essential life force, which has been animated in its physical form. Great scientists for instance Sir Isaac Newton recognized this realm, which he called the Ether. When there is a vibrational shift that will affect your thoughts, deeds, memories, and beliefs, do not be stressed. You can make a conscious alignment with each moment of this vibration from a sacred place, where miracles will happen. Each moment will be unique to you, to fit your wishes. They will be beautiful and felt the possibilities beyond your comprehension of your five ordinary states.

We live in a three-dimensional world, and everyone enjoys the power of thought through which they see the world. Words, thoughts, and feelings can be interpreted through one's outlook or state of mind. When you can use a different notion to meet all other thoughts, you are in a place called "the fifth-dimension", and from there your thoughts will paint anything so that it will happen instantly in front of your eyes, all ideas will come to you without limitations.

The key question is why we need a form to keep the true meaning of life. The answer is that we want the form to load up and host the spirit while we experience and discover new skills and learn lessons. However, this is immediately followed by another question, "Who am I?" The answer can be remarkably straightforward. For example, I live here, wanting to learn, explore, and experience learning about life on Earth. I am an author and I love myself. This is part of my physical self, through which I represent and introduce myself, to the impression that is the world. It has no volume and can change at any time as the situation and circumstances change. The complete solution to your asking is, however, that I am part of the Universal Source, the Mind of God. I feel peaceful when I consciously align with the Source, though I might not have seen, touched, or received it in the outer world. I know I will like it when I switch back to shapelessness from having a form. Hence, I am both form and formless and align with the Source represent Him on Earth, and, ultimately, I must return to the unseen someday.

Peace

Behold, it comes in might,
The power that is not power,
The light that is in darkness,
The shade in dazzling light.

It is joy that never spoke,
And grief unfelt, profound,
Immortal life unlived,
Eternal death unmourned.

It is not joy nor sorrow,
But that which is between,
It is not night nor morrow,
But that which joins them in.

It is sweet rest in music;
And pause in sacred art;
The silence between speaking;
Between two fits of passion — It is the calm of heart.

It is beauty never seen,
And love that stands alone,
It is song that lives un-sung,
And knowledge never known.

It is death between two lives,
And lull between two storms,
The void whence rose creation,
And that where it returns.

To it the tear-drop goes,
To spread the smiling form
It is the Goal of Life,
And Peace — its only home!

The poem —Peace by Swami Vivekananda

Introduction

Strength is an inner power that allows you to do something out of the ordinary, something that you would normally be unable to do. It is your ability, and you know it intimately; you know it is there for you all the time as part of your own being.

Struggle for change is undesirable and unnecessary if you have not first addressed the problem. It is like blaming others for the troubles you have created yourself. It is like standing in front of a mirror blaming the reflection you see before you.

If you want to win a martial arts contest, you must know yourself as well as you know your opponent. When you keep your mind at absolute peace, then you can attain absolute knowledge, not only on the next move your opponent will make but of each move of every challenger in the competition.

A quiet mind lives in a different world than a noisy mind. When the mind is silent, it connects with God's spirit, the force that created us; so, whatever you think is what God is thinking. It is the Divine shares His thoughts with you, so every thought or action you take leads to a win-win situation, and you will never stop developing the capacity for growth and abundance; this is the everlasting gift you receive.

Your inner strength is within you. Trust this inner power to sustain everything you do and believe. When you believe in your strength, you attain power; when you attain power, you have faith in yourself; when you have faith in yourself, you begin to trust God, who created you; when you trust God, you become free; when you become free, you seek and find; when you find, you know who you are; when you know who you are, you no longer need to struggle for material things in the mortal world; you do not need to fight with others, because you know there is no difference between you and them. There is but one source.

Your inner strength is your internal power that pushes you into action and enables you to meet spiritual success and achievement in every pillar of your life. It is the power presence in your mind that determines whether you are to fail or succeed in everything you do.

Inner strength can be attained and sharpened by anyone who trusts their inner-strength and inner-power leads them to the paths of success. In the past, people thought that strength and force could only be attained by successful people, because they have special abilities that enable them to develop inner strength and realize their goals. The truth is that inner strength is a gift from the Divine, and everyone can develop the willpower or the mind power to reach the heart's desire.

Constant development of inner power helps you fight or control any unwanted desires or harmful impulses. It also gives you the ability to decide and make the right decision at the right time and place to every one of your goals is accomplished. This ability gives you the strength to face and endure any challenge. It helps you overcome any inner and outer resistance, difficulties and bewilderments that confuse you.

Some individuals who lack inner strength finds it difficult to be assertive due to uncertainty of their inner power, thoughts, beliefs and faith. Some are scared to take action or make changes. They may have a lack of determination or do not know where their actions will take them, so they stop and are unable to see their plans to the end. However, a strong inner power can transmute all of this.

You do not need to be superhuman to develop inner strength— anyone can do it. It is not necessary to do any special practice, live in a forest, or undergo any painful physical mutilation.

Developing inner strength is a process that progresses gradually, and the more you carry it out, the easier it will be for you to reach a higher level of development to strengthen your inner power. The more you practice, the more it will help to drop your bad habits and strengthen your courage so that you can become more assertive than passive and continue to grow and change and be the best you can. Practice helps to improve your temperament, your job, your relationships, and your well-being and makes everything more enjoyable, cheerful, interesting and less challenging. You will gain inner strength and bring you things you feel deeply about; so, you can live a joyful and fearless life and continue to carry out your goals and meet change with confidence, hope and trust. Hope does shine all around.

Chapter One

What is inner power?

Inner power is a form of power within, which, when advanced, helps you think and lift up your eyes and look beyond your trouble; so, you act assertively. It also gives you the ability to exercise, and to avoid laziness, uneasiness, and lack of discipline. You take courage and the strength you have inside and every problem overcoming lie within your soul.

Inner power bestows you with the endurance to take steadfast action instead of fighting internal and external obstacles and harboring an unworthy that hinders success in life. There is no greater worry in life than worrying over something that may or may not occur.

The steadfast development of true inner strength requires a departure from your unwillingness to walk into the unknowable land of yourself. In other words, instead of allowing your mind to work against you, you use your mind's power to work for you. Just remember that you have everything under control; never jump to the end, or you may resist your own imaginative conclusions.

However, you must not confuse aggressive force with inner strength. Aggressive force is an intense force that can be physical or verbal. Avoid applying excessive force to meet your desires. Force is normally used by people with narrow-minded personalities. Conversely, inner energy is never aggressive; you must only use assertive and positive thinking to meet your goals.

Self-restraint is a family member and ally of inner strength. It has adopted the ability to control and avoid excessive force towards anything that could lead to a negative result. Self-restraint appears in many forms such as endurance and self-discipline. It is mindful: it is the ability to carry out one's plan and achieve one's goals in spite of the obstacles that can tempt one to abandon them.

One of the greatest aspects of self-restraint is the way it enables one to control oneself in any difficult situation or circumstance, and it gives one the ability to forego one's instinct for immediate pleasure or gratification to meet more satisfying results later on.

Self-restraint welcomes higher energy, yet we know that we do not spend enough time developing self-control or understanding the importance of self-discipline in everything we do. Due to insufficient information and research, it is often misunderstood; many believe that self-restraint is difficult and unpleasant to meet and requires a lot of energy surrender or sacrifice.

In fact, the truth is that self-restraint is the inner strength that allows you to stay powerful when dealing with day-to-day activities and achieving goals and denying unwanted impulses. Self-discipline helps you to develop habits that allow you to do everything right and be exact. It is true that a person might be talented; however, without self-discipline he or she might not get far.

You need inner strength to make the right decisions, and you also need self-restraint to work with your decisions until you reach and carry out your intents. Count the number of things you do only halfway each day without completing them, and you will see that half of your life leaves you unsatisfied and discontented. However, when you apply your inner strength and discipline, you can do much more than you think. You will not leave anything half-accomplished, nor will you become discontented, nor show a weakness of inner strength; instead you find other ways to satisfy your purposes and desires.

Trying to please everyone without a purpose is meaningless

and worthless: it only shows your lack of self-confidence, your weaknesses and your lack of self-discipline. Conversely, when you make the necessary changes and endorse your belief system with inner strength and discipline, you can avoid being pushed around, because you are consciously aware of what is happening around you and can automatically restrain your weaknesses and strengthen your willpower and self-discipline to prevent anything undesirable from happening.

The same applies to negative emotional thoughts: when you have too many negative thoughts in your mind, they will tear you down. Do not waste your time and energy on negative habits and feelings. The good news is that when you develop inner power and self-restraint, you immediately transfer your thoughts to a higher energy frequency to avoid further destruction.

Every time you think of achieving greatness, you should think healthy thoughts to shift your energy with the power of your inner strength. Your actions will increase the fuel tank of your inner power, preparing it for you to use at any time. Your inner strength stores energy and power, but when your inner energy is high, it has charged enough power for you to consume. It stores all the life-force for you to act when you need it the most. It is like an electric battery charge with full power: all things work smoothly and perfectly, but when the battery charge is low, all things work slower than you expect them to. Therefore, you must make sure you have enough rest so that you can charge your inner energy and allow it to work at full horsepower when you need it. (Life-force is also known as Qi. Qi can never create or be destroyed. With correct use of Qi, it can help you to better bring about beneficial influences.)

It is wrong to believe you cannot develop inner strength, or that it requires you to practice difficult physical exercises and always involves pain when changing activities. That is false. The truth is that the process can be transformed into a fun and joyful experience. You must be aware that everything takes time to process, that practice will allow you to progress gradually, and that, ultimately, you will reach your desired goal. You can practice anywhere at your pleasure; no restrictions about where you can exercise your inner strength. In fact, to some extent you do it nearly every day; you just do not realize you are doing it. For example, suppose you want to buy a high-tech notebook and are considering either an i5 or i7 notebook. The i7 has 17.6 inch screen displays, but it is expensive. You discipline yourself and intentionally exercise your will power, limiting yourself to the i5 notebook that has a 15.6 inch screen, despite you want to buy the i7 notebook.

In the above example, you act in opposition to your desire, despite a disagreement in your conscious mind. In this way, you have exercised your inner strength and have disciplined yourself not to follow your instinctive desire with your conscious mind. When you want a notebook, the mind suggests that you purchase the best. Your decision to buy the less expensive notebook is contrary to your mind's desire, but you abide by your decision, exercise your power of choice, and strengthen your will power and are disciplined.

It is not difficult at all; with simple exercises and practice, you can strengthen your inner power and restrain yourself. However, if you think this is an insufficient exercise, you can discharge yourself from any restraints and buy the high-end notebook.

You must practice self-discipline and inner strength with exercises so that you can have control over what you do. You must remember that they are available to you when you need them, and they serve a purpose and have meaning. With a deeper understanding of inner power you are growing into something more glorious, not just

I started reading spiritual books at a very young age. I tried to read as many spiritual books as possible to satisfy my curiosity about the spirit world, spirituality, and God. The books were very fascinating and always kept my attention and interest.

Years later, I had an opportunity to meet with people who shared my interests, and I learned even more about spirituality from them. As time passed, my interest in spirituality grew deeper, and now I am a spirituality author, which gives me an opportunity to write about what I learned and share it with others. In a search for knowledge and wisdom, I read books written by Dr. Wayne Dyer. I enjoyed his books. I also read books by His Holiness the Dalai Lama and Howard C. Cutler entitled The Art of Happiness. Dr. Dyer has written many books, but his book, The Power of Intention, especially caught my attention.

As I read their books, I started practicing meditation, mind strength, and mind control exercises. I realize that mind strength and discipline are very important for the mind. I can concentrate better, and they are especially important for inner strength, mind control, and development in my day-to-day activities.

One of the exercises I practice is that cooking without salt, and to this day I add no salt to my food. I have not added salt to my food for 30 years. I have sodium in my home, but I use it as a mouthwash and for bathing purposes. I believe I can endure without salt through discipline, will power and mind control. I have not had any difficulty resisting salt. I do not miss the sodium because I have become used to eating without salt. The success of not using salt in food for 30 years has made me very happy, because I harness my mind and do not experience any inner resistance. Now I enjoy eating my food without salt.

You may practice adding no salt to your food, but you have to sacrifice a bit of your pleasure and comfort; however, this is only temporary and serves a greater purpose. With a little practice, you can do it. By rejecting and denying yourself immediate enjoyment, you gain assertiveness and decisiveness.

If you refuse to try, you will never get what attained is. If you apply self-restraint and inner strength to everything you do, you can carry out everything you want and will know when to stop; by trusting your inner strength, you will know you are doing the right thing.

What this power can show you is that by applying inner strength and self-discipline, you can complete a task instead of having to abandon it when you are only halfway through. For example, one hot summer afternoon I was sitting outside on my balcony, reading a book. Due to the hot weather, after reading for a while, I became bored and put the book aside. At that very moment, I remembered the exercise I had practiced persistently; otherwise, I would never have obtained my goal. The more I practiced resistance and completing activities, the more I strengthened my inner power. This led me to finish reading the book without restraint.

This indicates that, in truth, you must complete something: you want to prevent inner resistance then you need self-discipline. You should always use self-inquiry to make sure you are doing the right thing and to apply the higher aspirations of inner strength to everything you do, which requires patience, discipline, and sacrifice.

When you apply inner strength to everything you do, you shed more light on every thought, notion, and action. Everything you do will last and be inspired. You can overcome your gloomy mind when you struggle: by using your inner strength, you can free yourself from your gloomy thoughts and desires. Surely and slowly, everything will become clear, and you will start to see that your inner strength has saved you from every trouble. You will begin to open your eyes and perceive your new conditions; even in the midst of your misery, you will suddenly see your life in a new light. In the whole new awareness of understanding, the knowledge of knowing the advantage importance of inner strength and self-discipline can overcome your gloomy mind. These things will continue to fill you with strength, support, and restraint: with faith, you can do amazing things by applying your inner power and effort.

Now you are aware that already dwelling inside you is an unlimited potential source of strength and power. It is your inner strength, your Authentic Self. You can use your feelings to tap into your innate power and channel the inner strength, wisdom, and knowledge that resides within you to connect to the Universal Source of God.

An inner power or inner voice is quite often called the 'Inner Voice of the Higher Self', which connects us to the Mind of God. Perhaps you will ask where and how you can connect with your Inner Voice, if the Inner Voice is so incredible. You might also want to learn more about it, so that the Higher Self can help you make a greater success of your life.

The Inner Voice that comes from deep within us works mainly to provide us with guidance. It guides you and walks with you in this life. It is an infinite source of wisdom that you cannot get from just anywhere, but only from your own Inner Self. It will give you advice and suggestions, through a soft voice that forewarns you that something is going to occur, so that you can prevent it or do something about it. Your Inner Voice is here to guide and remind you along the way, but never demands and is fundamentally different from the logical mind your use to analyze and that tells you what you should or should not do.

Very often, when you ignore, defy, or do not recognize something through this inner spiritual connection with the Source-Mind, then you regret it later. It would be very difficult to undertake damage-control for what you have not done according to the small voice's suggestions; you might wish to have a second chance to redo things. Thus, it is important to recognize the Inner Voice when it speaks to you and recognize that its inspirational messages come from the Spirit. Trust the information you are receiving and use it to guide your life.

An inspiring message is different from the retrieval of recorded data in the subconscious mind through memories. Retrieved data through the mind may be incorrect, and sometimes it hurts because it comes from a memory. A message of inspiration is the gut-feeling that occurs to you when the Source-Mind connects to your Higher Self, which brings you an instant message. Then you can act on it to improve your current situation or avoid a situation that is not favorable to you. Your life would be smoother and happier if you listened and took steadfast action. If you decide to choose not to listen, then you will move further away from your central code of the Source-Mind. Your life will gradually become more miserable, and more obstacles and reasons for despair will rapidly appear on your path.

Your Higher Self is connected to the pasts, presents and futures, existing beyond time and space. Through your dreams (dream believes to be a message from God), your Higher Self may forewarn you when something is going to happen in the next few hours or during the next morning. When you sleep, your subliminal mind becomes very active, bringing you messages from the Universal Source. When you wake in the morning you can apply your lucid dreams to your day-to-day activities. But it is important not to defy these dreams. To defy them is to discard important messages from the Source-Mind that wants to help you or even save your life. Do not let guilt, regret or fear that is reflected from your old belief system or an old condition that hinders you make a direct connection with your Infinite Soul. You simply relinquish the old by trusting and following this spiritual guidance: you will then see the miracle occur in your life almost instantaneously.

In fact, the Higher Self is always vigorously integrated with your daily activities. It is an ongoing communication that inspires, forewarns, and silently supports you without your knowledge, whenever or wherever is proper. You realize that the inspiring messages are concerned with you and your journey on earth and are often related to significant events, times and places.

Notice how often you hear your Inner Voice so that you can recognize it and not confuse it with the Ego's voice. If you listen to your Ego's voice, you could endanger yourself or bring unhappiness or harmful events into your life. Recognize what to listen for and do not confuse your Ego with the soft voice of the Higher Self.

The Inner Voice is easy to understand and it offers you a lucid message that you can easily follow, as it is expressed in the language or words that are most inspiring to you. The Inner Voice of your Higher Self does not have any agenda that requires help from you. It just wants to walk with you so that you can live in happiness and have more fun! The Higher Self dwells within you, and you must activate it before you can experience a quick consultation. Through inward meditation, you can trigger your Higher Self to do wonderful and inspiring things for you. It can always be fully trusted. The more often you connect with the Inner Voice of your Higher Self, the more it will awaken your consciousness, so you will go through life with awareness, and avoid making mistakes.

The Inner Voice is a gentle, soft voice you will recognize as you will experience a sinking feeling in your stomach (like butterflies), alerting you to the fact that you need either to do something immediately, or stop doing something that could do you harm. If it is something important, the inner feeling of butterflies in your stomach will be stronger. Your stomach holds the Solar Plexus chakra, which connects you directly with the Universal Source. That is the reason why strong messages are felt in that area of your body. If you experience this type of sinking feeling, you must stop your actions immediately until you feel comfortable, or suspend them until you have had time to consider things more deeply.

The Inner Voice does not only warn you of negative events and circumstances, it provides you with valuable information so that you can consider critical situations related to its directions and to your life experiences. With the help of your Inner Voice, you always do the right thing.

Often, people regard this Inner Voice they hear in their heads as abnormal, and they think that they are crazy, because they are talking to themselves. However, it is not the way people think it is. Instead, it is a voice that you hear when your Higher Self connects to the Source-Mind, bringing you an inspiring message, so that you can think about ordinary events, make proper choices and transcend them to what you desire. It is something you do not want to miss in real-time.

When the Higher Self communicates with the mortal mind by means of the Inner Voice, it is a higher communication between the conscious and subconscious mind, and is similar to telepathy: different messages can transcend to different people or different things.

With so many good messages transcending through this inner connection, maybe you should consider allowing it to happen for you, so you too can listen to and accept the Inner Voice's advice. It will bring a vibrant, good feeling to you so that you can do more to improve your life in the mortal world with the help of the Inner Realm. You should not treat the Higher Self as an occasional friend, but rather as a trusted friend to whom you can cling permanently. It is good practice to develop trust and faith in your Higher Self, which will make your life more alive, vibrant, and joyful. This will connect you back with the Source-Mind, knowing that you are an Infinite Being. As such, your life will be enhanced abundantly and effectively. In conclusion, each day you have this high awareness guide your life then designing your destiny is as effortless as you thought by mean of you have more confidence now.

I. You and Your Spirit

What are you? You are a physical self with a dynamic soul that connects with the mortal world. Your physical self comes with five earthly senses, namely taste, hearing, vision, touch and smell. These are the five basic physical functions that we normally apply to help our daily activities. Our physical body is a temporary temple for our souls. It is a soul-journey on Earth; however, the five essential functions in the body are to aid the soul to learn and complete an earthly journey without difficulties or barriers.

While walking on this spiritual journey you must admit you have experienced many scenarios, which make you feel fear, worry and perplexity: despite those ups and downs you have to pass through them and have used them. You wish that you did not need to go through all these unbearable times and experiences. You feel that you did not have a choice, other than to persist until such despair and adverse situations and circumstances left you.

We understand we have free will to choose all that we wish. However, it seems that we may not have a choice. It appears as if an invisible hand of the spirit has driven us into various unfounded situations unconsciously. You have unknowingly entered a different dimension or time zone and, being captured by a captor, you try to awake to do something to free yourself from the captor. You observed, you prayed and even chanted mantras that cannot help you. The reason is that you are still knocking into a different time zone unconsciously. For a while, an invisible intelligent of the unseen control all these activities; you have not realized that because you are asleep. You simply follow someone else's thoughts and the environment you are in. You want to escape these unwanted and undesired situations and free yourself from harm's way.

Why are there many uncertainties in seeking the truth in life? Why do we worry about many things that may or may not occur to us? What method do we use when we try our lives? Do we apply the method that focuses on the help of the Spirit? How do we live on Earth? Do we live a finite or an infinite life? Why cannot we choose the method that fits our personalities, whichever is more powerful and superior? We need the method that helps us to focus on the spirit, and not applying thought to the finite mind, which will not bring results. Make a promise to yourself that you will not recur yourself: you will not repeat whatever you did in the past. You will do something new.

When you use the limited mind to think, you spend more time than it takes to carry out your goals. However, the spiritual method gets results faster than you thought possible.

So, you ask, is that for real? Do not get excited? Even though you may craft what you want in a short time with a proper connection, you must know how making contact with the Spirit by using infinite thoughts through the latent mind to acquire the spiritual power the only power you need. You go beyond external power into the power of the Spirit: obey, realize and embrace the Laws of the Universe. The soul mystery unveiled: understand, acknowledge and practice, and, knows who you are as a spiritual being.

Once you have connected with the soul, all your pains, wounds and even a million sorrows transform, and healed your past. All pains and sorrows can be forgiven and dragged by. You should not fear the lack of enthusiasm effect of experiences, but accept and acknowledge that past actions will recur to hurt you. It banished all negative influences, thoughts and actions. Your infinite nature will not break or influence by pessimistic thoughts and actions.

To understand the spiritual laws of nature and to live in the Spirit will free you from fear, worry, despair, indecision and perplexing situations and will doubtlessly keep the distance from you. Understand that the Spirit will never change, as it is in the now, is what has been and what is coming; hence, you do not have long to embrace and enjoy the spirit. Ignorance of the soul will not relate to you at this time. You can connect with the Spirit now, at this instant, and benefit from the harvest of your connection immediately.

Enjoyment is your birthright and it ends your pain by knowing your spirit. All pain and sorrows have a beginning and an end. When the end is near, you begin to feel joy and happiness. You express a comfortable and cheerful feeling in your face to the outside, indicating that the outlook and balance of your internal and external emotions are in alignment with your soul. It confirms that you are one with the Universe and your higher self. Your physical pains and conscious thoughts may fail you, but the spirit will never lose or disappoint you. Once connected, your life will shine and glow forever. You recognize it is not so complex to live by the Spirit, but rather you cannot live without the Spirit.

When you deliberately choose to live a spiritual life, then you might feel that it is the most enjoyable thing that you give to yourself. In it you get an opportunity to manifest things that you have always wanted. Your body and mind are in alignment and that can help you do many things, but the most amazing and surprising things are the ones when you feel the calmness and peace in your thoughts: you can radiate these inner thoughts in your daily activities the moment you align with your soul. All things will transform into dynamic and emerge for you easily and naturally

Every human living on Earth has equal status: no one is superior to the others. You therefore should not try to select so, nor belittle yourself. Do not compare yourself with others. Comparison with others is psychological insanity. This is because everyone is unique. You can never get into the mind of other humans. Similarly, no one can read my mind, though they may imagine what I have in mind. Hence, do not push yourself to become somebody else, but simply be yourself and be happy. When you simply are yourself, you know who you are in order to acquire your power through the Spirit. It is the Spirit that gives you life and breath, and this is illuminated and vibrated through spiritual energies. You are born with a spiritual high power; hence, you should start to capitalize on it and benefit from it. You deserve it and live in it.

If you are wise enough, then you never pay attention to the thinking patterns of others. Be warned that your mind can be capable of crafting good and negative thoughts. Your negative thoughts will rise to hurt you when you pay less attention in your mind. However, when you are in the midst of difficult situations you still can stand firm; you do not get disturbed and it is at this critical moment that your wise thoughts are cultivated.

Think about this situation: if one day you were driving your car on the highway and someone cut you off, will you irritate by that person or will you cultivate a calm mind so you bless that person. Is it possible you could do that? Could you give blessings to a person who cut you off? Your Ego-mind screams at you that you are insane: the ridiculous person cut you off on the highway. You thought he maybe in a hurry and you wish him well. Of course, you are not insane. You definitely know what you are doing. You do it with a lucid mind. It is a practical and healthy habit you have been adept at for years, and you simply apply it to use it. You visualize your positive thinking and habit, and you have had it in you for years; you do it automatically with no hesitation. Your healthy thoughts have a profound transformation on you being guided by your inner self. It is unknown to you: indeed, you have shuffled off all negative thoughts before they penetrate the mind. You think optimistic thoughts and no other thoughts can enter to enter the mind. Even though occasional negative thoughts of your past will come to the surface, but you simply admit it and all will come to pass. You know what has passed can no longer be validated and cannot hurt you. You quickly recognize and acknowledge that and get going. Your positive thoughts, attitudes and habits are worth keeping going. You have confidence in yourself and trust that the

Spirit inside will help you to carry out your desires' impulse.

You fill the entire mind with thoughts. Thoughts influence you and your whole physical body. You are who you become in your thought. Your thoughts flow through you, your seeds transcends and stir into the thin air, into the deep black space of the Universe, and echo back to you what will become your reality. Though you may not see it, it is real, can get you out of this mess, and forever changed it.

Knowledge is power: if you know how to use it wisely it will lead you where you want to go in your life. If you have gone through a process steadily, then when you compare it from the beginning to two weeks or two years later, you might feel it is in a totally different dimension. This is because you get stronger as you are doing the same positive thing every day. Your personality and attitude towards life has transformed before you notice it. It is the hidden power that influences you and changes you with the divine essence of that great idea. You approach knowledge step-by-step and sought with patience; ultimately with bold and courageous you hold on to it but when the time you need to leave them then relinquish it when you are ready to move to the next level.

When you seek God, with your limited knowledge, you realize you cannot see God unless you seek God in the right place. There are many religions in the physical world: however, they teach the same thing about God. Throughout history there have been many concepts and mysteries built around God. However, if you can study step-by-step the mysteries about God, then there would be peace and harmony, a better understanding and respect for the creator of the Universe. Spiritual and religious leaders, and scientists, have their own concepts about how this Universe becomes existent. However, if we approach it through the Universal Laws, not as an event, then it will make us understand that everything is a mystery, which will continue to occur and keep us guessing. If we all simply remove our veils and accept that this Universe is created by an invisible energy, which we call God, through this love and peaceful energy and inspiration created all things and manifested to become what we have today.

Theory and belief created in our minds, which make us to believe. We do not need to prove that God exists or does not exist: All defined in our minds. We believe what we worship as oneness, the Universal God Source, who created humans and other living things on Earth through love and sound. We do not need to construct other thoughts or prove it. It is, "Believe and ye shall receive". Observe, follow and move closer towards the Universal Laws to meet peace and tranquility in your heart and feel the silence: after that you shall see God. You will never meet your God with a noisy mind. The moment you silence the mind, then God emerges. You are consciously aware of God and His omnipresence and know that He is God. Be aware that there is no other God, just one Universal source of God. You believe in this oneness, this energy, with faith and you never doubt it: when you have doubts, you lose all the good things about it. If you knew what faith could meet, then you will not talk insecurely about it.

When you know your true nature, then you might know you are an infinite being created by an invisible energy in the nothingness. Then it cleared all doubts and uncertainty from your mind. You are an extension connected to the Source-energy. You are no longer influenced by the external environment, events or concepts, or by thoughts in the Ego-mind. You must not wasting time asking questions that only the invisible Source can answer. It is all too complicated for our minds to answer. Do not think that you know the answer, for nobody has the precise answer to the mysteries of the unknown creation of this Universe, except God.

God is a connection. We are consciously connected and focused on connecting with everything through Him and not only are we here and now, we are all that ever lived on Earth. Be serious about the conscious connection with God. Let that be the first priority:

everything else secondary.

Fix your mind on God and be His devotee. You understand God and obey His law. You move towards God. You will reach God because God loves you. You cannot meet real happiness in the external world when you misaligned and unaware the omnipresence of God. However, when you consciously connect with God's spirit, all things will transform with no mental strain on you. You will feel energetic, fresh, and cheerful even after a long day.

Do not be afraid to talk to and to know your God. Have no confusion: if you did something silly and are in fear, God will punish you. You then keep distant from God. If that is the case, punishment could befall upon us for the silly thoughts that we carry out daily. Always follow, observe and obey the Universal Laws and live with them. Do not be under the impression that if we do not follow certain rituals or worship on a certain day, it will bring us harm. Cease this nonsensical thinking. God is invisible: it is difficult to see Him. He is inside and outside; about and below; beside and behind you. Yet He is nowhere, but everywhere. God's footprint is everywhere and we dwell in Him. God does not create good and bad things, we created them. In the physical world we have dual concepts. All things contain positive and negative, good and bad or evil. There are things that occur in this world for which we do not need to seek an answer. To seek an answer only God can answer is impossible, unless we combine with the Divine mind. To form one mind with the Divine is unlikely because we are in form, unless we transform to become formless; we would have to become one with the Source.

So, the question we ask is why we cannot just unmanifest from the formless to the formed and then from the formed to unmanifest again. It does not make sense. So long as the game keeps going, the beginning is the unmanifested, and then it is transformed to the manifested. Ultimately, we transform back to formlessness. You discover your own truth. The true nature of our Source-being is infinite Spirit.

When you connect with the Source, you stop thinking about your immediate problems. You know all things happen for a reason and all things do happen for the best. If things do not occur as expected, you do not omit anything, perhaps you will still find hidden power and peace within that carries you through the roadblocks that were hindering and frightening you. When you know something completely, then you no longer need to struggle or fight against it. Just try it with a lucid mind you will absolutely amaze by the results. When you know the Law of Karma, action and the response is effective. If you lack knowledge of this law of cause and effect, then everything will turn upside down and become ineffective. So the solution to your immediate problem is to connect with the Divine. When you connect with the Source, you connect with high vibrational energy, which makes you feel good, peaceful and content. Your thought energy comes from the nothingness, but not from the mental mind. You are thinking inspirational thoughts obtained from the emptiness. They are not as a result of your past thoughts or recur due to thinking in the ego mind. The high energy thoughts are complete from the Source and ready to use. When you are aware of immediate events occurring because of your past actions and that karmic law must allow you to carry them out without interference, then the Karmic law will make sure every subtle cause brings to a tangible result.

If you are intelligent enough, you should not interfere, but allow the karmic law to produce its results. When you have high vibrational thoughts, you do not need to worry about karmic law because you are always connected with the Divine: negative karma will not return to you. You control your destiny: connect with the Divine now. It is true that everyone has a unique difference karmic debt to pay. There is no escape from karma until it is repaid and completed.

You do not pay attention to current events or the attitude of the people around you. You pay all your attention to the direct connection with the Divine. You focus on your freedom and to liberating yourself as a free spirit.

Your ability to change rests on you; you should not rely on the external world to transform you. You need to grow up but not to pamper yourself with earthly desires, which arise mainly out of greed and envy. Look around: some polluted minds are everywhere with wanting to accumulate more power, wealth and possessions. Scam artists use the name of Christ to become super-rich and famous while the character of those con-artists bites the dust. Some powerful politicians may be able to influence the minds of millions, but their lack of energy to connect with the Divine energy that is working in the background.

When you are willing to change, you could be under the influence of something; however, if you are not influenced by anything, you can never make that transformational change. Think about it: we struggle every day to craft more positive thoughts so we can better express ourselves and attempt to overcome the obstacles and problems which we travel in our spiritual journey of life. We are trying to change. We change if we can; we believe in it and take action. Do not change anything by force; let the latent energy, which causes all change do it. Observe something that is real that you cannot change and something is noticeable which you can change by detecting it. Make your soul infinite with your Source that is real: what you cannot change, destroy or remove. You can enjoy it. Now fasten your seat belt we are all travelers on Earth. Perhaps we shall meet in eternity and exchange ideas — or for now continuously enjoy a journey. .

Your destiny is not engraved in stone: when you change your mind, you might have changed your fate. Your conscious mind loves to dwell in the past and in the fluid future. The past is history and the future is not coming yet. The Ego-mind can recall any of your memories at any time and there is no restriction or rule on how much of your past you can remember. However, if you are making that permanent change in your consciousness now, then you will displease the Ego. The Ego does not know what to do with your coherent and constant thoughts. Your immediate thoughts can manifest things almost at an instant and the Ego cannot do anything about it.

Your memory is not just an indication concern your present existence or destination. Perhaps you existed in many life forms before you appeared in the Now. What makes you seem in the now and where were you before you came to this human form? Life is a burning flame that it's burning and will ever cease. You must have existed somewhere in the past, but you just do not recall it, or after you have emerged in this world the past has hidden somewhere in your memory. Maybe it is too painful to memorize However, with the help of hypnosis, you can regain some regressions to your past. Understanding the past helps you to comprehend why things happened that were always unwanted and unforeseen. You thought you had not done anything to hurt anybody but, in this life, you have suffered many pains and despairs, one after another. It seems to never end. You wish to discover what makes you deserve all the negative karma that comes back to haunt you.

One needs aware that life does not just occur in one cycle. If you think your life began when you were born, then you think that when the time comes, it ends. It is your thought that there is only one life to live that is mistaken. This is only an Ego-concept. Life is a cycle, as spring changes to summer, followed by autumn then winter. At the end of the winter, it returns to spring again. Season and climate changes are and always have been a continuum and the same is true of our lives, that they are everlasting, ever-evolving and ever-growing. It is a burning flame; it burns endlessly. The Universal Laws of Nature have absolute power over, below and above of everything. Currently, we do not have the power or abilities to control or change the act of God. Obviously, we will never have such power as humanity. We embrace it with gratitude and live with it in harmony and peace.

Your time for joy and happiness will come when the time of your negative karma has ended. In a duo-concept physical world all things will not last forever. Similarly, if you think you can win it all at the end of the game, then you must think again: at the end of all possibilities nobodies wins it all even the devil will lose. Bear in mind when is in form he might not have all potentials to win everything until the sunlight hours has dawned.

Your despair and adverse situations will shift at the end of the cycle. Do not be fooled by your irregular conscious emotional thoughts that your life cannot change. Due to before the day dawns we do not know anything about an occurring event, after the day continue to unfold, then we become aware of all things. What you are thinking now will affect your destiny tomorrow; hence, you need to vigilant in every one of your conscious thoughts. Whatever you echo to the Universe it will return to you someday, and when thought returns, it might have transformed to become your actuality.

When you connect with the Spirit to guide your thoughts, you stop thinking but just follow what it guides you to do. You let the Spirit guide your energy where it goes. I am writing this text, but, in fact, the spirit guides me, and the Spirit is doing all the hard work: I just type it on the white page of the monitor. Seemingly, I am doing something, but actually I am doing nothing. I only follow the Spirit's direction and then it does for me. The Spirit within you is always waiting to help you. Allow yourself to receive this privilege today.

Karma has its own way of doing things. When you do a good deed today, many good things will return to you someday. You will never know when the auspicious karma returns, but when it does return then you might have all blessings befall you from heaven to say thank you for your good deeds and actions. You are bound by the Law of Karma and have to continue your truth on Earth. If you have completed all your karmic cycle of debts, you do not have to go through them again. You must stand your test of time, and then when that tragic moment has passed, the truth will shift you beyond possibility.

When a child is born, do we know what he or she becoming? Will he becomes the President of the United States of America someday, or just a common Joe, or a dark evil human soul? We do not know until the day has dawned, then everything will be clear. Parents, school teachers, or university professors know nothing about a person's future. However, as the person continues to evolve and grow, certain latent qualities and patterns start emerges and seen on the surface. The certainty of what a person wants to become will overcome all barriers that challenge him or her. The latent powers of a person gradually transform to become more powerful and, ultimately, as soon as all requirements and the right conditions blended, they will appear in a manifested form. Will you allow the favorable conditions, which are going to change your destiny? It is your destiny, you must do it and nobody can do it for you. You may not want to withhold an auspicious opportunity retrain from yourself: once that opportunity had left, it is very difficult to regain it. If you want to pursue that opportunity, you must make a steadfast decision, karma will vigilant over your action, and you may carry out your desires. Somehow, if you derail and change your decision, it is possibly not a negative thing: perhaps it is the right thing to do.

All things happen for a reason. If there is nothing lost, and it is not the end. It is our experience of the time makes it seem that way. You do not omit anything; you find peace inside.

Follow and connect to your Spirit to meet everything you desire. The Source-God is the only winning power that can fulfill your desires' impulses. When you make God's spirit the only supreme source and your goal, you know you are always on the right path; you carry out everything through the Divine with love. You do not feel hatred or envy towards others rather you may have a fantastic, great effect on those lives you touch; however, you get everything effectively through the Spirit.

When you start a project, first, it begins with an idea and then you transform that thought into an intention. You spend more time on that inspire thought; you do inward meditation to get ideas that are more spiritual and let the Universe show you how to make it work. Spend more time thinking about it. For example, if you are writing a book, the will to write a book should dominate over writing it. You are simply visualizing, outlining and gathering information, and not actually doing it. Your feeling is positive and you feel good about everything. More importantly, you need inspired by the Spirit. You know about inspirational success in your work; you have deep feelings and a love for what you do. It is different from want, as that drains your energy and makes you tired. However, when your work inspired and guided by Source; the oneness energy leads you every step of the way; you simply follow and the Spirit does the real work through you. You are actually doing nothing, but the work completed and will continue to fulfill.

You connect with the Divine then your idea is always inspired. Everything you do is full of positive vibrational and emotional thoughts even for a short time your heart is full of joy; you hear the song of your soul. You are full of enthusiasm, and eagerness, and for the moment you replace calmness for fear. Your positive emotions always show that you are on the right path and are doing fine; you do not listen to the problem instead go into the gap and connect with the silence. Your mind will not bring in any negative emotions to hurt you or discourage you. Because your mind is empty; you do not have thoughts, you look away from your problems even for a short time will make you feel joy in your heart, for a while the world seems to change a bit. Yet you do not know it is not the world change, it is you change inside. You know the past does not reflect your current situation for success. The past is insignificant because it knows little about your real nature. If you had no luck in the past, that does not mean that you cannot do well in the Now. You simply tap into the Divine connection through the invisible energy lying dormant within and that will open a channel for your connection with the Divine. The connection is inevitably open. Your own past thoughts, experiences, and acts are obstacles, but not the Source. Hence, you are free to connect with the Spirit to get inspiration and success.

When you are not inspired, success is a problem; you doubt your work, you have no self-awareness or confidence. You do not trust yourself; you drive yourself in the wrong direction with painful experiences; you abandon projects before you start.

Your mind is vulnerable and hard to control but with practice you can harness the mind to do your bidding. When you connect with the Spirit you need no thinking mind. When you stop thinking, you have a peaceful and calm mind. When the mind is quiet then you take control of it. The mind will obey you. When your mind, spirit and body are at one with the Source-energy, there is nothing you cannot have or be or do. You live an infinite life; you live by the laws of the Spirit; everything you do inspire.

Even though your inspired success comes with everything you do, when the time comes that you need to relinquish it, you should do so according to the Laws of Detachment. Your knowledge, your wisdom, your aptitudes, and your possessions are temporary and come from the Divine. You are a gatekeeper. You do not own what you have now acquired. God's spirit gives it to you; so, you can use it temporarily. Hence, do not get attached to it all and you should share it with the less privileged.

When you detach from what you have, that does not mean that you lose everything you own. In fact, you gain more because you let the Universe know that you have more than enough; so you share with others and the Universe is glad that you did that and grants more to you. You simply obey and observe the Laws of Giving and Receiving.

Whatever you accumulated over the years is only an illusion. It is not real and you cannot bring it with you when you return to the nothingness. Whatever you do, you must act according to your life's purpose and meaning. If you lose your purpose, you lose your balance and your life becomes meaningless and purposeless. Ask the Universe to guide you towards your life. God is the center of your Source-being: when you lose God, you lose your balance and you cannot stand up. God is inside you and you must activate the power to help you. You practice inward meditation on God and on God alone. You must use your inner vehicle to make your success. Without the coherent connection with God, all your success is only an illusion and is not real. Simply, a desire cannot be accomplished. When you connect with the Spirit, you use the higher consciousness of the mind, but not the lower mind. You can get things done faster than with your finite mind.

With your lower mind, be aware that whatever you do will take more time to manifest what you desire: with the higher consciousness of the mind, you can meet your impulses within a short period. The reason the lower mind works slower is that, when you want to manifest something, there are barriers surrounding you that may hinder your manifestation, despite the thoughts that control and discourage by the Ego-mind. It may bring in many of your past negative emotional thoughts, fears, worries and untrue beliefs to hurt and track you. The mind tells you that, if you do that, you can never have success because you are a loser: you have not had success in anything in the past, so why do you think you will be successful now? You are wasting your time; you will not do it.

On the contrary, when you connect with the higher consciousness of the mind, you inspired for success. Your ideas, thoughts, and intentions are purified and you inspired to do the thing you admire. All feelings and emotions are positive, and auspicious: none is negative. Negative feelings and thoughts are not able to enter the mind and they are eliminated on arrival. In addition, because of inspiration, you can do things much faster because you are using a supreme vehicle connected directly to the Spirit; hence, this enables you to carry out your impulses in a relatively short period. You do not need to force it to happen, as all things just happen naturally and, more importantly, you see results.

After years of accomplishment and achievement, with success in your heart, you realize that your success is not due to you but comes from the Divine. You discover yourself is a greater person than you were before. You are more compassionate and kind to yourself and others. You see things from a different perspective; you do not hold the ideas or arguments that you used to. You recognize your true nature and beauty, and humbly accept the opinions of others with gratitude. Whatever you did before it transformed to become meekness through the conscious awareness of the Spirit: your interest in sharing your wealth with others is getting stronger, as is your eagerness to move ahead to do more humanitarian work for the world. You no longer only think of yourself as an individual, but you think of the world at large because you know you are at one with the world and with the Universal Source. Shift to the Spirit to enable yourself to experience more joy and happiness and an opportunity to practice forgiveness. You become truly an addict of God's Spirit, in that you do not define others in your judgment; you simply define yourself with people as one. Therefore, there will be no value in people needing to judge.

Unlike those who have not yet awakened, you have armed yourself, but not with lethal weapons. You shield yourself through inward meditation solely on God's Spirit. You become divinely discontented with traditional religions, and robotic, conditioned human lives. You change the way that you perceive religion. Though you neither follow the old pattern nor renounce religion, you know you will survive like a stranger in a desert, but with an awakened mind. You do not have negative feelings or fear. You know negativity or fear will hurt you. This is because you follow your heart and the Divine energy guides you where you want to go. You do not struggle or fight with anyone, nor explain to anyone the way you do things, though you may find people do not understand you. You separate yourself from all dilemmas, seeking the harmonious event, which is real, and yet is the genuine truth: that is, to consciously align your soul with your creator, the Mind of God, the creator of your existence and every living thing on Earth, in the entire Universe and the Cosmos.

That time has come. One day you know that, whatever you have achieved now with great success, at the end when you need to take a round trip back to the nothingness, you will not carry back: even your wisdom and knowledge. It is only an illusion, so do not push it and always share your wealth with others and follow the Laws of the Universe. You will feel more joy, more fun in your life. This is your life, you know how to take care of it until you return to the void and reconnect with the Source and Oneness.

Chapter Two

Everything in Life is for Something

One is a lonely number, but two is complete. When two things combine, the combination meets the need for you to have something that transforms the singular into something that is whole and complete. Do you see that? Everything in life intended for something. Your existence intended to help to fulfill another human life. Your life on Earth has a higher purpose, but it depends on the actions you take to fulfill the higher consciousness' intention. Our lives may not necessarily be parallel to that higher consciousness. If they were, something different would certainly have occurred.

However, when you look inwards, you realize that, to find things in life, you must connect with something or nothing happens. In other words, if you want a special event to occur in your life, a new channel needs to open. In your inner vision, you perceive that you need the wind to blow your way before you can expect those real rewards in life.

What do we need rain for? Rain helps bring nutrients to the soil so that farmers can grow crops that benefit us all. So then, what's the tree for? Trees offer shade, shelter for the birds, give us fresh air, and benefit all living things. What about bees and flowers? Bees pollinate the flowers, and, without them, the flowers could not survive. You can always find something that is in a relationship with something else. Humans, bees, flowers, trees, oceans, mountains and everything else is all here for each other, whole and complete. No one thing can survive without the aid of the others.

When you are doing the right thing, you still need the other side to make everything complete. Therefore, you always need two elements that are combined to complete the circle.

When two things together meet your needs, you have something that is whole. In the same way, life has multiple parts. It is completed in the invisible world before it transfers to the visible, so it continues to evolve and thrive. The spirit will reward us when we help, love and depend on each other. When you are ready for something, go for it, but don't forget that you are only one part of the whole. You need another part to make everything complete. You must either wait for a portal to open, or you can ask for help. That's the way: it is the only way. Be patient! You are never alone. Help is always on its way. Your thoughts and the invisible spirit are always guiding you and helping you, only silently. You will always find what you are looking for when your intention is clear. You knock and ask at the right time and place; then something happens that gives you the feeling that everything is right within you because you have done the right thing. Even though you do it for yourself, you are also doing it for God. The supernatural spirit will then start to dwell within you and help you to do things that you have never been able to do for yourself.

Remember, every moment is the right moment. You can always do something to enhance your personal reality. Thus when you are walking, jogging, driving, washing dishes, or anything else, keep a small prayer with you for inspiration. Even when life seems like it has nothing special to offer you, you can still keep your prayer running. Keep it on your monitor, so that when you need it, you can use prayer to refresh your mind and make yourself feel better. Your life has a higher purpose. Remember that you are here for God and not for yourself. Live this truth by doing more for God and less for yourself.

Chapter Three

The Master View of Life

In this go-getting, illusory world everyone creates his or her own master view of life. However, everything on Earth is provisional, not permanent; even your favorite toys that you think will last, will expire or be retired someday. Each person requires self-mastery in his or her own life, and everything remains a mystery until that day dawns; then every conflict, and problem becomes known. The person awakens and is able to be still. This stillness enables a person to realize that he or she should not blame anyone else for the troubles created by the self, but should take responsibility for his or her own blunders. Then that person can abstain from using the wild and uncontrolled mind and instead harness the mind so that it is tamed, still and silent. The wildest beast knows its master. The mind surrenders to you; it listens, cooperates with you and follows you. The power has given to you to dominion over all territories and boundaries.

You control your mind without using force and without fighting. You succeed in harnessing your mind without violence because you are a good soldier; you can conquer difficult and complex situations without a struggle. You succeed because you guided by your thoughts inside. You are not a dictator because you are using your intelligence non-aggressively to harness your own power, so you feel satisfied and contented.

A person who speaks from the heart of compassion will always be humble and realize that he or she does not know everything. This is because inner wisdom and intelligence come from the spirit and cannot be achieved through reliance on the outside world. Similarly, if you want to conquer any complex situation you need to know the circumstances surrounding those particular conditions thoroughly, just as you need to know yourself well become enlightened.

If we refuse to listen to the demands of the Ego, we move towards the Source of our own being. We know when enough is enough and that we do not need to accumulate more than we should. More abundance will always come to us. Because abundance might not always seem as money, what we enjoy will join our abundance. Riches dwell inside your central core, so if you believe you are rich, you will be so someday. Money comes to you when you need it. Most often, it emerges when least expected, but it always comes at the right time and place. However, bear in mind that not everything you have and you enjoy is abundance. You need to focus the vibration energy of what you desire where you are and cause it to exist in the here and now. Where you are (and who you are) in your life now depends on your thoughts and actions. You can always change your future by changing your feelings, thoughts and actions. When the fluid future finally arrived, it was actually your present. You should not get upset about your past results, because you can inevitably do better now. The difference between the past and the present is letting go and knowing the past no longer needs validation. The past has many lessons and experiences to teach us something. We may not know what that 'something' is, but rest assured that you will be stronger and better for it.

Life is a process of searching for something unknown. Because we are curious, we will not stop searching for an answer until we discover something new to satisfy us. We begin seeking a particular understanding to fill the void inside. This helps us understand why part of us is missing and makes us want to comprehend more.

We are seeking the true purpose life is offering, which will allow us to live better and happier. You can circle around the external world to look for an answer, but that will not show the missing puzzle piece. You see no answer. You did not align with the Source within, which is the gateway to all knowledge, wisdom and comprehension.

Your being and nonbeing should connect to and support each other.

When you seek fulfillment in the wrong place, you look outside of yourself for a sense of purpose that you will never find. Therefore, your search for real purpose in the external world is painful and eventually affects you mentally, emotionally, psychologically and spiritually, because you are seeking a purpose that can only manifest itself inside you. You are one within yourself, but you must be aware that all things manifested inside before transferred to the mortal world. You will discover that this purpose found inside us is God's seed, which allows us to face difficult, complex and adverse situations and find solutions to our external troubles.

Your infinite soul is like a well that will never go dry. It is filled with infinite possibilities; it is hidden but always present and ready to aid you on your life's journey. In addition, your infinite soul does not distinguish between good and bad and welcomes both the positive and the negative. Therefore, the more you listen to your small voice and focus on your subliminal thoughts, the more your soul turns them into reality. Your soul has no desire for itself, yet it is present in all things.

Although you may not realize it, you always create reality in your life. In fact, you are creating the real reality of your future as you read this text and apply it to yourself and the choices you make stunned. You receive instant positive experience as you continue to read.

Understanding this allows you to unlock the actual reality of your true self and gain power over your mind and the abundance that you cannot get elsewhere. Only you can decide your destiny and happiness. However, your unhappiness has a temporary effect through the work you do, the attachments you cling to, yet you refuse to relinquish your current situations to the Spirit to help you. You can transform happiness into a true abundance of infinite life through your own efforts. You need to stay lucid and purify your Inner Self until you see nothing, but God's light.

You patiently wait with yourself to connect with your Inner Self. You hold the key to your inner consciousness. All you need to do now is open the door and find what hide inside. The notion that you want to discover this sacred place comes from a higher consciousness derived from the Source; therefore, when you trigger the sleeping giant inside, you can do or be anything you want or need.

You are seeking an infinite life, which is quite different from a finite life. You should aware that uncertain times and unreal moments will make you feel confused and perplexed about what you are doing. You may even want to quit. However, these feelings of uncertainty are normal. You just need to realize that an amazing time is about to emerge. You simply have to bear with the uncertainty a bit longer before everything becomes clear, and you can enter your own truth. Eventually, you will understand that the part that confuses you most seems right somehow, which is genuinely new to you. The gateway to your infinite life is that you seek and change, so you will feel better. You will feel more hopeful and empowered and think more clearly. If you persist with your journey, you will pass through this test in time. Nothing, not even your Ego, can prevent you from making this inquiry, nor can it tell you what to do. When you take a moment to seek the truth authorized by the light, even dark forces cannot stop you. You simply have to continue your quest into the unknown until you find the answer to your inquiry and acknowledge your real self, and have faith in the goodness of the Universal Creative Life Force that created us, and you will win in the end.

We have conquered many of the forces that surround us, yet when it comes to invisible forces, we are still living in the dark and cannot understand the unknown nature of the mysterious energies that dwell within us. However, some people find it difficult or troubling to admit that this subtle force exists, since there is no solid proof that these invisible forces work in our internal worlds and determine events occurring in the outer world.

With so much to gain and nothing to lose, some people seek out and explore the essential inner world. They try to look at each layer deeply, venturing into the internal world of their own secret, sacred and empowered innermost selves. They meditate inward, delving into the subtle world and communicating with their souls through silence, connecting to their innermost thoughts and feelings. They feel inner calm and peace. They understand that through the powers of thought, they can take possession and command of their lives. Life does not need to be determined by the opinion offer by others. These seekers believe that once a person gains this inner power, he or she can reprogram his or her own destiny. Life is not predestined; you can change your fate by changing your thoughts.

Sometimes it seems that, no matter what we want to do, have or become, something new and different come up. We almost wind up achieving our original plan, but at the last moment we change our minds, either doing the opposite or abstaining completely. We cannot blame anybody else for our own blunders, because we resist our own goals without resentment or remorse. We resent our own weakness. Instead of walking on the right path, we walk in the opposite direction and think we are still on the right track without the ability to leave it.

Then, we play the blame game, and not accept the fault ourselves. The Ego believes the "I" or the "self" is always right and can do no wrong.

You have enough Ego control that you decided to do something different and call upon the strength and source of your inner power take us to the heights of success. You want to regain command from the Ego and master, and consciously decide your own destiny.

It is a life choice, allowing this invisible Inner Source to guide your daily activities and ultimately direct your life decisions. As you make this choice, you become conscious of its presence. Since you let the Inner Source influence your life, you are on the path to determining your own destiny. You become an individual who always knows exactly where you want to go, what you want to do and how to be yourself. It reflects a true understanding of your real self, a willingness to see who you are, a gentle free spirit, a compassion, kindness, and unselfishness caring Source being.

Everything on Earth is dynamic and has a living spirit inside. Every living organism, animals, plants, and even rocks and flowers have a spirit. It is an expression of God and His created energy that everything has an active life force. However, the life force of a common rock predetermined; this means that it does not have choices. It is determined by the natural force of the Universe. The rock has no choice in where it wants to transform; that again, it's determined by the force of nature. One day it will return to dust, as will we all. The difference between humans and rocks is that humans always have a choice and do things freely. Human spirits are eternal and have no beginning or end. The rock's nature cannot change but human destiny is not fixed and fluid. That's why God places humans above all His creations. Furthermore, each human has unique aptitudes, and a unique character and temperament. We have thoughts and ideas along with the power to decide our own destiny. We choose to evolve or regress.

Your being is in the constant process of unfolding and changing from moment-to-moment. Achieving clarity will not be your choice. You will never know the unfolding moment until it is opened to you.

Your own Source of being is a gift that came with birth.

You do not know how your life will unfold; however, you are a part of creation, and you can influence your life and figure your future by changing your thoughts. Your future is not cast in stone, and you can choose to make changes at any moment. To influence your future, you need to tap into the sacred, still, silence place within where your future make it seems.

All of your life choices and decisions made in the present. You live in the present, not the past or the fluid future. The past is history. The present is timeless. The future is unknown. You decline to stay in the past or future because they are not timeless. The past always has a time stamp, and fill with bad psychological, social, and economic memories caused by illusion of fear regarding what is coming and that hurt you and everyone. We have no real choice about how our fate unfolds. When your consciousness is in the present, you are full of energy, which means you create and complete everything based on your present experiences.

Intelligence is also a gift given at birth. We have abilities to think to decide what we want and do not want. Thinking is the only way we get to know our true nature. Many interesting things created, re-created and manifested now or will emerge in the future because of thoughts. Because of our human nature, we think all the time; hence, an individual cannot see that some thoughts are negative and harmful to himself and others. For instance, you might think you are always healthy and strong, but your physical body tells you differently deep inside. Later, you shocked to realize the reality: you are weak and need a physical checkup. You possibly deceived by your own thoughts. A thought has no strong hold, unless it transferred to a reality. Thoughts are images created in your mind; they have no foundation or real strength until you transform them into truths in the present.

When negative emotional thoughts become embedded in your consciousness, you can always substitute optimistic thoughts. Recurring thoughts should be as clear as possible. Because of our nature, we cannot know if we have reached a bad decision because we are too busy creating the things we want at the moment and cannot see the truth until everything has unfolded and is validated.

Things would be bleak if we had to live out our lives under the conditions imposed by this limited awareness. It would be like driving a racecar without brakes. You could go anywhere, but you would not be able to stop or easily change course. You would be nervous and fearful over where you headed; you might even doubt that you would ever arrive anywhere. Your thoughts are like wild beasts bearing various sensations and memories. You must focus on changing your thoughts from desires to actions. You must understand that your desired moment occurs in the present. Be aware of the present and manifest everything in your consciousness. It is as though you are outside the world, but you are still conscious of anything and everything. You are conscious of all sounds, noises, smells, feelings, visuals, thoughts, textures, conditions, and activities around you. You can hear sounds from outside you, your awareness internalized, because you have practiced this higher consciousness. You can deal with everything without leaving this internal consciousness, because you have worked with your Inner Being. You know which direction you will go, and you go towards it without hesitation.

You know. You see it through your inner vision.

Do not worry too much, about how your life is now; it is better for you to drop all negative thoughts and emotions. It is better to continue with your life without the heavy burden of negative thoughts and feelings. If you keep dwelling on your current chaotic situations and the despair you feel, your life will never be transformed. First, empty your mind of the junk and nonsense, and then fill it with positive thoughts.

You will awake and become aware of yourself and your surroundings now when you are without thought. This self-awareness in the now does not come from thought. It arrives through higher consciousness that you meet when your Inner Being aligned with the present moment. Since you align with your Source of being, you do not need to think about which direction you are going. Just follow; the Source sees and knows what is best for you. Self-interests blinded your finite nature; your Inner Source represents your awareness so you can see them for what they are. Your Inner Source is guiding you even when you are unaware that it is occurring.

The presence of your higher consciousness keeps you from defeating yourself, instead making you victorious. Each time you refuse to follow the old patterns produced by your limited way of thinking, new and better alternatives emerge before your inner eyes. At this very moment, new messages are rising to greet you from your Inner Being.

When your Inner Self assists you in designing and guiding your life, you cannot fail. With the Inner Source as your guide, designing your fate is effortless, as long as you are full of confidence and believe that you cannot fail when reality itself navigates your way. Your finite level may not understand it, but you know deep down inside what you should do to gain your new higher consciousness. You need courage to take on this challenge; you must look down beneath you so you can see beyond your present level of understanding. Ask the Inner Source if it is possible for you to see the strength of your wish, limitless in the timeless present.

Have you ever experienced a conscious moment there are so many things that needs to complete that you felt overwhelmed and almost did not know what to do? Usually, when this happens, your mind flooded with 10, 000 things and your life feels unmanageable.

Here are some of the things that can weigh on your mind:

- Worrying yourself sick about how you can continue;
- Feeling fatigue even before your work begins;

• Worrying you cannot finish your work on time or get anything done;

• Worrying you may lose your inspiration;

• Your mind feels congested and cannot stay focused;

• Worrying that you will lose your income and cannot pay your bills.

These are just some of the 10,000 things that might seem in your mind, making you very worried, but things might not occur the way you think. Sometimes your thoughts do not show the truth and therefore deceive you. You allow these negative thoughts and emotions to continue without taking the time to doubt them. In fact, it is not just our own thoughts that betray us. Other people deceive us, too. Maybe you see a person smiling and assume that he is friendly, but he actually has an agenda to scam you. What you really experience is one thought and then you continue with too many negative sub-thoughts and emotions; before very long, you have burned down the forest.

What are these negative thoughts, so powerful that they can stop you from thinking positively? Who are they? They are invisible resident evils: fear, worry and indecision. They grouped an alliance housed in your mind, when activated it becomes your instant nightmare. These three terrible thoughts and emotions team up to keep you off track and forever running to catch up. They hide themselves behind your mind and project-horrifying image makes you feel more intense than real experiences. For instance, try to think of a terrible event in the past. The resulting mental image is a single copy with a thousand loose ends, which causes negative impact of your emotions and feelings!

What happens next is that one image spreads into multiple layers of unwanted events in the past that emerges one by one and infuses with anxiety and pressure-filled negative emotions parade in your mind. Now in your mind's eye that image (which by now is impossibly complex) not only looks real, you feel it too. Your heartbeat is faster than normal and your blood pressure starts jumping higher than it should. Your breath is heavy, but not light and easy. You feel the tension in every cell and organ, and feel as if there is a weight on your shoulders. You feel pressure circulate through your whole body, as if a volcano is about to erupt beyond control. Then you hear a gloomy voice say, "You are hopeless." You say to yourself, "It is just too much. How can I get out of this? How can I see this through?" You need to find a way to see through it, instead of looking for an exit. You can resolve this by imagining that the person involved in that event is standing in front of you. You face him or her with whatever he or she has done to you, but now you want to end the past event by saying to him or her, "I wish we had never been through this, but I want to end this and I wish you well. Thank you and goodbye." Now you have seen this past event through to completion and you do not need to revisit it.

You lose nothing, but you do not afraid to take risks. Fear will never be your source; you do everything fearlessly. Whatever you do, you cannot be the source of your own fearlessness. Whenever you see in your mind — good or bad — if you believe it with your whole body, mind and spirit, it will happen.

Life is a series of choices; including every risk you are willing to take soon, you are on your way to success, but except risking your life for any unwise, harebrained stunts. This kind of activity is not risky at all, other than to endanger your life for a superficial thrill. Yes, it satisfies you temporarily to push yourself beyond the limit, but so does sticking your finger into a powerful electric socket. So, stop chasing the impossible and push yourself to limitless as an alternative put the risks out of your mind. Real self-improvement changes you permanently. It goes beyond the external limits and makes you feel good inside, and expressed to the outer world. It gives you a permanent inner boost and is a real transformation that frees you from low self-esteem.

If you allow transformation and liberation in your external world to come from within, you will not have to go through painful experiences and make mistakes to progress; hence, you will learn that you can realize these changes in a decisive, safety, audacity and free way. You will gain the secret knowledge and wisdom that will allow you to choose the best moment of self-transformation, and all will happen in the visible, timeless present. The Innate Source will not let you go through anything that is self-destructive or perilous. When you make the right choice to allow the Inner Source to take charge of your life, you will in the end to create your own fate and spiritual success.

With everything, you do consciously, you change yourself. You are presented with the unique opportunity to fortify yourself with self-wisdom and inner-strength.

When you have the Inner Source to guide your life, it refuses to let you go along with people who has potential destructive risk to you and it automatically ends your association with their self-destructive behaviors. It removes you from that dangerous situation. It separates you from those people or makes them leave you. Therefore, you win your life back. These people are not worth keeping nor should you fear losing them. In fact, these people are not even missing you. You do not want to become a slave to your own nightmare, even though you may fear to find yourself alone. You may see their destructive power overwhelm you. However, when you disassociate yourself from them, you realize that all you lose are unconscious painful experiences due to your conscious mind improperly misguide you. What a relief! Now you trust your intuition leads you to the right spiritual paths of peace and love.

You trigger your Inner Source to deliver into your hands a personal invitation to discover a free and fearless life. In fact, your connection with the Inner Source has no conscious threat or risk, but you must willingly face those fears, whatever becomes possible.

Think about this scenario: The moment your life is at risk is like entering a tunnel with no light at the end. Since the Inner Source and you connected, each time you choose to enter a tunnel, a light turned on, so you can clearly see between your fearful life in the past and your new fearless one.

Every one of us has the potential that there is an urge written deep within us in our genes and spirit, to grow and change, given with a unique opportunity, and become the best we can deal with daily events. Each event hides inside a central code. It connects to a new secret of inner-wisdom, inner-strength and inner-intelligence. The inner-strength gives you the courage to say "no" to something you normally would say "yes" to (out of fear of resentment). It makes you bold enough to say "no".

Trying to fill the void inside you may still make you feel empty. This is because emptiness is nothingness. Just let it be unfilled. Let it fill up by itself. You cannot simply decide to stop feeling empty. The truth will win; you do not need to fight to defend yourself, so put down your armor, shield and sword. Criticism cannot hurt you if you know yourself and feel content. Be meek. The wise speak only when necessary. It is fine to say, "I do not know." Softness is not weakness; bending a little when necessary allows things to move smoothly. The weight of any trouble can possibly determine by how much you fear it. If you do not give your fears power, you will amaze by how light they are.

Consider the phrase "Yes, we can." Words have no power until one empowers them; then the words become dynamic. They become a self-fulfilling prophecy.

You cannot wear a mask or hide behind a curtain and still be real. Life is real only when you act honestly. Your life cannot be part of a drama and be real at the same time. You do not need to be somebody else. Just be yourself, and then everything will follow. As you think and believe; so, it becomes.

Chapter Four

Life is an Undeniable Miracle

There are some moments in our lives in which we experience greatness; unfortunately, there are moments that are not so great. However, it is unnecessary to feel upset, or despair all the time; similarly, it is true that every present moment possible joyful, cheerful and blissful. It is down to the thoughts in your mind and your imagination in every moment. For example, it is unnecessary to persuade everyone on planet earth to believe in God, as it is against the Universal Laws of Allowing; however, that cannot prevent you letting others know that the greatness of God is higher than anything humans can imagine and that He actually dwells in everyone's heart. I believe even a person who denies God will ask God to aid him or save his life, particularly when he feels his life is in jeopardy or when exhausted with every option. This occurs often because it is natural human instinct that we remember who we are — a spirit and a part of God's creation. God is our savior; God is our heavenly father; God is our protector; God is our adviser; God is our healer and many other attributes you can use to define who God is in your heart and mind.

I remember reading an article about a scientist who did not believe in God. He had always denied God's existence, and everything he did had needed verified through scientific evidence. One day, he received a call that his wife was in an intensive care in the hospital. The hospital asked him to come right away. In immediate response to the phone call he said, "Oh, God, please save my wife's life. I will do everything I can in my power to broadcast your glory. I believe in you. Please forgive me for denying you. From now on, I will do everything I possibly can in my power to compensate you for abandoning you when I have not recognized you. I thank you, I love you; I will make changes and become the best I can to serve you, God, please save my wife." After he hung up the telephone, he went to the hospital to see his wife. At the hospital, he saw a miracle. His wife had improved from a critical condition in a matter of hours. After this incident, he accepted God. He never mentioned a word of denial toward God. He kept his word and told everyone about the unexplainable miracle that healed his wife. He believed it was God unconditional love — a force that has existed time and space with love that cured her.

We may not understand why things happen the way they do; however, this we know if we trust the Great Spirit with faith, we persist, the dark fields of life eventually will guide into the abundant fields to see the light and splendor.

Miracles occur every moment in our lives; however, we have to awaken in the Now to feel and receive them. There is a moment in our lives when we misunderstood the greatness of God and continue to deny Him and His existence. We forget we are a piece of God's creation and consciously connect to everything on earth. We are one with all things; we breathe and are light up by God. However, because of our limitations, we have forgotten our Authentic Self; everything changed after we were born on earth. We thought we could do everything by ourselves and replace God with the gloomy Ego. We go our separate ways and believe everything bend to our way or the highway.

This denial and separation, however, cannot last long because we always feel something is missing or is bigger in our hearts. Even a person who has a loving family, a powerful career, and abundant wealth and possessions, is not genuinely happy and feels the void in his heart. He tries to suppress and forget this feeling; however, his attempt is only a form of denial that keeps him from discovering what is bothering him and makes him feel sadness and pain inside. He thinks he has everything this world can offer: health, love, wealth, power and prosperity. "What else am I missing," he silently asks himself. The Ego replies, "You have to work harder and accumulate more possessions so that you are not hopeless and helpless. That will fill the emptiness in your heart." "Yes, you are right. I should work much harder and get more possessions. Maybe that is what I am missing. Thank you very much." Unfortunately, it satisfied him only temporarily. Now what? The Ego said the same old things again. "You need to continue to work harder; you must discard your rivals. I guarantee that you will feel better soon." However, he knew in his heart that he could not believe the Ego. It is not material things that he seeks or does not have. It is rather the truth and happiness that he has spun around trying to figure out where the missing piece is. Therefore, he changes the direction he is facing, regardless of the way this world is turning. This choice changes his relationship with his internal and external world. He realizes it is the right choice. What is the right choice? It is the choice that he makes in, instead of looking for something from the external world. The answer never seems coherent to him. He finds the direction that he is searching for comes when he adjusts to and welcomes change. He finds courage, comfort and support and the still, inner voice within; he continues to look inside for knowledge and wisdom, and inner strength fills the void. He realizes that, in order to solve his problems, he needs quiet, alone time so he can hear the quiet voice whisper and direct him to the path of greater fulfillment. He has all the time in the world to make it right, but needs the silence on his own. Hope does shine all around him. However, he also realizes that he should not make the mistake of jumping ahead to any conclusions, such as, "He already knew that." He knew that if he did, it would close the door to this completely new understanding about to open to him. Although, at this stage, he did not know where the missing piece of the puzzle was, in his mind he knew there was a higher potential. It is a potential higher than his perception. There is a great feeling that comes with realizing that life is always open, and this allows him to stay open to developing a relationship with the higher power, the Great God. God is always waiting for us to develop an intimate relationship with Him.

"Follow your heart to do whatever you desire, for everything else is secondary" Steve Jobs

As we have learned through our personal life experiences, the secret life is not the destination but it's the journey experienced within. Life has always been and continuously influenced by our inner relationships through the flame of energy inside. These interplay mastermind everything before anything transpires in the physical world. Therefore, one can always change the occurrence outside to bring into fruition that which a person chooses. You can transform circumstances, if you so desire. Our feelings, emotions, thoughts, notions, and endless energies are responsible for everlasting life, and you are responsible to make your own choice and once choice determines the Universe move to bring into a final result that which you choose. It starts to change things in your life. If you aren't pleased with the script, you have the absolute power to change it at any time... You are the author and the editor.

The Innate Being that lives in us is powerful and everlasting, unlike our physical body, which will perish someday. Our souls not only navigate our journey, but they also hold a divine connection and are aligned with God. The greatest being dwells within us. This unseen, Innate Being is a part of God. It is the true nature of God: spiritual energies that are dwelling in us and are omnipresent, although we cannot see them due to our physical limitations. This relationship with the Divine being serves us well in everything we pursue. It is the Innate Being that has changed us, so we do the right thing. It is the awakening of our Spiritual Beings that changes our awareness to do and see things differently. First it shows us we are in a relationship; then it empowers us to change and a chance to show us its magnificence in our lives.

Think a moment. Every lesson we have learned and every trouble we have experienced in relationships is from investing ourselves in an opposite direction because we did not follow the inner advice. Rather, we listened to the Ego-self and did things recklessly, without considering the welfare of others. We learned some, but then we unconsciously repeated the same old mistake again.

We think our external world relationships are perfect and all things are under our radar's scheme. We believe we can master our own lives than seeking advice from an unknown source that we cannot see or feel; we abstained from listening to the silence, small voice within giving us the guidance we need. We decide to go our own separate way without listening to the Inner Self, thinking that the external world is perfect even without seeking advice from the Source of being within.

We attempt to change the force that created us because we refuse to listen to the force echoes to us. Do we need more proof to show us its existence inside? Then we start to understand what we have to lose by applying the flash of tremendous power and the gift of overcoming recline within to guide our souls. We want to recreate an inner relationship with something that we have missed for years. We are here, and we think we are here permanently, but our time is only temporary. Our destination is taking a return trip to the nothingness and blending with the Divine.

What a relief when ultimately we discover our relationships is not connected with the external world but with the inner realm. The inner world directs and manages both worlds. We thought we could depend on the external world, but our calculations were wrong. We experienced disappointment, but luckily we realized it now instead of regretting it later. All fears, worries and anxiety cannot bind us to our own without being made consciously by our Inner Self. When we feel emotions, it is our Inner Self informs us something is wrong or warning us to change course before it is too late. In fact, it is our physical being that makes us unaware of the hidden relationship with the Divine within. As we awaken to this truth, we should pray to God and lift up our eyes, and look beyond our troubles; all possibilities and thank Him for everything that we receive and will continue to receive, and we should ask Him to guide our lives until eternity.

In fact, we have been driven to look in the same senseless direction during our lives without being aware. We discover that we no longer seek because we have seen a whole new, fantastic day right in front of us. It is at this point when our true relationship with God begins. This longing never stopped; it was just waiting for us to invite its power into our hearts. When we walk away from life's false relationships, we receive the return of the charming relationship we have with the Divine. It's your life ...Go for it!

Our hearts have the power to transform everything we desire. If a person had a set of relationships on the exterior that provided emptiness and longing, he will come to the point of longing for a special relationship that he only knows from within. It is one he cannot receive in the mortal world. Then, he will not need to seek any longer. No place he has been can give him the peace to fill the gap of his emptiness. He has been seeking in the wrong place and has made many mistakes. Life has had ups and downs. He does not need to be at this stage anymore. He can relax now as he discovers a place that can give him love and peace. This place is within the core of his heart. Now he is singing his song to the Divine, knowing he is no longer isolated. The gap inside has been filled. He knows it is not an act. This truth is reflected from his heart to the exterior world. It is a relationship beyond the influences and distractions of this world.

Before you awaken, you are blind, but the inner eye allows you to see the subliminal relationship that you are unaware of during your spiritual unconscious. You must awaken your sleeping self. Although you may believe that your conscious self is more powerful than the sleeping one, this is not true. You have unconsciously refused to accept the Inner Being that is actually stronger than the self.

God is always present in our hearts. He may be out of sight, but He is omnipresent, inside and outside you, above and around you. When you feel the silence in you, you see God's omnipresence. On the other hand, He will not emerge when there is conflict and strife in your heart. You have to uncover yourself and remove the veil … only then shall you see God. There is no separation. God is not missing from your life; instead, you have to eradicate whatever is standing between you and God's presence.

Our lives are not clear until the end of the day. Within each of us is an inherent guidance system helps us walks through a temporary, uninviting journey; however, we are not thrown in this journey alone in a cruel world without the proper tools for taking care of ourselves. A person in his lifetime does not realize the power is ready at his command. We are continuously part of an ongoing soul journey, representing God and do God's work here. We are not alone because God has never forgotten us. He has bestowed every one of us with blessings. Our circumstance possibly different, but our soul purposes and meanings are the same: to be content, confident and complete, fulfilling each moment, guided by a compassionate, invisible Spirit and feeling truly happy.

The spirit can reach and teach you in the way beyond words and comprehension, but you need still, in silence; so, you can hear the quiet voice. It concerns your health and happiness; the message comes to you from deep within, from your deepest thoughts and beliefs. It allows you to receive the message as you think and believe; so, it becomes. This inspirational message is intended to change your life please claim and unwrap your gifts.

Do not be afraid to allow the truth to strike you. What does the truth mean to you? Whether it is a simple story you hear or something you read in a moment of personal crisis, do not panic when you learn what life is trying to show you about reality and about yourself. When this spiritual lesson strikes your heart, it is intended to tell the truth about your current situation. You cannot deny it. Accept it. It is a guiding light that will help you, doesn't harm you.

No harm can occur to you because what you will do inspired by the Source from above. From a physical perspective, you may not be aware that you are being guided by the invisible Spirit, but, in fact, you are standing in the right place at the right time to do the work that you long for. The reality of your life will just spring up before you, and joy and happiness will start to overtake you so that you feel a contentment and stillness in your compassionate heart like you have never felt before. In fact, it is guaranteed to lead you consistently, with no struggle or fight; it will leave you full of hopeful expectation and meaning. You think that everything that occurs in your path is supposed to be within reach, which is why you must not be afraid to let this inner truth strike you. Truth reflected within you so that you like what you do; it restores everything you thought would confuse you or make you afraid. Once you have settled in an unknown, shocking environment, you probably felt excited and scared at the same time, but that's your normal response to the external world; you can always wait for that desired moment to emerge, even though you see the problem, but you are not too shy to ask for help. You know you do not know everything unless everything is revealed. When you ask for help, your prayer can begin to be answered. When you receive the help that you need, you will see beauty and will see there's such a thing as unconditional love around you, as well as truth and compassion. You know these wondrous things exist above and beside you, and then you look at the world inside you. What do you see? You see inner peace and contentment. You must not turn away from the problem as it is part of the conditions you must walk through before you see the light transpire. You must tell yourself before you see a colorful landscape that there are missing puzzles to be filled and other things you have to do before the transformation. Then, when you look at it again changed, you will not feel pain anymore; you'll feel complete and will no longer be lonely.

At any age, when you look at your world, you can have a conversation with yourself: "I do not like the world I see. If I could be somebody else, I would be happy."

A voice replies, "Why do you want to be someone else instead of yourself?"

"I don't know. I guess being someone else will make me feel good," you say.

The voice replies, "You don't see yourself well, do you? Otherwise, you would never imagine you need to become someone else."

"I thought... Maybe I could do better," you reply.

"You thought! Do you really think you can do better when you're in control? Do you think you can get organized?" You have not seen the whole canvas. You continue debating with yourself when you know these inner conversations will not be over until you change your inner focus and you understand your true feelings about the world around you. Stressful moments do not come from the outer world but are produced by your own reflections. You see the reflection of your image wherever you go, which offers an important lesson: can you handle looking at the world you have created? Do you think you are important and that people have come to see you? The world you feel within is the world you reflect on the outside. You create your own image through inner awareness, such as "I am poor," "I am a millionaire," or "I am nobody." You know the drill, but do you let this self-proclaimed and self-created image trap you in the world you made? Do you feel trapped in life? You are trapped in the world you made in your own self-image.

The worlds a person experiences reflect the moment of awakening that he or she feels in their consciousness. When a person lives in a world where they feel confined, hatred, full of anger or envy, they perceive themselves as being betrayed by others; they need to run for their lives. They fight and struggle with everything and every person they run into. These internal struggles are projecting to the outside world. They condemn the disharmony and misshapen world that they have made for themselves. Because they think the world is unfair, they turn it around and perform some unclean acts against other folks and take what is theirs. Perhaps they have become so adept at trickery that they give them what is theirs and thank them for it. They become aimless, run faster, but do not get anywhere; they accumulate more, but have less. Being a cuckold and a rogue to others does not mean that they are smarter or more intelligent than their victims. They continue to go deeper into deception, using people unconsciously for their own gain and joy and to ease feelings of incompetence. They feel no remorse. Why should they care? They are living large: or are they? They thought the problem was solved, but do not see the hidden problems. They build their happiness on the backs of other people. They are not solving the problems of their world and cannot see into their world because all they care for is to gain more money. They do not recognize the real problems as they continue to live a cunning life. They think they are smart, rich and successful. They have no regret for what has been done; the egoistic mind has deceived them. They persist, but this con-game won't last: one day they bite the dust and lose it all and close the curtain.

This kind of person forgot he is an infinite being in the mortal world. He uses his own selfish mind to trick others. He carries the ugliness to the outside world to deceive people; unrepentantly, unknown to him he does it to himself. He observes the ugliness of the world inside and passes it onto others and believes it is just. His prayer is answered. He robbed others and will be paid back by his own karma eventually; the negative karma will be returned to him threefold. No one can escape this individual cause of action. One must pay a price for what one causes to happen to others. This is a dual world in which we dwell; hence, everything is two-sided. We will taste the negative as well as the positive. If you do a good deed to folks, you will receive a higher return from the Spirit.

You are always creating your own reality; you are the world of your individual truth. You are the observer and the observed at the same time. You are also being observed by the invisible world of the spirit. Illusion is reality when you believe it is so. Whatever you do, think three times before you act on it. Do not go rogue; you are under observation by the spirit in the spirit realm, and you will regret yourself. It will not rid you of your self-created nightmare. You must be vigilant about what you do, and maybe your next prayer will be answered in a positive yet productive way. You should only pray for something you need and appreciate everything, but do not be stressed and frustrated when the event seems out of control is to stop and review of where you are and who you are. Your own deep awareness of your world is selfless, and you see your condition begin to transform you. It brings you slowly back to your original Source of being and look deeper to see through that thin veil. Listen to your heart and let the spirit show you and still, in silence, gather all the information, and let the Universe show you how to make it work. Then, you make all progresses and changes within. If you trust, believe and expect you will receive it shortly.

Can you help me, my soul? You will be able to see what you wanted to see. Because you humble yourself and ask, the spirit helps you. When you ask for help, you have asked sincerely and have spoken from your heart. You submit and confess that you need help. You do not know how to convert your dual world into the one you want to see. What happens after you ask for help? The moment of you surrender your inner and outer worlds converge into one. Help is on its way. You see the way you want to see. Any compliance is accurate from the moment you ask for it. You cannot receive help without inviting help from the Spirit and being willing to receive a special relationship. You must cast away your pride before you can develop this relationship. You ask for this pass is you wish to change. Because of this change, it is acted out in that moment.

You brought into something that you were not in a relationship with before. Now you have created a beautiful relationship with your own inner world, and you see continuous changes. Now an answer comes to you. It becomes: yes, I will help you.

One of the unseen barriers is that you do not understand every aspect and create problems in the world. Thus, you are the problem. However, you can find a solution and break the iceberg apart. No one in the physical world has a solution better than yours. You know you hold the answer inside.

A positive aspect of the spiritual approach is that although you aware your physical limitations, but you consciously connect with your Authentic Self within, which can help you solve every problem. Every thought turns into logical and you consider all options before transferring the solution to the physical world; hence, as you think and believe, so it becomes.

Prayer works because it comes from your spiritual heart. In your prayers, you admitted you need help and relinquished your power to the Source, immediately creating a closer relationship between the Universal Source and you. Because your troubles become the Source's problems as well in this intimate relationship, the Source must help you through your prayers. Thus things will begin to transform. Your adverse situation will get better and this signifies that both the work and words of God are good. You find guiding light even in the midst of the dark situation.

However, prayer without a conscious connection to the Source is not authentic. Although it appears genuine, perhaps you should infuse your prayer with emotional thoughts and feelings, but not read from notes. Find a quiet place close your eyes you will hear assuaging voice of the Spirit speaking to you, and you can discuss whatever it is that's bothering you. When you recognize the omnipresence of God within you, look around you will see signs and symbols; you will hear inspiring ideas urges you to do something, or calling someone, or sending an email, but whatever it is you must take action. This is the quiet inner voice speaking to you. It shows that you are aligned and in vibrational harmony with God's spirit; thus, the Universe respond to your prayer request and you get answers.

The reason your prayer is answered because you related to God. Being submitted to God means you obey and follow the Universal laws. You no longer experience fear and worry. You talk to God for direction and guidance directly. Since you and God are consciously connected, you feel calm and peaceful. The connection with God's spirit provides you with wider approach through which you can discover many wonderful things and receive inspirational messages to dissolve your troubles at any time and place. The true nature of prayer has two steps: first, you say a prayer at a low level through your conscious mind; second, the subliminal mind automatically translates your message into energy and echoes it to the Universe. Remember the second stage is a higher level of spiritual communication between the Source's mind and the higher mind. You trust the process that has sustained you until now. Let go of everything. You know that when your mind is at peace and silence your prayers answered and will return to you, and your outer-world seems to change.

You know where to submit your prayers to the Kingdom of God, the dwelling place of God's spirit. But, truly, do you really know exactly where the King's Kingdom is? Don't you know that the Kingdom of God is within everything? Do you understand that the Universal Creative Life Force is inside you? You dwell within God's spirit. If you do not know that, then you do not know God.

Perhaps you thought God dwelling place is in the fifth dimension, which is distant from all of us. No, it is untrue. God is never separated from us even after we came here. God is visible, invisible and omnipresent, though you may not see Him; however, when you see yourself in the mirror, it reflects the God you perceive.

God is all understanding and omnipresent, omniscient and all-that-is powerful.

If you are contemplating how God is still separated from you, now think about your ten fingers. Your ten fingers are seemingly separated from each other; however, in fact, they are closely connected and related to each other like every cell, blood vessel, organ, and heartbeat; your entire body must be connected, so everything will function correctly, so you can live.

The limited idea and sense in the physical world that has been mistranslated by people in the past and in the contemporary world has then been embedded in our belief system to become part of the whole untrue story that God is distant from us, leaving only the memory that God is beyond reach and nowhere to be found. In fact, when your mind is at peace, you shall see God. God is who you see He is. The translation is depending upon your perception and definition of who He actually is. I said earlier that when you stand in front of the mirror, God is who you see. Each individual has different translations regarding what God is and who God should be. It is your imagination in your mind to feel get closed in on Him. You stand firm with strength and in stillness you feel His presence. You do not to analyze God simply go into the gap, and invite Him into your heart. You will live a whole new world and always be inspired. And in inspiring and changing a new world full of joy and happiness is born. It brings into your life of everything you wish for of which you enjoy.

For you to understand more about God, you must know where you come from. When you were in the spiritual realm, you dwelled in nothingness and were always with God. You always connected to God, so you must like where you came from. You flew freely in heaven. You had no attachment and emptied everything. No ego will bother you. You are absolutely a free spirit. You dwell in a place every moment that is perfectly presented.

However, things have changed since you converted from nonexistent to being. You see that all things have been changed from invisible to physical. Even how you approach things has become more intense. You no longer approach things with ease and love like when you were a spirit living in the nothingness, but deliberately want things have a tremendous, beneficial effect, despite things sometimes having no meaning and purpose.

You realize that physical life on Earth has limitations; the moment life is gone, it is gone forever. You observe people grabbing as much as they can because they have been told that what they see is what they get, and they only have one life to live. Do they know what they are doing? Why do they need to accumulate so many things that they cannot take with them at the end of their journeys? They do not see the truth about the physical world; all things are illusions and are temporary. We are guests living on Earth. All things are loaned to us by God. You are a temporary keeper of his things. When the appropriate time comes, we will return to nothingness and convert back to a spirit; hence, we do not really need anything on Earth but enough to live comfortably and happily. .

This is the truth. We see our physical world. We observe everything happening in the Now. The present events happen in the moment, and we understand our present moments through our senses. You know you exist and are real, at least for now. The infinite soul exists forever and has no end and no beginning. God created Heaven and Earth completely and perfectly. Nothing else needs to be done or undone.

So, God's world is all-that-is. God created all possibilities includes the past, present and future. The time is eternal and the place is nothingness. They are created for endless purposes and everlasting extant. They evolve by themselves within the consciousness, in the here and now.

Everything in the physical world has gone and will never come back. Maybe it is true. It is possible that we do not see this with our physical eyes. But, in a spiritual sense, it still exists. You do not receive the signal in your brain telling you the thing exists, because you do not see it. For example, you see the birds flying in heaven when they flow through you to another dimension. You aren't seeing them anymore does not mean they are not there. The signal in your brain and eyes was disrupted; hence, you did not see them. You just feel a sense of losing it. But, the reality of who you are cannot perish and will last forever.

When you feel calm and content in the immediate moment, you are connected with God. You know God is within reach because He always dwells in our spiritual hearts. The next time you feel angry and agitated; know that God is not there. God is consciously present when your mind and heart are at peace. You will reconnect with God whenever you want to, at any time and in any place. You will never lose that relationship with God. How well you connect with God depends on the relationship you build in conjunction with yourself. If you love yourself, you also love God and everything God creates. You build a relationship with Him and then in Him. You must continue to invoke, invite and welcome God in.

In the beginning of this relationship, reunions with your inner self were just an exchange, where you humbly submitted yourself to the inner world to ask for help. However, the moment you admitted you were incapable of handling things, you could see the possibilities of the real world. Though you may not see this new transformation instantaneously; you get to see a revision. Your life is shifting in a way that works, and your understanding is deeply strengthened within. This is only the partial truth until you transform it to the physical world so that it becomes the peaceful ally of your life.

You still remain the way you are because you think your way works. The notions come to you; you are the one who made the world, and you see it work. In other words, you are the one responsible for your own script; no one can write that script for you. You may be reluctant to see that through all these years, you have created many canvases that were unpleasant; after everything you have done for yourself, but you still can see what is unpleasant and unwanted on the landscape of your life. You should look away at your problems even for a short time, generate joy in your heart, you know that all things begin to change; you do not really need to know why this is so but one thing you do know is that the Universe is always appreciated a grateful heart.

However, let your fears be calmed if you are smart enough, a certain point comes where you no longer want to see or endure that ugly landscape in your path. As that path reverses, you begin to see the truth; a new vision emerges, so you follow the source whose light rescued you by reversing the notion that you have been unconsciously captured by an invisible, unconscious false strength. That false power was you thinking that you could depend on whatever you needed.

Pause a moment.

What good is finding the strength you think can help you, when it turns out to be the opposite? It does not solve your problems, but is it rather another form of self-deception? What good is finding strength if it leaves you disappointed? Of course, it can help you temporarily, but it is not a real solution. You must be aware that you are seeking help from the dark force that guides you deeper into the ocean until you no longer can see the light. The dark force then tells you to hang in there: very soon you will do better than you ever have before. It is just another endless lie to satisfy your eagerness and to guarantee you that you will do better later. Hence, for a short period you trust the devil; you have not called upon your inner-strength to help. However, the more you chase after solutions, the further away the answers seem to be. In fact, you do not rush; you miss much in life. What you need to do presently is to stop running and put the problem out of your mind and the answers will come to you. Are you still thinking about where you can get that answer? The quest becomes wearisome to you. Just look at what you have been doing repeatedly and that is not the worst part; you start running out of things to fill the gap. Remember that your true nature has been activated, and you have not closed the part of your inner self that can offer help. Your inner self cannot help you unless you invite it. No matter how cruel the outer world is, you can seek help from your inner self at any time and place. You have confidence when you seek help from your Authentic Self, but you must ask. When you feel you're exhausted, you can always go back to your own source; you are always welcome, but you must trust the process that has genuinely sustained you until now and hold onto it.

The request must be genuine, not full of hopes and dreams. It must not be based on wants and desires. It must come from your compassion and kindness heart, the heart that speaks the truth, and the heart that cannot be lied to by your conscious mind, saying, "Someday you will be wise and powerful." What amounts to a genuine request for help? Should it be like that "knock and the door shall be opened" that Jesus talked about? Ask and help will be given. Jesus cured the blind man because he asked Jesus to cure him. This miracle had to do with a sincere request for help and coincides with the Universal Laws of Allowing. You are free to do anything within the law of the physical world, and no one can interfere with what you do unless you ask for help. So asking means you genuinely ask, "Can you help me?" You surrender yourself at the point you ask. You will begin to see signs that thing will start to take shape, and you will begin to see a transformation in your life. You have sincerely asked for a new, changed life. However, you must continue to work with your higher self until you see the truth within yourself. Now you can ask a simple question, such as "I want to change the world I created. Can you help me?" Your higher source is waiting to help you, but you must ask. Similarly, God is waiting to be asked.

When God rips away your old life, this does not mean that you have a special power or strength to do whatever you want to rather than building a special relationship with God; you cannot go back to your old strength or follow in someone else's footsteps. You leave behind all your weaknesses, including negative thoughts and emotions, and lean on the full power of God's strength and breathe and shine through God. You continue to grow and evolve and live an infinite life rather than the finite life in the material world. Real spiritual life means casting off the old and substituting it with the new spiritual growth; you no longer want to be what you once were. Whatever you do now, you do it from within, even though somehow it may be seen as unrealistic or beyond reach. Do not doubt, but remember to knock, and the door will be opened. The option is always open to you with no questions asked. You will get through that door; if you stand there, you will receive the help that you need, and all will become transparent. That's the spiritual path. It is your spiritual life, and you do not need to consult with anyone in the physical world about it. You can do it on your own accord; you do it from within because God is within you.

You learn to surrender your troubled life to God. After a while, you will begin to see that surrendering your life to God is essential. It is the only way; there are no other ways. When you see the way, it goes far beyond the mere appearances and the rest will take care of itself.

Most people do not know that they have an innate nature that walks with them and guides them in a spiritual journey on Earth. This innate nature does not want anything from you. It simply navigates your journey silently and advises you by issuing an invisible invitation as it sees fit. Souls that are cooperating will reward for eternity after the journey here ends.

That said, each person walks on a different spiritual path though it is unknown at every moment; however, success of knowing increases amazingly when you still the true nature of your being and it is then that you see the unfolding events being opened to you. The journey to fulfillment continues as each person embraces and expresses the possibilities in his or her own life. Connecting to

God's gift of this individual spiritual experience happens through one's awareness of it, as the traveler is willing to transform and assume responsibility for his or her own actions. Fasten your seat belt and enjoy the journey. If you have faith, it leads you to the paths of peace and contentment.

In life you will walk on many pleasant and unpleasant paths. What does that mean to you? It means that life is not going to be easy. Reality is not knocking at your door, giving you everything while you do nothing. The truth is, life is a journey of learning and exploring. You are a student of lifetime learning and never stop learning. Your life itself is the center of this audacity experience, whether you are dealing with relationship, health or business issues it carries you all the times and moving you forward. The Universe wants you to do "well", to get "better" and be the "best." The Universe wants you to have the "Best." What is your choice? The choice is yours to make. Will you willing to accept the utmost "best" where life offers to you for your own Source of being? Give yourself an opportunity to receive the "Best." You deserve it.

Can this be fair? Absolutely! It is fair, and it is just. God treats every individual equally and fairly, without judging. He gives each individual soul freedom of choice and free will. What the spirit requests are what a person will receive. There is no reception outside the scope of any requests that you make. Hence, if you are angry, if you are stressed, or if you are frightened, you are stepping outside of your spiritual zone. You carry these feelings with you at your own risk and of your own accord.

You have asked what pain comes with these requests; you do not know what you are manifesting.

Each of these events comes with a story created and wished by you. God will not condition them for you or make these pains go away. If you work with your Authentic Self and see each event with your spiritual eyes, these undesired events shall not occur due to the fact that you are within the net of the Universe. You are within the guidance of your own Source of being. But you do not understand that what makes you dwell in the misery Land of Pain. You want to take a break from being living in the Land of Pain in the Land of Abundance and Happiness. You then send your prayer to God and ask God to remove your pain, which God cannot do. God cannot change conditions based on the scenario that you create. You must make changes yourself to your current situations and see your life improve before you send your prayers to God so that He can continue to change you and improve your life. On your part you must do all you can to remove constant pains. The River of Life flows better if you improve your life with self-knowledge.

Knowledge is wisdom. Lack of self-knowledge is unwise. Hence, if you continue living in the dark, you ask God to change you that will not happen. God cannot create something that does not already exist. Your ignorance keeps you doing things that are spinning. There are no excuses if you choose to continue living in the dark or sleeping with the devil. You can't say you do not know what you are doing or that you do not see where you are mistaken. The truth is you always know absolutely what you do. There is no denial of you created the pain that leads you to walk on the Field of Thorn. To deny you have created your own pains are delusional. Hence, the pains must be removed by you. The good news is you can relax now if you are willing to make changes in yourself and God will never defy you; so, your River of Life runs smoothly and fully through your being.

Could you be excused if you kept on taking illegal drugs, knowing that they will kill you someday? The answer to your prayer is no. You die at your own peril. You are sorry for your own cause of action; it is also outside the net of what God will help you with. You manifest this condition yourself, and you receive what you ask for. At every moment, you do thing recklessly you will lose your insight. You cannot blame anyone but yourself. Actually, you see it all in your own inner world, but you do not want to change it. You activate this unwanted, undesired condition, and you understand it. You do it every day without changing the role you play, causing conflict, confusion, and misery. Wake up now!

The answer to your prayers is that you need to make changes. That brings a very clear message to you: it urges you to take steadfast action to improve your life. If you close your mind and think that you know that already, you may miss a little point that could have saved you from all your troubles. It makes your life easier, not more complex or difficult. When you start generating feelings of peace, joy and happiness, suddenly magic starts working in you and the subconscious starts finding the ways and means to bring you the things you deeply desire.

We are unique individuals; we create our own landscape and canvas. So, if you ask God to change your life, then you must know what is in the life you now bear. You should give God thanks for a good life. Your life is improving and you are in good shape. You have formed your prayer into what God wants to hear from you. The Great God will then send more of the good things that you deserve. You get what you ask for, an answer that you promised yourself, and will see your condition change and improve. You accept yourself as already being in a decent condition, and from that decent condition you can grow a secret extension of that optimistic confidence to bring to fruition everything you wish for with success. Hope gives you expectations and is the most important ingredient in your life: even in the moment you lost your faith, you should never give up hope. Hope is the fuel for faith to light up your life again!

You pray in this way: Every day, in every way, I have more and more confidence that my life is getting better and better. I enjoy everything I have received and will receive. Thank you, my Great God. I appreciate you.

This shows that you allow your confidence to draw from within to improve the conditions that you bear in this life. This is a petition that you submit to God so that God knows you are good instead of complaining or submitting to an adverse situation that you cannot live with. This prayer, along with your work on inner self-help, will put you into a perfect relationship with the things that you hope for.

When you begin to love and embrace life, you will realize that that is what your life, being here, is for. You are here because your infinite self has a mission on Earth. There is nothing truly real but your soul. Your current state awakens your soul to begin an inner journey. You are possessed of something that is temporary; that something, your body, is your refuge that you possess. However, there is no difference between you and that temporary state. That state and the real you (your soul) were created at the same time. The soul and the state are one and the same.

Would you like to receive miracles from God? First, you need to know that God's spirit is eternal and His miracles are eternal, perfect and permanent. If you understand this, then you can expect and experience as many miracles as you like, within yourself. Careful observation of all incoming and outgoing visitors to your inner self is your own personal miracle.

What is a miracle? According to the Encarta Dictionary, a miracle is "an event that appears to be contrary to the laws of nature and is regarded as an act of God."

A miracle is something that we cannot comprehend, and no human language can explain exactly what it is. For example, your cup of tea in the morning is an instant miracle because in your inner state you want a cup of tea. That miracle just happens to pass through you. It happens so quickly that you did not recognize that a miracle was occurring. You are not aware of it because it processes and manifests at the same time. It travels through your inner self and is transferred to your external self so that you can enjoy it. Think about it. Isn't that what you want?

Miracles can also manifest through the emotion of joy. Joy is only temporary and evaporates quickly once it is achieved. For example, buying a new notebook computer can bring you joy and excitement, but after a while the feeling disappears. The temporary condition that created it has changed, as it must eventually do. You are left wondering "Where did my joy go? What happened to my happiness and excitement?" It's gone because the Authentic Self that was connected for a time and created the feeling has disappeared, too. You find yourself trying to recover that feeling. You want to get back that joyful moment. You want there to be more.

So you look for it again. You start another cycle of accumulating more stuff and more money. If I have more, it won't leave me, you think. Yes, it will.

Do not forget that you are living in a dual world; you always have the opportunity to taste two sides of your life. Do not be afraid to go along with that negative presence that you feel even if you consciously refuse to accept it. As soon as you experience the negative, the positive will emerge. When the good times come, you forget what had upset you in the past because life moves on and changes all the time; it won't stay at one stage forever. It has to change to fit into the dual world system, and the wheel of fortune just keeps turning, as the world continues turning, too. No one knows what will happen next. I don't know; only God knows. That's the truth. Do not give up what you want in your life. Take the time to look inside yourself to see what you like; if you do not like change, you won't allow it inside you. You should start every moment conscious of your inner state. Your consciousness of your inner state allows you to express yourself to the external state but not be dominated by it. It is the same as if you are asking God to allow you to dwell within Him. To this request, God will always say yes. You stand on firm ground until you return home to God. Your soul will then return to eternal nothingness.

Your life now translates into the realm of the infinite from finite. Your soul is forever set free.

Chapter Five

The Meaning of Your Life

Life is trying to share its secret meaning with you, but you need to know how to decode the meaning in order to fully enjoy and embrace life. You should ask yourself several questions. For instance, ask "What is my goal here?" or "What am I doing here and why I am here?" To answer these questions you need to empty your mind. Focus on who you are, where you came from and who sent you here. Once you know the answers to the questions, you have probably started to transform and change. These changes will eventually fill your life with meaning and lead you in a purposeful direction.

The first shift we make is from nothingness to form; we transform from invisible spirits to humans. This has taught us to view the world as a place where all things originate from invisibility and become visible. When we reach the end of our life story, we return to non-being from being. We know the history of the spiritual master that spreads from the Far East to the West, in both ancient times and contemporary times, who explored many truths and believes that our origin state is the spirit form. Our origins became confused and complicated in recorded history when we first began our journey here. The mystery of life remains unknown, exciting and fascinating to us all. I think we all enjoy questions about the unknown and the unanswerable; however, we also feel peaceful and safe with the material world around us.

Now the big question is "Who am I?" The answer is that I am a body with certain characteristics. I have a name, temperament, personality, talents and accomplishments. However, my identity also includes the invisible presence that I know is also a part of me.

The latent part of me does not have any boundaries, limitations or a visible solid form. You can call this latent aspect a "soul" or "mind," which our endless invisible thoughts get into within the physical mind.

Although the latent part of me is invisible, but I can feel it intact here and recognize I am a part of it.

I am a part of God's creation, a source for all. That's why I must like where I come from, which is formless converted into human form. Therefore, I am both human and spirit. Spirit is my source, and the destination that I must return to will be nothingness at the end of my voyage on Earth.

Some other questions remain unanswered, such as what happens after the death of my form? Who is God? What does spirit life look like? What is my purpose? I do not believe it is easy to answer these questions. Perhaps the invisible God's spirit clarifies all these mysteries, and someday we will know.

When I think of the events that happened and the people who existed prior to my arrival on Earth in 1957, I wonder what determined my showing up at the exact time I did. Where was I before 1957? I believe it is beyond my ability to answer these questions because I do not know and have no way of knowing. I believe it must have gone through some procedures, and unfolding could have taken place in the formation of who I am as a mortal being.

Our definition of who we are can be explained by our accomplishments, acquisitions, and net worth as others see us. When we fail a test, our sense of self makes us feel like we fail the whole world. Because we think we are observed by others, failing is not an option. We do not want to be labeled as losers. Nobody in his or her sound mind wants to bear the mark of the "failure." The notion of being a winner enters our mind sooner when we enter preschool. In reality, we love to win, as it represents that we are doing well. This is invariably perceived in our ego belief. It is engraved firmly in our minds and our consciousness. The idea of winning affects every aspect of our evolving ego. It is as if winning speaks for itself and makes a loser out of the competition.

The beliefs that are produced by the ego lead you to consider life as being full of competition and that the winner always takes it all. However, can we really win it all? It is unlikely that we can win every time we enter a competition, because there is always another champion emerging to challenge you; one who is perhaps better than you, so at the end it is impossible to win it all. We do not know the result until the last moment of competition is revealed. Therefore, winning or losing is only temporary; hence, you do not need to feel stressed or judge yourself to be less worthy, because an opportunity will always be open for you to try it again. You do not need to do anything in order to validate yourself as worthy and valuable. You just need to let yourself be and practice doing nothing; it is then that things will be done for you. You are always guided by the invisible spirit. This spirit ensures that you get thing done; your tasks will be diminished and decrease daily until you have accomplished your goal. In other words, you submit your works to the invisible and let things take their natural course. Do not allow the beliefs that are embedded in your ego guide you, and always remember: It is only when you let go of your desires and exist in the present that the miracle begins to take place. When you pay attention to the spirit, you will always get things done to your satisfaction.

In the physical world we create our own reality through thoughts and actions; hence our thoughts, feelings and emotions affect our present and future; therefore, they must be in harmony along with our actions. If they are not in sync, they are not harmonized and your present and future will intersect and they will cancel each other out. Now you know why it is so important to decide what you want in your life.

The key is to accept where you are in your present situation without resistance; don't lay back and accept what is, instead, keep your intentions clear. This prevents our false notions, generated by the gloomy ego, from invalidating our self-confidence. Only our thoughts that come from the Authentic Self are reliable and can stand the truth. Our Authentic Self connection is healthy as long as we recognize, and always make conscious, the connection. We must always remember to repel the ego's teachings and the false concepts which result. These are unreliable and undependable and cannot withstand the truth.

Unfortunately, it's the truth that we do not always listen to our own inner self and rely more on the opinions of others. This was taught to us by the Ego. It told us to believe that the opinions of others are more valuable than our own opinions of ourselves. We simply follow the old belief system that our parents, friends or teachers held and apply it as if it were our own beliefs. We convince ourselves that if any of these people hold these beliefs then they cannot be wrong; hence, we should respect their opinions rather than our own. We never cast doubt. We never question that some of their beliefs could be wrong, outdated or no longer valid. These false beliefs gradually affect our self-esteem, and sense of worth, causing us to doubt of our own Authentic Self.

Self-esteem stems from internally held positive beliefs about ourselves; however, it does not, come from the approval of others. The ego-concept beliefs guide and dictate that we are physical beings, but without a spiritual core. They tell us that the physical body is all we have in the mortal world.

In other words, what we see is what we get in the mortal world, and we have only one life to live. Our value is always judged by the opinions of others, which is what others choose to think about us. We limit ourselves in every situation that we encounter.

That's why we fail in some aspects of our lives, because we

follow the old formula that contains all old theories. The best path is to change our old belief system now and replace it with one that truly suits our social climate. You need to shift from relying upon the opinions of others to relying on the power within, and without hesitation and doubt. This will also trigger the awareness of our own innate power that can direct, navigate, and show us that we are spiritual in nature. We have the spiritual power that can give us inner wisdom, and we do not need to spend a lot of time trying to win the approval of or please others to receive their views and help. We begin to internalize that external situation through internal assessments. We stop expanding our life in an attempt to be somebody, doing things others want us to do, and to be what others want us to be. We will do things that suit our own circumstances and meet our goals and impulses. With the help of the innate power, you will succeed in every aspect of your life, and that is the most successful form of power that we obtain within. It is easy to develop and to be accessible and limitless because it is your own unique power, and it does not take long for you to identify and use it whenever you need it. When we give more credence to our own assessment rather than other opinions, we recognize the wisdom that created us.

The more we use this innate power, the more we tend to believe ourselves and want to stay connected to our spiritual self to retain this power. You can practice as often as you like to connect to your Authentic Self through inward meditation. You make real change through the way you project yourself, so you will have zero difficulty in applying the innate power that you were born with; you have a gift from the Divine that actually benefits your entire life.

The invisible source is responsible for all the creation in this Universe and on the planet Earth. However, the ego has a vested interest in our believing that we were separated from God at birth, and that's the most important thing in our life is missing. Because we thought God was separated from us, we also lost our meaning and purpose in life. In fact, if we believe we are permanently attached to God, the ego's reason for existence disappears immediately. The ego has no place in us. If God is omnipresent then there is no place God cannot present. God is in each of us, and in everything that we sense is missing from our lives.

The secret of the meaning of life is: You do not need to struggle, stress, fight for your life and become discontent. You can live every moment of your existence with peace and tranquility and spend quality time with yourself and just be.

Say this to yourself today: I give my gratitude to the Universe that I am grateful for everything I received and shall receive. I have superb health, and abundance flows to me through the Universe. I am grateful for my life filled with love, peace, and joy. I am relinquished and open to Divine guidance.

You may not always have the ambition to be better than everyone else, win at every pursuit, accumulate more belongings and be seen by others as incredibly successful. Obviously, the ego wants us to believe that our friends are actually rivals and competitors, challenging us so that we must either beat them or lose to them. Our infinite self knows that we do not need more stuff or competition in order to be worthy. There are no scarcities in the Universe; however, the ego wants us to believe wealth and contentment are not readily available. The ego also wants us to believe that accumulating more is a healthy and normal way to cure our discontent about all the things that are missing in our lives. As far as the ego is concerned, chasing goals means spending a lifetime struggling to get the things we believe are missing. From the ego's perspective, we need to constantly improve because we want to be successful or else we are nobody. In fact, the truth is we are nobody because we are spirit. We do not need any material attachments. However, when we are being competitive, energized by the idea that we need more, there is never enough to fulfill our needs.

Nevertheless, we can override the ego concept and senseless ideology of striving and instead live a life of contentment. In this case, when we focus on our contentment and connectedness to the world, everything will be clarified. Because we are connected to everything, God's spirit becomes one source, connected with everyone. As soon as we align with God's spirit, whatever seems to be missing begins to appear.

Life is not meaningful without serving others and the world. We serve others and consciously align ourselves with God's spirit. The direction we take in life is far more significant than the ego's desires in the present. For instance, the path you take is more valuable than a focus on how many possessions you have accumulated thus far. Therefore, it is important to make a commitment to transform your self-destructive, negative, emotional form of life into something more productive and meaningful so that whatever you do is significant and reflects your current environment and circumstances and bring beneficial effect to folk's lives you touch.

If we permanently listen to our inner self instead of following the demands of the ego, our own Source of being will become closer to the Source, and we will not constantly pursue the material objects demanded by the ego. The ego constantly seeks more favor, fueling the endless striving with a false promise of favorable outcomes in the future. However, attaining these goals simply increases these desires, unless we reach a point where we decide to change the direction of our lives. As this transmutation begins, we shift away from the stimulus of ambition and self-importance provided by the ego; yet, we must make sure we proceed on the right path and do not become derailed and move in the opposite direction. This is not a warning that we will definitely derail; it is just a precaution so that we remain in the driver's seat without losing our motivation. We must realign our lives based on our current individual situations in order to experience a meaningful existence.

When our motivation is fueled by our inner being, we vibrate in the higher energy field instead of staying at a low frequency with no strength as when we are fueled by the gloomy ego. Because we are returning to our natural origins, our way of life is supported by oneness with the Source; our authentic selves will support our potential to reach this wholeness.

The sooner we follow the guidance of our inner core; the ego's influence will diminish and become less attractive. We begin to notice that our lives have changed for the better. There is less stress and struggle, and we realize that what the ego has previously told us was a lie that was guiding us in a negative direction. It was telling us what life is about, what we can accomplish, and how to get more possessions. We now know that life is not about achievement and accumulation. Rather, life is about meaning, directive, letting go of desire and—more important—relinquishing our attachments and always remembering to avoid being challenged by the ego. It tells us to do more, instead of giving more. You will start to notice that you have more by detaching yourself from the need to acquire more possessions.

The shift from desire to less desire does not mean we can no longer attract abundance into our lives. We must simply let it come naturally and feel the bliss of being aligned with the Oneness. We must be aware that we may seemingly do nothing; everything is done for us, because we are guided by the invisible Spirit. We do not need to purposefully look for it; even if we do, we may not receive it. Only by surrendering to the Source will we gain everything. In other words, we achieve our goals without paying high costs. We can attain a wonderful position, accomplishment and importance without forcing ourselves. We learn from the ancient teaching that we must "let go and relinquish to God." We neither sow nor reap when we believe the Source will supply everything to meet our needs. It would be meaningless to accomplish and accumulate everything if we then lose our souls. Our lives become out of control; we become compromised by the gloomy ego and the dark force. That is not what we want to focus on, and it should be avoided. We do not want to live in the dark shadow, which is filled with negative emotional thoughts and notions that the ego is the "greatest of all." It is false.

Imagine the difficulty the ego has if we refuse to cooperate with it and begin to practice detachment, relinquishing ourselves to the invisible God's spirit and meekness. The ego will disappear and bother us no more.

When we diminish our self-importance, we rely on our inner decisions without relying on the opinions and beliefs of others; we become independent and do not judge the good or bad thoughts of others. This belief comes purely from our own authentic selves; we are all special, and no one should be defied or compared to one another. We should not compete for what we desire or fight to sustain such unnecessary notions. Fighting to sustain our notions is simply ideas and beliefs of the ego. The ego believes the ideas of separation, and to control and dominate others, are all part and parcel of this way of thinking.

When we return to our original state of spirit, we recognize that we come from nothingness: an infinite being. Then, a sense of oneness begins to replace separateness. Through our authentic selves, we are reminded that we are connected. Thus, we need to dominate others vanishes into thin air, and we stop thinking about the need to conquer others. At this point, the need to satisfy the ego's desires will soon disappear. When we replace the need to accumulate more possessions and treasures, we feel the peace and tranquility within; we feel content and conscious that the Source unites us. We realize that everything on Earth is connected, such as trees, animals and all living organisms. This even includes mountains, oceans and anything else we perceive as having a spirit dwelling within. As we are connected, there will be nothing missing in our lives. As we all know, the invisible God's spirit is also trying to tell us that He has never separated from us and that we can relax now. We are spirits; this truth has been revealed to us, and we begin trusting the Spirit that created us, the infinite God.

All living things are breathing through Him, and the whole Universe and Earth are also illuminated by Him.

There are many mysterious things happening on Earth that we do not understand or are unknown to us, so we seek and hope to find an answer to the true meaning of life. Because of this longing, we feel something inside—a course of fire that awakens us to new thoughts, a nameless but sacred need to seek and discover more.

As we look inside, we realize we are not alone; we follow in the footsteps of those who explored before us. However, the answer is shocking: They have awakened to the truth that we are human beings, each with an infinite soul dwelling inside. At the moment of truth, it becomes clear that each of us is something that that was unknown before. We consciously awakened to a higher consciousness that was a gift from birth, an infinite soul that will never perish or be removed from us. The soul contains limitless inner wisdom that we can apply, the wisdom we cannot discover anywhere in the outside world. It helps us obtain many amazing things we could never personally imagine.

Our lives on earth are always seeking something new, but the sacred answer is inevitably waiting for us. It is sacred simply to initiate the search for inner truth. We are individually sacred, because this search is initiated and driven by the higher consciousness; we are stimulated by its call.

The secret meaning of life can only be discovered through awakening within. We need to trigger the power so that we can seek the sacred words that help rewrite our lives on Earth. There are many ways we can discover how to do this, such as meditating inward through the silence so we retire to our Divine realm, and have the opportunity to receive guidance from beyond ourselves. We can perceive what life is like on a daily basis before we project, transfer, and manifest to the outside world. It is never about the ego. It is regarding a life worthy of celebration, which is full of harmony and peace: Everything and everyone surrounding us is calm and content. However, these peaceful environments cannot be adopted through the ego notions in our conscious minds. In order to achieve and accomplish an infinite life we need to detach from everything, relinquish our life problems to the Divine, and invite the Divine spirit to give us grace and help us to dissolve our problems, because no one knows us better than the Mind of God.

Now relax all tension in your whole body, mind, and spirit, becoming more present to the Divine consciousness that is in the here and now. This will expand your awareness.

Perhaps you are thinking about what you are doing with your life. Why are you doing what you are doing? Is this what you really want to be doing? Do you really understand why you are here at this moment? To answer all these questions on a personal level you have to look deep inside your heart, which is pure, lucid, sacred, and Divine. Looking within and seeing who you are will not hurt your life or make your current situations worse, but will allow you to explore your awareness and understand yourself intimately. By knowing yourself better, you can overcome any unwanted behavior patterns that attempt to drag you down along your life path. Knowing yourself better allows you to harness everything in your manifesting journey.

How you are going to manifest your journey? Buddha said, "Fearless, silent and loving." Follow this advice and you will experience the everlasting present moment of your journey, no matter what happens later. When you align with these three qualities — fearless, silent, and loving, you break through your fear to bring excitement instead. A young boy left his bicycle key in the house; however, he was too afraid to go inside to get the key because it was dark. However, he was determined to challenge this fear and did not think how scary it was, but how excited he would feel once he got his key. Your life is exactly the same. Look at how many challenges you face every day. See which one challenges you the most; then determine to conquer it fears, with silence and loving in your heart. By embracing your fears you will actually transcend them because you know in your heart, fear is only an illusion. By driving through fear it becomes powerless. The day you overcome fear, more success, happiness, and abundance will unfold from every aspect of your being.

If you find it difficult to approach fear due to your experiences, you can change that by realigning with the Divine, so you are connected to the all-powerful energy of love that enables you to create anything you want in consciousness. Take a deep breath now and relax, knowing that fear is an illusion that soon will vanish. Negative emotional thoughts in your mind are about to retire and be shifted. You must admit you have given too much power, credibility, and authority to your ego mind for too long, and become out of control. Sometimes, you just let the mind go wild without paying attention; eventually the mind controls you. You will do whatever the mind tells you to do. You feel indecision, fear, and worry, because you have chosen to live by the ego bidding and demand environment, and have not realized you still have a choice to realign with the authentic self and live in a no-fear, non- demanding environment. No surprise then that these negative emotions create pressure, anxiety, and stress, leading to pain and suffering in your physical body. These negative emotional thoughts in your mind are real, but they can be shifted to positive ones! Harnessing your mind is always a challenge but you are the master of your ego mind, not the opposite. Regain your control! Whatever you think about will attract the energy back to you and will become your reality. The choice is yours!

Like any venture before it begins, you may think it is impossible to accomplish. However, when you take a closer look, you may notice it has been waiting for you to do it for years. Some days you may find it relaxes, while other days you ignore it until inspiration comes, and you continue with a high spirit. There are many paths to take in life; all are guided by God's spirit in silent consciousness. It is important that you choose the path that feels right for you no matter how wrong it may seem to others. You carry your karmic lessons and life's purpose to learn these lessons, whatever you can in consciousness, here, now.

Perhaps you are constantly thinking about that moment when you will see the effects of your manifestation; however, some blunders are bound to occur. You are still not manifesting what you want. Relax now. Anything you acquire is already within you. Imagine all the beautiful flowers waiting to be watered to grow. In the same way, you too will evolve and blossom. Let them inspire you. You already have the power of that genie within you called energy. Just look inside yourself. Look for those forgotten seeds and find Divine effect and inspiration! The inspiration will reconnect with your inner being and allow miracles to effortlessly emerge in your life.

You do not need to force things to occur; just relinquish control and let it transpire deeply within and then transmute. God provides for the birds that fly in the sky. He does not force them in their efforts to search for food. In the same way, your spirit will be fed.

The shift that you make is silently inspired and directed by your authentic self. It helps you to achieve impulses that have not arisen from your ego and its selfish ways but through the part of yourself that is selfless. You walk on the right path freely without judging and discriminating; you walk with the joy of knowing that you are fulfilling your distinctive life's purpose.

Life begins very simply, then gradually become more complex and transforms to become difficult. By inspiration and awakening you can reverse and make the end the beginning. This process is invisibly guided by the intelligence and inner wisdom of your authentic self. Your inner wisdom derives from the nothingness and comes through the Divine. We are energized by a sense of the spirit that navigates us through what we need to do and removes the complexities and perplexities that the ego has imposed upon us. The reverence we feel is similar to the sense of awe that experience when we observe the beauty and the force of nature.

We appreciate the sunny day, and then the rain comes and we enjoy hearing the thunderstorm and the wind howl. After the storm, everything returns to normal, and we are delighted to see butterflies and honeybees do their jobs pollinating the colorful flowers and blossoms.

The virtue we see in life is love and respect for ourselves and other beings. This can be reflected when we reverse to spirit, and the desire to dominate anyone becomes diminished. Spirit has no desire for success, does not need attachments, and expectations simply fly free in the Divine realm. Spirit is the original part of us and we must love it. No ego tells us what it commands us to do.

In the material goal-getting world, things are totally different from the spirit world. You want to climb to the top of the pyramid and feel you must be the best, until one day someone knocks you down and that person provisionally becomes the best. This causes a problem, because it creates conflict, fights and constant struggles. We do not want our accomplishments compromised and diminished by others. This is the way of the ego, with no loving feelings for others. To contest is the goal, with an ego on the lookout for someone to fight with and overpower.

So, if the gloomy ego is so bad, you ask, can one drop it? The answer is that it's doubtful, because the ego is attached to your conscious mind, in a way similar to how your soul has always been there, until someday you reverse to spirit. Everything will be undone, and the ego will be set free. You will return the ego and the constant thoughts in your mind to the Divine source. These thoughts, which represent the "I" and the ones that say "I am this or I am that" create the ego's entire belief system.

When you say, "I am this, but not that," you create an attachment-limiting idea that causes you pain and ego-created suffering. Everything we have is an illusion, but the truth is we are still one with the oneness Source, the Mind of God.

When you can see two sides of the coin and know your spirit dwells in a mortal body, and then you will know you connect to the all-powerful, loving, infinite God. When you create the illusions of fear, you are misaligned with the Divine source. You believe in the illusion, so you become confused and stuck with everything in the mortal world. When you are still living in the world of illusion, it is impossible for you to remove the ego, until some day when you return to the nothingness and reverse from being to nonbeing. Then the ego leaves you. Now, you will continue to experience the ego.

The ego always tells you there are golden opportunities that may not come again if you stop working and refuse to surrender your freedom to accumulate more abundance and possessions. Do not listen to the mind. The mind lives in the duality world. It believes the opposite is also true. But this is subject to change. Only you can harness the mind. You tell the mind and make it believe that you are the master. Then things begin to change. Amazing things will happen when you soften things and events and live in the present that arises from higher consciousness itself. When you are conscious of the ego in the present and can bring loving awareness into it, you can immediately dissolve it. You feel aligned with the Divine source and everything is perfect for your source of being, and the ego has no chance to contest again.

When you open the channel to the inner world, you open yourself to love and respect for each of God's creatures, including every living organism. In the meaningful phase of life we substitute our usual struggle with just being ourselves —living in the Source of oneness.

Now ask yourself, what helps you come alive? The answer is truly living out your individual passion in a way that improves other peoples' lives. This is when you live well and get in touch with your authentic self. The inner being is honorable and faithful, the quality that you can trust most.

Gentleness and compassion are part of a meaningful life, pointing the way to offering kindness and consideration to others. The inner being embraces only oneness, not the concept of separateness. Separateness is a concept of the ego. This feeling of unified flow with other beings fit into the concepts of compassion and meekness and kindness because we remember and return to our original nature. In other words, whatever affects one directly, affects all individuals indirectly and the world surrounds all of us.

When we live guided by the Authentic Self, we support each other. We relinquish the ambitions imposed upon us by the ego and relax into the meaning that supports our particular lifestyles. Supportiveness means providing a service to others without expectation of anything in return. It is a way of life that taps into the mystery of learning to think like God. Try to imagine how God would think in a difficult situation. When we see ourselves as God, we begin to know how the Divine force operates. God operates in an unconditional manner. He did it all by Himself with His hands and has never complained, but continues to offer us everything, repeatedly. That's it.

What you desire in life is already embedded within you, and you do not need to desire it or intentionally look for it any longer.

It is always within and arises at exactly the right time and place. In order to receive your desires, you just have to sit quietly, be still, and listen.

In order to live the life you want, you need to forget your past. That will open up the gates of your greatest dreams and desires, and you will enter the land of imagination and fantasy. You probably notice how blocked your mind becomes when you feel depressed and down. It becomes consumed with how things are limited, difficult, and perplexed instead of creative and possible. To get out of this unwanted situation put your attention and energy inside your center core. Your heart is where your impulse desires abide. The key to opening your dream desires is to feel the joy in your heart. Ask your heart if it is able to handle more joy and laughter in the here and now. Of course it can. Your heart is your center core; it can handle every ecstasy, situation, and circumstance, but will continue to eliminate or discard anything undesirable.

As you become open to the power inside, you probably notice your life beginning to change, and you experience positive coincidental events. These coincidences come from the higher vibrational energy from the Source. It helps you to meet the people you want to see and improve your relationships. Positive events occur because you are vibrating in the higher energy field, and your conscious mind is aligned and cooperating with your subconscious mind, so everything becomes perfect. It is the Universe telling you that you are on the right path. Just keep going, and you will reach the Promised Land. Awaken now because you are consciously resonated with the infinite being you truly are.

Be as authentic as you can, and follow the path to what the Divine source has in store for you. It is then that you are ready to take on the challenge you see everywhere arising from this vibration and taking you to the energy of Divine love. You were indeed born in the appropriate time for you to experience the spark of fire in your life and do exactly what is needed to be done. The moment of the discovery—the unveiling of the truth — is ahead of you; you must deliberately choose that experience, and continue to explore and to help others through your compassionate heart. You will experience more joy than you thought possible.

If you cannot find joy within, then you will not find it. Your joy and cheerfulness are always reflected from inside and projected to the outer world. However, both your internal and external countenances must be matched and balanced. Your inside world must resonate with the mortal world; it is then that you are aware that everything is radiating positive energy. It pours out from every cell in your body. It shows that you are truly cheerful and content.

As your joy extends through your heart to the mind, you will begin to feel that your dreams can also be transformed into reality. You will want more of this energy in your life. You now know what is like to be living with optimistic thoughts and energy in the illusory world. By listening to your heart it guides you, you will see all your impulses transformed to become bigger and bigger every day. You will turn your desires, intentions and passions into the pure reality of truth, and you will live a meaningful and purposeful life. That's why we are here— to explore our dynamic journey and embrace life on Earth. All embark and enjoy!

Finally, no matter what happens in your world, you can always find meaning in your life within, but not in the outer world. You can find infinite joy, health and abundance inside.

All you need to do is disconnect the ego mind from the mortal world. Relax in a sacred place of silence, quiet the mind and make a conscious connection with the Source.

Our objective is to live every moment in this way, permanently connected to our authentic self and in oneness with the Source, while connecting internally with the Source.

This is the true reality from which we must evolve. We must also bless the outer world, continue to evolve from within and continue to express unconditional love, respect for each other, compassion and service. We are here not simply to celebrate ourselves but to provide our services for others. We have always been connected with the Mind of God. We are one people.

Mind, consciousness, and spirit are our reality. All events occurring in the physical world are only an illusion. In the end everything will return to nothingness in the Divine realm and transform from form to formless. We will surely end the cycle of physical life and the spirit will be set free. However, life will never end; it is a continuum with no end and no beginning. All things and living organisms ultimately return to one creator, the Universal Mind of the Universal Creative Life Force, God or the Source.

In closing, most stress results from dwelling on the past and outdated beliefs that keep us struggling for more. Because of our ego, we believe we do not have enough. When we make the change and discard the ego to embrace our inner authority then the ego vanishes into thin air. Instead of chasing, fighting and changing, we must attach to our Source of being and whatever we do will satisfy us at our soul levels. Everything we have fitted into our true nature. All our attachments, ambition, and desire are nothing. All are only shadows in the mortal world. The physical world is not real!

Chapter Six

Gift from the Divine

Everyone on this planet received a unique gift from the Divine before we come to this plant, Earth. We are all aware of this unique gift; however, we do not recognize how to harness this precious gift that we were born with or the best way to utilize it. That said, we need to recognize how deeply we are the Divine dwelling in a mortal body and walking on a journey (our mission) on Earth.

The more we know the Universe, the more we realize how little we know about it or the mystery of the Divine kingdom. It makes you realize how little we all know, and it humbles us before our great and infinite God. You feel this world is full of wonders, interests and sensation; you realize that, in the world in which you dwell, everything is possible through the power of thought and intention that triggers the Divine within. Later, you cast the seed that lives inside your heart and mind to the Universe; you project it to the mortal world where it becomes dynamic action. Consequently, when desires or impulses return, you have the power to act upon them; you know they will become your vital deep experience, and impulses and desires will now lead to love, health, and prosperity.

You might or might not believe in this gift; however, you can explore it and experiment with it as a scientist would. You have the power to discover your own gift and no one can snatch it from you. However, if you do not discover this ability, you will never know what this free gift is about. When you see an apple, you know it is an apple and you might even have heard about the many benefits of eating apples and how they are good for your health. However, you still will not know this personally without eating one. Similarly, you might be conscious of your innate power, but you need to trigger the

Inner Source before it can serve you. You may or may not awaken your Authentic Self in one go. Do not get frustrated or abstain if you have difficulties; you know it is best for you to keep trying. You need to attempt it again and again until you feel the power inside is activated. It will come little by little, beginning with the feeling that the genie inside is awakened and whatever you do will be directed by your Inner Child. It will transmute your wildest desires into reality and you will have a better understanding, wisdom, and knowledge of how to realize your impulses that lead to riches.

Do you know that it is your unique inner gift that helps you on your journey on earth so that you can harness anything you put your heart into? This Divine gift is the collection of your unique talents which come in diverse forms and distinguish you from others. They are different because you are a unique individual who is fundamentally dissimilar from me in terms of personality, temperament, what you like or dislike, how you talk and converse with others, how you respond to and handle a crisis, pain and sorrow, joy and happiness, how you use your abilities to survive as your mind is bearing fruit, and how you project your energy as you live life successfully, fearlessly and abundantly.

How do you take matters into your own hands? How do you introduce yourself to the world? You can introduce yourself this way: I am a writer. My ability allows me to write books, and I enjoy it. Perhaps you have many aptitudes; your abilities are not limited to writing books. You can paint, cook and become a natural-born leader. You begin to notice, as you start to discover your burning desire, what it is you want to become. Then, something will happen to enable you to concentrate on the desire to develop your short- or long-term career. It comes from an entirely unknown source, and these are innate abilities that will guide you in harnessing that particular career.

When you accomplish one stage, you move on to something else that brings more joy and satisfaction. This will cause you to do good things for others through your changed world, or perhaps what you wish for will flash through your mind. You may call it an inspiration, a desire, or a hunch.

Our free gift allows us to create material things in the form of thoughts that distinguish us from other living organisms. The Divine gift also allows us to have the power of dominion over all animals. We can manifest anything through deliberate delivery and the power of conscious thought in the here and now.

Many of us might not know how to harness this gift and replace it with the driving force to survive, which feels like the opposite of being powerful. The reason for this is that, throughout ancient history, we lived according to our heritage of always being told what to do and to disregard our own thoughts. For centuries we lived like robots, just following a bunch of protocols, rules, and regulations dictated by our leaders and government with no feelings or notions of our own. These old concepts lead to a society ruled by laws controlled by the government or a dictator. This type of society easily falls into self-centered, ego-driven concepts, without being aware that this is happening and being unable to repel it. These old beliefs lead us to believe that we need to get as many things as we can, even if they are unnecessary, all because of the subconscious idea of scarcity and the illusion that we must maintain perfection, that we have only one life to live, and that we only need to care for ourselves. We have forgotten the gift that we were born with, which is to help each other, because we are united with the Divine in one source.

Take a look at yourself in the mirror. What does your reflection tell you?

It does show what you really are, whether you are a caring, loving, and compassionate person or a selfish ego-minded person who cares only for himself or herself. However, you may not be aware of how far-reaching your ability is and how it manifests into your own true reality in all aspects. Everything begins with our thoughts. That is why it is critical that we become vigilant, control our thoughts, and use them wisely and positively to avoid harming others.

When you can control your thoughts, you can manifest anything your heart desires. However, if you cannot control your thoughts, anything that will manifest to you will randomly come to you in your consciousness, which is not really what you want to receive. Knowing when to send and receive will bring great success in life.

Happiness is a great success in life. When we can harness this precious gift from the Divine, given at our birth, we can make the kind of life we want to pursue manifest so that we can live comfortably and abundantly without fear of what tomorrow will bring. We should not lose sight of this source of happiness through habit, culture, and belief. We should respond to life through our Inner Source, not the Ego-self, which prevents us from using our gifts and thus manifesting our desires.

Finally, there is incredible radiating energy at the center core to assist you. This is what and who you really are: a Divine being. You can discover everything in your life, given the amazing power dwelling within that will forever change you for the better. Now is the time to surrender your life's problems to the Divine. Ask the Divine to give you grace and good health, so you can live better and better every day without strife or fear. God has never separated from you and will always dwell within you because He cares for all your needs and loves you. You are part of the creation of God that will never change. Now open your eyes so you can know and see that God is invariably with you for eternity.

Now take the direction in life that is right for you in the present moment. Inquire within about what direction you should take, and focus on doing good for others through the power of the gift that you adopted at birth. Make a commitment to transform a self-destructive way of life into something purposeful, meaningful and significant.

You should always refuse to listen to the gloomy voice and instead seek the Divine Source. You will be vibrated by your Divine Source of being, vibrating at a higher frequency than the fake ego. Remember you are a spiritual being; therefore, you do not need more than you have. So, return to your original status, detached from the need to acquire and accumulate. You should focus primarily on humility. You can use your inner power to tune in to the oneness of the Source through conscious connections with others. Use your power sincerely, genuinely and joyfully and service to all mankind. That is the purpose of your gift and your awareness of the oneness that unites us. You will soon discover that you are connected through God's spirit to everything you thought you were missing in your life.

Chapter Seven

Transformation

Transformation: it is an attempt to change and get one's life in order to gain more power and principles. From ancient times onwards, we have never stopped searching for real importance in our lives in an attempt to make transformational changes. We seek these virtues for tranquility and mental peace. Our true nature within is always guided by the Source. By knowing your own standards, this should allow you to confirm your heart's impact on peace and happiness in life. However, our soul wants far more than just to be blissful. The greater the peace and blissfulness in our lives, the greater order it will certainly bring to Earth, and that is our primary goal. When we go easy on life, we attain real inner peace and a profile of change to increased confidence, earnestness, and kindness.

Without a doubt, we need fulfillment and meaning in our lives. However, how do we transform ourselves, knowing that our egoistic mind might lead us down the wrong path, causing us regret? Perhaps we need conscious understanding unwavering of what we need to do and experience in order to continue. Hence, to achieve our goals and desires, we need to work on our harmony with the innermost view that the invisible worlds of spirits harnesses within, from which all things come to exist, so everything can possibly accomplish easily and effortlessly.

Our long journey of experiencing life on Earth began the moment we entered into adulthood, when we made some changes in our transitions during this trip to Earth. We have to examine properly various stages, learn, and meet with many hard lessons; then, finally, we begin to awaken to the wisdom that leads to a life filled with joy, tranquility, and peace.

Life begins in the realm of the invisible spirit, from which material formed. We have an enclosed spirit dwelling within; at the end of our last trip, we will revert to the atmosphere and return to the black, vast nothingness of the void, from whence we came.

When we are spirit, everything is free! "Okay, tell me, who am I, will you?" You are a divine reality formed in the image of the Divine. You were created in the emptiness of the void. On one side of the disc, you are an Infinite Being; however, when you look deeper, you realize that you have a presence that stays within your temporary material body. It is a haven for your soul. Because you are perfect, this is where all creativity comes from: it is inside you! It is futile for you to consider going anywhere else. You just stay where you are. You do not even need to seek counsel! It is already inside you. The sooner you are willing to sacrifice everything, then the sooner you are liberated: what occurs is just a stimulus that fills your life, The spiritual part of you are no longer bound by the earthly limitations of time-space boundaries and you know exactly what is happening.

You have a brain and an Infinite Spirit in physical reality. Thought impulses originate from the spirit in nothingness, stimulating the conscious-mind directly, and then you work on it and make it happen in the material world.

Spiritual Being is our true nature. The Authentic Self and you mix to complete your trip on planet Earth. Your real identity is an Infinite Being, but you are having a life-experience in the here and now. We recognize the Divine Consciousness through the spirit in our physical body. Then, we know God is omnipresent. Life is dynamic, and soul is infinite. Life is active by itself, and just keeps going, everlastingly, and ever-evolving. God loves to live in us and see us continue to grow and develop. He serves us, and, in return, we express our gratitude to Him for His grace and miracles.

When the mind is caught into being, it gets jammed. The painful emotions that arise need to be managed and switched about to turn things around. Who should take responsibility? Is it you? Obviously, it is not another person who needs to fix you! The reason you are jammed in your dilemma because the Ego is harness you, and it became dangerously selfish and ambitious. You should have listened to the Authentic Self within that guides you. Then, you might have acted differently. However, you did not pay attention, to the inner power; so, wherever the Ego goes, your troubles will always follow. Therefore, you must consciously stay alert every time you have negative emotional thoughts. The update is that you can request the Inner Source to help dissolve the difficulty inside you before you stop it in the physical world. You can always get an answer to your troubles, but, then again, that does not mean that the problem will not return: you must be vigilant concerning every one of your thoughts and actions. Furthermore, you must concentrate on dissolving your problems before you plan to do something else. You can always ask the Spirit for help. Do not get frustrated and angry; patiently wait to solve everything, and all will come to pass. You inevitably work with energy until it clicks, and then you know the answer; you dissolve and materialize all things. You listen to your Inner Source, remove yourself from the Ego, and cause no conscious thoughts in the consciousness.

Now, see in your mind that you have returned to the void and are realigned with the Source, from whence you originated. It is formless, pure, and divine, so you know you are nonbeing, feeling no pain and no-thing, just pure formlessness. You know all of your troubles, worries, and all fighting occurs only in the physical world. The whole purpose of this journey on earth is for your return to the spiritual realm. However, while on earth, you must stay away from the Ego's dominance and avoid being tamed by any negative force. You must choose to move towards to the Source, God, and transfer to oneness and wholeness.

As you avoid the negative Ego and start to lean in the direction of the Source, your conscious life will refresh and change: it will become one with more general and objective purposes. You will be fulfilled and know that, when you use the positive energy for your body, mind, and soul, it will certainly be recommended by the Universal Source. In addition, you understand the structure of the illusory world does not always deliver the things that you want: sometimes it can be quite different from your desires and expectations. Only when you find meaning and purpose in a lifestyle that supports you as you cling to the Source, will miracles and a sense of purpose occur. You accept that point in life is aligned with the conscious, present moment of your existence. You must not follow the Ego's dogma, but continue to make transformational changes, be released from the Ego's comforts and ambitions, and return to zero where everything is available, and free. Your subliminal thoughts will allow you to connect with your inner energy and that can truly set you free. We can do that with certainty, fulfill our greatest duty in our journey on Earth, and influence the development of this planet for the best possible outcomes for many years to come.

Chapter Eight

Transmute Your Fear into Happiness, Peace, and Inspiration

Before you prepare your mind for its successful use, you obviously must be prepared to receive it positivity. The preparation process is not difficult. It begins with research, study, analysis, and comprehending the three illusions of the enemies you have to conquer: indecision, doubt, and fear.

The power of one's sixth sense will not function if any of the above are present and remain in the mind. The members of this dark force are easily found, and the rest of the undesired forces are close at hand. However, fear may also be self-created because we are simply overwhelmed and made anxious by the situation, even when we logically know that no actual harm will come to us.

Remember that indecision can easily transform into doubt; when the two blends, they formed together become your greatest fear. This will start slowly and then progress into being your deepest fear of living, bringing hindrance to your job, family, relationships, and life patterns. Along with these fears come mental depression; you will bind yourself in your own small world and make contact with nobody except your family.

Fear is one of the reasons people withholds their dreams. Even if they intensely want to carry out their goals, they might struggle with the possibility restrain of being overpowered by failure, as they do not want to endure the outcome of their choices. Hence, they abstain before they begin. They also fear that, once they become successful, they might not be able to handle the situation responsibly, as the responsibility will be great and cause them more stress and pain. Hence, they hold back and choose to do nothing. However, they do not realize that success comes at a price: no pain, no gain. Nevertheless, the fear is great enough to cause paralysis, if we allow it, whether the things we think are real or imagined.

The basic causes of fear are poverty, loneliness, death, criticism, poor health, aging, and losing a loved one. In fact, fear is nothing more than a state of mind. Our state of mind is set under our control and direction. A person cannot conceive whether they created a thought. In other words, our thoughts transform into impulsive desires; later, the thoughts that you think most turn into your profound experiences.

When you create fearful thoughts in your minds, these thoughts will be mirrored in your life's experiences. This is so especially because the people you meet will also be very negative and will not have clear minds. This is because your own mind is shadowed by your own illusion of fear, limiting and restricting your opportunities. This reduces your self-esteem, self-trust, and any feelings of being abandoned. You fear being alone, abandoned, and unloved. You have a difficult time trusting yourself, your abilities and strengths, the Universe, and others.

The good news is you can overcome fear and rise up to the horizon by simply changing your negative thought patterns and having lucid thoughts. It just takes a bit of confidence and determined effort. Some of your efforts might take a bit of time before they come to fruition, but you must not give up on change. Believe you are doing better now, even if it takes some time to see results. You must believe you will reach the Promised Land with no destructive fear, so transform your life and live fearlessly and abundantly.

You can do this with the help of affirmation and prayer, which will increase the positive energy of your thoughts and shift them from fear to love. Affirmation is simply repeating the words you use to assure yourself that every day, in every way, you have confidence that you are getting better and better. You let go of unwanted thoughts so that inspirational ones that will inspire you to do well can enter your mind. Your inspirations come from nothingness and do not rely on recalling memories from the past that are stored in your latent mind.

One of the most relaxing ways to cast out fear is to become aligned with your inner self. When you spend more time with your Authentic Self, you will have more purified thoughts, strength, and energy. By practicing inward meditation, God will bring you joy and happiness. You feel you are in a state of contentment and tranquility. You see everything inside that is peaceful and project the same to the world. You begin to enjoy the sunshine and the sounds around you. You breathe deeply and enjoy the silence and stillness, and that God is omnipresent, allowing you to relax fully in the now. Now you know there is no reason to fear; fear is only an illusion. In addition, fear does not coexist with love, because God is love and peace. You live within the Universe, which dwells within you to bring your heart everything it desires. These things are love, health, wealth, and success in the mortal world. So, you keep going and always keep up positive optimistic thoughts; everything you touch transpires. You continue to explore your thoughts and imagination in your mind now. Remember this: you deliberately choose the higher-energy thought in order that you are inevitably connected with God's spirit to attain inner peace and tranquility.

Chapter Nine

The Mystery of Pain and Suffering

Suffering is the most serious problem in life. The important question is why suffering comes from the many pains and diseases in life. What is the purpose of suffering in one's life? What about a person who born with a genetic disease that has had no choice simply to accept the misfortune. One may ask, "Where is God? Is that God's will?" Surely there is no God will, because He never intended to see His creation suffer from any pain. God could not bear our suffering. God simply wants us to get close and remember Him. He wants us to cling to Him for everything in our daily lives. However, if God prevents diseases and illnesses from forming in our mortal bodies, then why does disease occur in some lives, in some hearts, so it seems never-ending? In other words, there are instances of different kinds of disease occurring in one mortal body at the same time. Why does disease occur in one's life? One may cry out, "Why, God, have you forsaken me to allow this awful unbearable disease that is upon me? What did I do to deserve this disease?" Jesus said, "Disease occurs in one person so that the work of God can manifest in him." Hence, it allows each human to help another, so that someone in pain can find relief, release his suffering, and heal his heart. God intends disease to happen so that every human can help another. Thus, a man's misfortune can be transformed into a miracle of mercy on Earth. In other words, if there is no pain or suffering within us, then there can be no opportunity for God to show His power and we will be withdrawn from God.

His gospel would be missed. Every time we meet someone who is suffering or in pain or sorrow, there is an opportunity for us to manifest God's work so that His will can be done on Earth as it is in Heaven. This allows us to show kindness and compassion to others by offering comfort, or whatever else may be in our power to help. Your presence to help sick people get well is like God's omnipresence; this is the reason suffering is allowed.

On the other hand, it may be God's intention for us to benefit from our own troubles so that we can do better. We cannot benefit from anything without learning through our own mistakes. We will miss many fine opportunities for spiritual attainment if we are not willing to suffer. However, are we willing to suffer and pay the price? We cannot become stronger without facing rocks in our lives and then finding shelter from the storm, or facing extreme heat without the experience of suffering. We learn beautiful life lessons through self-denial and mistakes, which allow the healing transformation to transpire.

If everything happens for a reason, suffering occurs in human life because God has a reason for it. This is an especially good belief to hold when we find ourselves in trouble. God has his reasons for sending trouble to people's lives. There is always a mystery, perplexity, and heartbreak, and we do not know why. We do not have the answers, because we are not meant to have them. The answers are for God to give, and only He has the answers to our queries. Let God answer: the "why" belongs to Him. Let us trust Him and be still. God makes no mistakes.

Chapter Ten

What is Intuition?

Intuition is the ability to predict something you feel in your subconscious. It is a psychic phenomenon. There are two functions of the mind: one gives logical reasoning and the other provides sense perception. The latter is the one on the left side, providing logical thoughts, and the right side provides the right side of the brain with intuitive functions.

The right side of the brain gives you thoughts that just pop into your head. These thoughts come through intuition, without prior knowledge of where they are coming from. You simply feel and sense an immediate danger, so you retreat from the situation. This is your subconscious mind giving you a warning and recognizing the danger of the situation. With the key patterns of the dynamic situation, you make a steadfast decision to withdraw from the situation and, without conscious thought; the subconscious knows to move you to a safe place. This is your right-mind intuition. Such decision-making may come from earlier involvement and experiences, about which the data is stored in the subconscious mind. When a similar situation occurs, the subconscious mind automatically retrieves this data and sends it to the conscious mind, which moves you out of the dangerous situation. For example, you might pick up the energy of a person. From his or her bodily gestures, breathing, and tone of voice, you might sense a variety of cues giving you an indication. However, these subconscious phenomena, such as feelings, skills, knowledge, perceptions, habits, beliefs, and desires are unknown to the mind. We are aware of that the left side of the brain controls the right side, while the right side of the brain controls the left. When you concentrate on impulsive thoughts, giving them your full attention for ninety days, this will cause things to occur through your subconscious mind. The subconscious and the conscious mind work together, increasing the energy of thoughts, transforming them into your reality.

In reality we do not apply intuition as a reliable source in our daily activities. We tend to evaluate information based on accuracy, logic, the facts, and the clarity of our conclusions, as these have become dominant forces of our daily living.

When you realize the limitations of the conscious mind and choose to rely on the subliminal mind, you will appreciate the power of intuition. Everyone, in fact, has intuition. That is, until we allow our minds to take over and we forget how to use it. We can learn how to use it again, though.

You have feelings and senses. When your subconscious mind processes data and responds with an answer that seems to be out of the blue, you deny it. This is because this answer cannot be explained until later, after the events occur. The mental mind can never understand intuition, which is more powerful than the intellect. The intellectual part of your mind wants validity, but your intuition is absurd. When it tries to explain, things become difficult. Events you see in your intuition can still be possible, though, without causes. Our intellect might dismiss our experience with intuition. Those people who accept the existence of intuition, however, allow it to become their reality. It can be validated through a personal experience that is true. This is so vital to you.

Perhaps you have, at one time, experienced something that felt right and dismissed it, only later to discover that you should have trusted your intuition. The mind just cannot accept what is not logical. It is for this reason that intuition has been dismissed for centuries and is not accurately used in mainstream thinking.

Your feelings of intuition come, in fact, directly from your heart. When intuitive insights are detected, the electrical circuits near the heart are activated before the ones in the brain. This indicates that the heart plays an active part before the mind processes anything. You cannot always believe the five physical senses, but you can trust your heart, for it is there that intuition begins. Intuition shows us things that can save our lives. Our spirits have both external and internal perceptions. The external perception works through appearance, while the internal works through intuition. Although we may not know how intuition works, we do know that it is not limited to one's race, culture, educational background, geographical location, or religion. In other words, it works well for people of all ages. Anyone can apply the free gift of intuition through practice.

Chapter Eleven

Wheel of Fortune

Life is like a revolving wheel of fortune. You do not know your life's destination until it reveals itself. This is because there are visible and invisible forces that are in control and shape the Universe that governs us, above and below. Hence, it would be difficult for us to do things according to our hearts' desires. The moment we think of doing something, the next moment arises to challenge us, unless we have clarity of mind at that same moment.

One cannot resist or reject difficult situations: however, a person still has to face them and resolve them in the pain of this continuing creativity. One must think of all events as learning experiences. We are students who continue learning for life. Once a person accepts that he is a life-student, then this person's life possibilities are good, as all bad things are over.

Resisting anything that is within oneself will only bring more resistance, and that makes things more difficult to endure. We live in a dual world on Earth. Nothing can guarantee that it will transform or that its negative effects will stop and fade away.

One cannot get any positive results unless one understands oneself and sees that negative situations will soon be over. It is unnecessary to talk with others about an adverse situation. Others may not want to hear you talk.

Comparison is a form of psychological slavery. It is not wise to compare our situation with another's. It will complicate things and continue the captivity. If current events upset you, then it is your responsibility to find a way to turn the page: believe in yourself and change things.

Chapter Twelve

Yes, we are Empowered by God's spirit

Very often we say we cannot do something because it is too complicated and impractical to make it happen. However, we do not even try. We easily conclude that our abilities are limited due to a lack of resources. We rely on our belief system and learn from past experiences, which are stored in our subconscious minds. We head to an unsolved problem with a tied knot. Then, we give up even before we begin. It is true that, from a physical perspective, our abilities are limited to the five mortal senses. However, we can go beyond these limitations by delving deeply within our soul to ask for help. We are aware that our infinite soul resides within our mortal body and guides our incredible journey on Earth.

We think it would be nice if we could reach deep inside and talk to our soul, which is willing to do our bidding. In fact, our infinite soul is forever eager and ready to do things for us; however, we must invite its presence to assist us. In order to do so, we need to practice inward meditation to awaken and acknowledge the giant inside us. We need to talk to our soul as we talk to a friend. We have to respect and trust the unconscious part of us to help us, not only in times of difficulties and perplexities, but also in everything that happens in our lives. These events, as we perceive them, unfold when they are guided by our infinite soul. They come about much easier because our soul empowers us the moment we need to make right choices and big decisions.

Being guided by our soul, we should always see this moment as positive. In this way, we will not fall into negativity and into the hands of the dark force. As guided by the Infinite Being, we recognize our true nature: who we really are. Ultimately, we can do everything with love because we are a part of a Divine creation.

Who we really are in our soul can never be denied or separated by our thoughts in the conscious mind. Our Ego can bring in many negative thoughts to trick and limit us to believe it is unlikely we can fulfill our desires. The Ego insists we have only one life to live and that what we see is what we shall receive. In fact, we believe in God, yet edge Him out of our consciousness. We become disconnected from our creator and allow the Ego to take control of our daily activities.

The Ego insists that we should grab everything for ourselves and that others are our enemies and rivals to be defied and ignored. We should work harder to make more money and accumulate more possessions in this life because there is no next life. Meekness is unnecessary because it shows weakness and can easily be defeated by rivals. These egotistical thoughts continue into adulthood from childhood and are often integrated into our self-concept, current belief system, and also become part of our personality and character. You undoubtedly believe it is better to achieve and acquire more.

The truth is that we do not need to do a thing to validate our belief systems to prove that we are worthy and valuable. We have to do nothing but allow peace to flow through ourselves naturally. All things will take care of themselves. You simply let go, and let God guide your life, just as your heart, lungs, and blood vessels in your circulatory system work automatically. You don't need to worry about a thing. Let yourself be. There's no need to think big or set goals. Just follow and listen to your infinite soul that guides your daily activities.

Perhaps you are thinking it is unrealistic, but it is the truth that all things are caused by the power within bringing itself to the forefront. All things are caused by God working through you to get everything done.

Our belief system encourages us to do something and dismisses our belief that all things can be completed automatically. We are accountable for our achievements in everything we do. In school, we need to score higher grades to graduate with distinction, while at work we feel gratified with accomplishments. How successful we are depends upon how much money and how many acquisitions we possess. We evaluate our own success by comparing ourselves with others. We were taught that failure should not be in our dictionary. There should be no failure in our vocabulary; otherwise we cannot face friends, family, and ourselves. If we do not do well, we are labeled as a "failure." We cannot experience God and others in our own consciousness.

However, when we change our old belief systems and relinquish ourselves to our higher selves, things begin to change supernaturally. We no longer follow an anchor that is old and outdated; rather we choose to believe something solid within that can help us to grow and develop and to attain the life that we want to enjoy. When we surrender our lives to the Divine, we know that we have freedom that takes no mind away.

Now, who we really are cannot be interrupted by thoughts in our minds. We have 60,000 thoughts per day and two per second, so not all of them are positive and optimistic. Therefore, it is dangerous to listen to the Ego; instead we have a choice of listening to our higher selves. Every time we fail, it is as though we have failed as human beings and it feels as if we cannot face the world, as when we are sick and cannot perform our work to the required standard. We become a victim of mental depression, which causes a combination of physical, mental, emotional, spiritual, and psychological misalignments.

Ultimately, we no longer enjoy the outdoor activities we once did. These scenarios will only become true if we listen to the false self, our Ego.

I live and breathe within my higher self. I listen to my higher self, who guides me on what to do. I do everything according to the guidance of my higher self and replace desire with nothingness. With less desire in my mind, I will not be controlled by the Ego. Then, many amazing things spring up and come naturally to me.

In fact, we are human beings with a soul guiding us. We have everything in our possession, but our soul needs the right season to manifest itself in us. Think about when we design something originating from nothing. After that, we transform our thoughts into what we intend to do. Subsequently, we turn our intentions into acts of faith and take positive action. From this action, we will transform something into our actual reality. These are caused by God's spirit and we simply follow His invisible hand to do so.

By radically changing your cause to the invisible power of God's spirit, you have taken a step forward in your life and will change your life for the better. You are no longer stuck with your old belief system that caused you pain and many sleepless nights because you know that you are moving forward to the life you love and enjoy. This life is a life filled with success and happiness that you treasure, as you follow the guidance of your higher self.

For a while we listen to our authentic self, but then the Ego tries to ward off our awareness of our spiritual nature. Unconscious of its influence, we spend much time trying to win others' approval. We try to be a person who someone else wants us to be. We want to be that particular person, so we can gain power, talent, and appeal. However, if you listen to your higher self, you will be completely unaffected by these external judgments. If you follow false self-guidance, you will be miserably affected. This is how the false master lures you into misguiding your higher self.

When seeking approval is the guiding principle of your life, it's impossible to develop loving relationships with others. This is because we cannot abandon what we have. We cannot give love and respect to others when we have to find it for ourselves. Nevertheless, we are so judgmental of others. The Ego contributes to our constant state of confusion, fear, and unhappiness.

So, as we always seek to pursue approval ratings throughout our lives, we learn to please our parents, teachers, professors, or any other authority figures. This is done through ranking their opinions above our own. This process occurs day-by-day, month after month, or year after year, and often at the subconscious level. The results are based on the Ego-concept.

When we treasure others' opinion, we deny the wisdom that created us.

We fulfill the false-master's plans and prophecies. But, behold, we can transform this from relying on others to trusting our own higher self that directs us. We can have faith that God's spirit is always there and ready to help us.

The Ego's program encourages us to believe we are separated from our creator and everyone else. Just as it seems that when the water makes waves in the ocean, the water and the ocean are divided. But, when the waves return, the water and the ocean are once again united. Water is never separated from the ocean. The two are as one source.

Separation is the concept of the Ego. We are misguided and confused when we allow the Ego to convince us to fight, struggle, control others and win every competition. We must preserve our illusion of separateness. The belief of separation from God and everything has a long history. Our ancestors believed they were separated from the Divine infinite power.

Now is your chance to shift this old outdated belief to a contemporary one. Become aware that you are spiritually connected with everything including trees, animals, oceans and mountains. You are a divine being that dwells in God and breathes through God. God breathes in men then men have a living soul. The Universal Source is Divine, and you combined with it will bring joy and happiness. You will receive the assistance to fulfill your heart's desire.

The truth is that you have walked this life and many lives in the past. You are always connected with the higher spiritual being in the astral Universe. To say that you are alone is an illusion created by your mind. Everyone you met and will meet in your life is connected to you.

The idea that we are separated from each other is only an illusion subconsciously programmed by the Ego to confuse us. We are a part of this mysterious Universe and part of the whole. Like the organs in the body, which only seem to be separated, we are interconnected with each other. We need every organ in the mortal body to function and live well. Look at your fingers. It looks as if they are separated, but, in fact, all the blood vessels are connected inside, even though we may not see it. When you think of separation, it is just your mind not focusing on unification. It is focused on what is not connected instead of what you feel you are connected with. When the mind is calm and refocused and returns to the focal point, then the mind will agree to be united with the Oneness of the Source and will rests deeply to heal the core of your own being with one mind and one source. Your thoughts of solitude instantly dissolve into the all-powerful, the one source, the Mind of God, the Divine. The oneness is the treasure of this Universe that is all things: the omniscience of God.

We were united with the Source in the nothingness and, when we live on Earth, the mind experiences many pains and sorrows. Because we experience troubles alone, it makes us think that there is no one for us and that we are not united as we once were. However, your higher self can help you overcome this illusion of separation and become aware that there's more to life than fighting with each other. At the end, we realize that we actually fight our own shadow at the express wish of others.

We accept that God is actually dwelling in our hearts, both everywhere and nowhere. Then we know all is well. We feel the peace and calmness within. When everything is still and tranquil, we feel God's presence. God cannot emerge when we constantly fight with ourselves. We hear God talking to us in silence and stillness and feel inner peace.

There were times when the Ego had no influence on us. During the waking hours of consciousness, we are under the influence and direction of the Ego to do things that are unthought-of and possibly reckless. We do things without consideration for the welfare of others. However, when we yearn for change, we begin to search for the reason for our existence. We move to something concrete. We move into the core of our soul to find purpose and meaning in life, rather than continue to listen to the Ego and feel we have no existence. The soul guides us back to where we came from, toward a fulfilling life satisfied with purpose. The soul guides us toward the right path, which is full of meaning and purpose. We are guided in a direction more valuable than any concern for other things. We make a commitment to life rather than sabotage our lives in a harmful way. We are here so that we may head towards a more meaningful and purposeful life.

We do not need the world to be in our hands to prove we are capable of doing powerful things. What good would it be if we gained everything but subsequently lost our soul? King Salomon cries out to God to save his life and soul. The best strategy is to relinquish ourselves to God and let Him do our bidding without struggle, so that we may achieve things at all costs. We attain the wondrous situation of accomplishing more, and we ultimately treasure the significance of life.

Chapter Thirteen

Peace in Your Mind

How do you achieve peace in your mind? It is perhaps a question that you ask yourself frequently. Most of the time, you are trying to achieve inner peace and tranquility in your life so you can relax and accomplish remarkable things for yourself and others. However, do you know that both internal and external tranquility must be balanced, so you can attain the greater peacefulness you desire in your life? One pillar, with no support, will fall easily, but two pillars can support each other and can withstand any external forces. This makes life more relaxing and creates a feeling of peace and tranquility.

Your innate power has no desire, but it will assist you in achieving anything you desire so you may live a better quality of life. Because you want to have a higher quality of life, you have not stopped desiring many things, and you want to be satisfied and have instant bliss and happiness.

A longing for things is not bad. However, it creates a false feeling of scarcity and makes you think you need to accumulate more. There is nothing wrong with making more money so you can pay your bills, go on vacation, buy a house and live better; however, that desire in your mind is not your ultimate goal that drives your life's purpose. It is not your true mission and reason for existence.

Perhaps you should consider taking a step backwards and contemplating what you truly desire in life. Observe what you have already achieved in the here and now. What have you created within your dimension of consciousness? It might be a feeling you can use instantly for yourself. Think about who is actually in control of your mind.

In fact, you are the master of your own domain. You control the ups and downs of every stage of your life. You should possibly focus less on gathering more things in the physical world: instead, hold on to the nature of your inner spirit that is your higher self. Be present to get the maximum energy, the consciousness and spirit of your powerful Inner Being, which is capable of manifesting everything that you truly are.

To find peace, you have to start somewhere, but then you reach nowhere. You do not have to go anywhere to find serenity, because you might seek it in the wrong place. Forget about finding the way; you are already there. All you need to do is tap into the inner feeling that dwells within, a feeling that creates the source of energy, creativity, love, and peace.

If you believe that what you are going to receive is real, it will become your reality. If you disbelieve, your uncertainty is also real. Therefore, what you believe and disbelieve are determined by you in your mind. It is best not to let doubt sink in. You will win everything that your heart desires.

More importantly, you will emerge at the right time, in the right place. The true objective in life is not to prove ourselves, but rather to discover the truth, come what may. What you are now experiencing is a healing touch to your soul and a continuation of your walk on your spiritual journey through to its end. Experience it and enjoy it, and then you will gain it all. You will know the truth, that this is all part of this beautiful journey on earth.

Chapter Fourteen

Peace and Tranquility

What is peace? Where do we find peace? Peace occurs when you recognize that you are infinite and capable of living a spiritual life: you find peace within. You can't find peace anywhere in the external world. People often spend time traveling the world, hoping to find a peaceful place to dwell, but they are always disappointed with what they find. They realize that the physical world is not equipped for absolute peace. In fact, they don't realize that the only place they can find eternal peace is within. They have been searching in the wrong place, and therefore they can never find the results that they are looking for. The peaceful mind is always within and not far away. As soon as you recognize that peace is found within, then you start perceiving the eternal light that comes to you from the nothingness and that light fills you with peace and tranquility.

Peace is achieved through an inner state of mind that extends to external consciousness, as projected in this material world. This spiritual peace is God's infinite love for you. God gives power to you that open up your heart to His guidance.

When we spend a lot of time on average things, sometimes we rely on the training that we have had, but somehow events still happen and we don't know what to do. The best action is to be motionless and still. You should leave that screen that doesn't speak to you, so you can observe what a seer has seen. Then everything will be clear in front of you. However, sometimes you might wish that you had fewer activities in your mind. At that point, it is wise to listen to your heart and resist the temptation to rush. Empty your thoughts from your mind and let nature guide your mind to where it needs be.

Be conscious of how you think in different situations and try to keep a record of your thoughts. This might be difficult when many things are happening at the same time. When you don't know what to do, know that the best action is stillness. Pay attention to how physical stress and your emotions affect your mind and be aware that you are vulnerable during times when you are tired, hungry, or agitated. Consider what you have been reading, watching, and listening to. Does it bring you any inner bliss or joy? If not, why you are continuing to give it your attention? Ask the Inner Source to help you select better readings, sounds, visions, and activities to feed your mind. Stop going to places or meeting with people that are a bad influence on you or lead you to unhealthy thoughts. You should spend time solidity and purify your mind with thoughtlessness. Your Inner Source can offer you greater power of positive thinking and peace. Believe that the way you think will influence your actions. You should practice emptying your mind and letting the energy guide your thoughts. Ask God to help you absorb the truth in His word so He can begin to transform your life. The best way to achieve peace and harmony is to be unified with God.

When you feel that your life is exhausted and that there is nothing worth living for, then you should turn to a sacred place for help without further delay. The silence of a sacred secret place is the only place that can offer you help. It is a place where you can seek peace, inner bliss, and tranquility. The Inner Source will not reject you: in this way, it is unlike the external world that discriminates. When you acknowledge the Inner Source and are united with the spirit, you live a spiritual life and you will transform yourself towards joy. Life will never be the same again.

When you live a spiritual life with spiritual peace, then you recognize that any idea, plan, or purpose that you hold in your mind will bring you tranquility. Your thoughts become more attentive and active in the now. You are concerned only with the now. You always know that the moment is filled with tranquility and peace because you have opened yourself to the Source's inflow: all your thoughts are healthy, constructive, and productive and you continue to live life with meaning.

The sooner you come to the realization of your oneness, the sooner you no longer fear that external forces can affect you. You know the external factors are there, but you can quickly return to your senses and you are consciously aware that things will be resolved soon. Since the external chaos does not affect you, you will not be upset for the whole day. You have the power to see through the storm and are able to stand calm even when lightening strikes. When we have the Inner Source within us, nothing can disturb our harmony and peace, especially when we are truthful in every aspect of our lives. The Source unites us and governs the Universe: this power will always prevail and, in the end, we will always have tranquility and silence.

In the past, you thought you had attained enduring peace, but then something occurred that disturbed your mind, so you were upset by the chaos of external events. We are emotional individuals and it is very easy to be affected by the external factors that cause fear and turmoil in our minds. You ask yourself what to do, but you have lost your sense of balance. Your mind starts to create many upsetting thoughts and you are infused with negative vibrations. You can't think of a solution, and you feel helpless and powerless. You wish that you could crack the code and dissolve the problem. You realize that there will be an extraordinary impact on your life, at least for a short period of time. However, when you open your mind to look for a solution, then it will come to you. If your mind is closed, then you can't receive help, because the Source won't interrupt your life without invitation. Then you begin to sense the memorizing influence that you have on your surroundings: on different people, and on events. Results and changes that you have been longing for ages now suddenly occur in the present and you deserve them.

In the natural world, after the storm passes and the trees return to their natural state, the trees are in harmony with nature again. But, in your mind, you wish for peace: however, it seems that peace doesn't want to settle within you. The peace that you have inside you is being compromised through the news that just arrived by email. However, you heard a voice speaking to you, telling you to relax: a great wave of renewal, which shall bring with it hope for a better future, is on the horizon for you. You pause for a moment, and then you start to feel the calming energy within: the storms have withdrawn and only peace remains. The voice continues that you should do anything to stay attentive. You must not let external events bother you or overpower you: your problem could just disappear by the grace of an instant-produced miracle. If you let the nuisance overwhelm you, then your whole day will be affected and you will be disharmonized by the Ego. You must approach these undesired feelings as calmly as possible so that you can be in a state of consciousness: gradually, all negative emotions will fade away. The voice carries on, saying that you must relax and have a lucid mind. You must face the problem and surmount it. You must face the problem and be aware of it every moment. Once you deal with it, then you don't have to bargain with negative emotions again! They can't disturb you or bring discontentment to you because you will pass from a state of an effective life of solitude to the one surrounded by people who appreciate, love and respect you. You will pass from a state of misfortune and incessant trouble and ever mounting worry to one of bliss. In fact, you stop worrying about how things will turn out, as the problems resolve by themselves. Since there's always a light at the end of the tunnel, you will find it much easier to manifest something that you wish for right before your eyes.

Let the awareness that God has given to you become your inner wisdom. If you do this, then you can make transformational changes immediately via the peace and consciousness of God's omnipresence. But I urge you to remain and see it for yourself.

Chapter Fifteen

Hope

Life involves choice, that is full of hope for infinite expectations. You can refine your hope for joy and happiness and see things beautifully, but you must believe you deserve it. You must view your current situation through the good side of the lens. If you always examine your life from a negative perspective, it will always be full of clutter and chaos. However, if you allow yourself to have a positive outlook on life, beautiful, gorgeous, and tremendous things will enter your life. You will be surprised at how your life becomes enlightened with shininess and hope.

Hope is embraced with grace, faith, and love. God shows us grace and love because He is peaceful and merciful. Things that seem impossible become possible with the grace of God, even if you do not believe you deserve them. God said, "I will allow you to have whatever you hope for. Believe in it because you deserve it." Your faith gives you an opportunity to trust that God is loving and that He will bless you every day. It is God's love that you receive everything your heart hopes for and you believe that you can get it and you deserve it. Through His compassion, kindness, and mercy, God wants to heal all your illnesses so that you can live well again.

Your troubles and problems will cease when you believe in God. Life is a choice you make, and it allows you to continue to have hope, which will allow you to see the rainbow at the end of the rainstorm. Your disorders and unfortunate conditions will be washed away when you have hope. You will remember the good things, and all your negative thoughts will fade away. Hence, despite what happens in your life, you should never surrender hope, because God is hope. He resides above, beside, behind, and within you to fulfill all of your needs. As you ask, so you should receive. Trust in God with tremendous faith to receive the remarkable hope of success and abundance that you expect every day.

Chapter Sixteen

Human Desire

The modern world seems chaotic, including financial crises, battles within countries, struggles to maintain power, and poverty. It is like a ball rolling downhill that cannot be stopped until it reaches a dead-end. However, there is no foreseeable destination. You might wonder if your conscious self would listen to your Inner Source, you would have the answers to many of your troubles.

We can overcome many of our current disorder and reducing the chaos by working within that we change without. What stops us from preventing the continuation of these crises and using our abilities to solve global problems, such as economic difficulties and conflict between countries?

The answer is one remarkably easy word – greed. It is easy to understand how this concept can cause many problems in the world today.

People have questioned the impact of human desire from the time of the Roman Empire to the present day. However, our lives are affected by more than greed. When combined with jealousy, greed becomes the most poisonous component of today's society.

Greed and jealousy have a long history and do not merely occur by accident. Thus, you might ask from where jealousy originates. It results from a person's eagerness and desire. For example, when your desires have not been met, you might become jealous if you see that your neighbor has many things you do not have. However, someone with ample wealth who lives across the country will not bother you because you do not see him every day.

However, you might see your neighbor almost daily and that can make you wonder why you cannot have what he has. Your mind might lead you to think that you are more sensible than him, and so you should have more of everything. But, the question is, can you afford to have what he has? Possibly you might not be able to afford to buy the objects that he has accumulated so far, because we are unique individuals. Everybody's circumstances are different. So, with that said, there is nothing to be jealous about. Greed and envy will only bring hatred that could subsequently cause many unhappy occurrences, such as turning friends into enemies, conflicts arising and the possibility of war between countries. These problems just keep growing, without any apparent solution.

We allow the dark force to control our minds and cause us to do negative things to others. We have forgotten our main purpose in life and the reason that God sent us here. We have discarded our original infinite state, which was filled with love and allowed the Ego-mind to take control and dictate our lives for us. We do what this false self tells us to do. All we care for and are concerned about is ourselves and we view others as rivals and enemies. Hence, the Ego-mind believes that we should eliminate our rivals in order to win this competition and destroy our enemies to take what they have and we are anxious to receive. Our mind's desires make things appear not to be right and we view them as unjust. Our entire lives can change and many evil things can happen. We need to cast away all of the evil, negative thoughts and replace them with positive desires. We should never allow the Ego-mind to take control of our lives.

We need to apply our great wisdom in an intelligent way and not act with a jealous and greedy mind. We need successfully to follow the Universal Laws of Nature, which allow things to be set before us that do not bring us harm.

Our wisdom and intelligence come from the consciousness of the Universal Source and do not live in the shadow of our Ego-mind, which has no discipline. When the mind is out of control, we find many horrible, thoughtless ways to attain whatever we want to accomplish, refusing to think about how our actions can harm others. The mind can even fabricate falsities so we can defeat our rivals. The more we act on negative thoughts, the more we distance ourselves from our original state of Infinite Being and are separate from the Oneness Source, the purpose and meaning of our mission, and our destiny. We cling to ambition.

There is nothing wrong with being ambitious, but do it in a positive way; humbly help others to succeed instead of hurting others on your path to success. Your accomplishments will never be great if you harm others; by doing so, you will definitely see results, but you will gain a bad reputation.

Therefore, you should examine your actions before you perform them. Considering the consequences two or three times before you take action makes a huge difference.

This also reminds you that every action you take could cause harm to others and you should stop and practice self-control and mindfulness in order to avoid any possible conflict arising from your reckless actions. When your life is run by your Ego-mind, false belief and fear can rule and you only do what you have been told to do and nothing beyond that. The option for self-directed action is non-existent for blind followers and the obedient. Therefore, practice moderation, flexibility and meekness when making pronouncements about how you want to do things.

The best possible answer to our problems is to practice virtue. When you get into the habit, each and every day, of giving something away or sending a prayer to bless this world for peace, you will achieve positive feelings of peaceful contentment attained both inside and outside. This is because internal and external circumstances must be balanced before you can know, or feels, the peace and tranquility within your soul. Your calmness and inner emotions and feelings will also indicate that you are aligned with the Oneness of the Source. Because you show joy and happiness in your face, people will know that you are happy.

Change the thoughts in your mind by moderating your Ego. Seeing yourself as a being who gives, rather than to get endlessly, and only lives on what is needed, you will begin to see that your purpose has moved so that it is aligned with the Source's consciousness and not with the Ego's directives. When you acquire the only resource you need, you will gain virtue. This is the key to long-lasting success and the only vision that will stand in your life.

Chapter Seventeen

Forgiveness

As Jesus was dying on the cross, being crucified by the Romans, he cried out to God, "Father, forgive those who have hurt me." In our own lives, we have many unhappy and painful experiences, but how do we erase the pain and become healed after those awful events? We don't want to carry those burdens with us throughout our lives. Those tragic events are like nightmares that stalk us in our subconscious mind, day in and day out. When we are sleeping, our memories recur in our dreams, resulting in a restless sleep that eventually affects our mortal health and well-being.

However, through forgiveness, we can eliminate those unwanted events from repeating throughout our lives. Forgiveness will open a flood-gate of relief by helping us to eliminate things and events we want to put behind us, but not suppress within us. Negative emotions, such as anger, frustration, hatred, jealousy, envy, fear and worry, that we have stored in our minds, cause us pain and sorrow and never seem to go away.

When we are hurt by someone, we should forgive them and ask for blessings for that person. In return, the Universe will bless us. The Universe knows we no longer carry the hatred within us; therefore we deserve a blessing. We should do unto others what we want others to do unto us.

In other words, when we forgive others, we actually forgive ourselves. We forgive that we drove ourselves into such unforgettable events subconsciously, without thorough thought. The sooner we let go of past events, the sooner we lighten the burden on our shoulders. We have to accept that certain past events were beyond our control and are not our fault. They have already been experienced and the sooner we forgive, the sooner everything will return to normal. This is a dual concept that we have adopted on Earth.

All things come with positive and negative consequences. The sooner we experience the negative, the sooner the positive will emerge, because no tragic events last forever. When we experience positive events, we are filled with joy and happiness and all negativity fades away. Hence, when we forgive others and bless them, we bless ourselves. All negative things can be forgotten and put behind us: there is no need to mention them again. Positive events allow us to be inspired. When we hear God's voice speaking to us in silence, we ultimately remember our original nature as Infinite Beings who are full of love. God dwells within us, and we live and breathe through God. Our life is illuminated by God. We understand God is always forgiving, and with His unconditional love we no longer feel pain inside, but are combined to attain joy and happiness, so we can carry on and complete all His works and missions on Earth.

Chapter Eighteen

Liberate Yourself and Relinquish Yourself to the Force of Nature

When you live a life filled with lies and deception, you cannot determine what your reality is; you merely act. Indeed, you are never alone, especially when you are surrounded by negative, discouraging and opposing influences, feeling sorry for yourself and not knowing how to escape from that dark tunnel. You give up, but continue to dive deeper into the severe pain until you cannot take anymore and, eventually, you close the curtains of your life.

Whatever confuses you, can you be selfish and take your own compulsive behavior, suffering, frustration, sadness and misery and toss it at others? In other words, when you take your own pain and insanity casts it at others, so that innocent people have to suffer with you are not just. You are doing thing which has made no sense of what may be considered nonsense.

You must be aware of that: no matter how painful and sorrowful your life is, you have no right to do so. You can celebrate any moment of your life, but never do things maliciously to other people. Get the inspiration and guidance for your life through the Universal Source. You must believe, whatever your troubles, no matter how large they might seem, that they can be resolved in a peaceful way. Listen to your heart and soul in your quiet time and think the power of your choice.

In order to melt away your problems, you must know exactly and for certain what you desire in life. Merely knowing or letting go what you don't want in life is not enough to eliminate your sorrows and emotional pains. Dropping one bad habit, only to pick up another, does not end the trouble but only drives you into another dead-end with no exit. You are simply searching for another excuse and manage to put the problem on hold, or so you think: yet the problem remains unsolved.

The truth is that letting go is not that hard. It is about the fact that all is natural. It is as natural for you and as it is the same principle of the old palm tree. When the wind blows, the old palm tree bends slightly, standing up again when the wind stops. It does not force its own weight against nature, because it does not always need to win. Give something to yourself by not pushing it; just wait a little bit longer and stop interfere the nature causes. When you lighten your burden, you will continue to be productive, wealthy, and rich in the eyes of others. Swap your burdens with an internal assertion that allows you to access the Source. Affirm now, "I am a part of the Universal Source. I am sure that I am able to support myself, those around me, and the world. I retreat into silence, knowing that all is taken care of by the Divine Light."

When the fruit matures, it naturally falls to the ground rather than being forced off the tree. No strange force is necessary. Natural forces are willing to act on its own without waiting for you to think about how to do something if you are unable to do it yourself. You need to break focus, allow calm, quiet, and hope to flow through and let go of sadness, regret, anxiety, fear, and negative thoughts. You need to think more clearly. You will hear the inner voice inside giving you the guidance you need.

When you follow the power of letting go, you will not have to fight and disagree with it. You will know all is well and know exactly what needs to be dropped, and will never look back. Life moves on without strife and allows for flexibility. It is the higher consciousness of the Infinite Self that is acting when you know you are in the energy field and launch your new life: this is the rise of a new nature. You have no need to hold onto any old thoughts, people, or events because you already have everything. You live in consciousness, in the here and now, which allows you to live wholly rather than be dominated.

Chapter Nineteen

Healing Heart

I have been to many places and gone through my share of tough times and misery. Let me sing this song to you express my sorrows and regret over not listening to you. Now, I no longer need to be on the stage or in the spotlight and I no longer need applause. I know that you and I, together, would be enough for me to feel happy and joyful and live a healthier life.

There are some areas in my life in which I feel powerless and I don't know how to resolve that. However, I refused to listen to you and walked on my own path. Now, I turn around, change the direction I am facing, and see a bigger picture. Although the unwilling world may not change, as I myself change, everything has transformed to become a much better and clearer picture. My choice changes the relationship between me and the world that I am facing.

Ultimately, I have found the relationship that is—and always has been—within me. I guess I already knew that. This realization will open the doors to the higher consciousness of awakening that I wish to begin and that will enable me to engage in true prayer: one true relationship with God to help me open my inner eyes to see better than before. Once I was blind, and was kept in spiritual unconsciousness. I believe in the higher power of God, who wants to develop an intimate relationship with me. He wants me to be aware of His presence within me and see that I am living within Him. I think for a moment and then I relinquish all my impulses and desires to the supreme power of God, for He knows what is best for me even before I pray to Him. He always knew all of my needs without my having to express them to Him. This is because

He understands me better than I know myself. Some may reject me, but He will never turn me down. I then know I should invest in something that I can depend on; as I awaken to this, I know how to pray to help me to do what is right for me. It is at this point, as my broken heart heals, that I indeed long for a new level of relationship with the Oneness, the Source of the Universe.

Chapter Twenty

The Power of Thought

You are a free spirit: say it to yourself in the next ten minutes or so. You are not bound by any earthly actions or thoughts that force you to experience negative emotions and low vibrations. When you connected your thoughts with the spirit, you might have dwelt in the higher vibrational energy thought field. You stay in the higher frequency and always feeling good. You no longer live with the illusion of fear, or feel anxious, or constantly doubt and are indecisive in life. However, take courage and go deeper connect with the Divine spirit, activate the inner code lie within your soul, you will be amazed at the tremendous power you made to yourself.

So, you search for this Divine one and hope that you are connecting to it. Again and again you look around and you do not have a clue where and how to hook up. You stand on your feet and hear the quiet voice that spoke to you. But, then the voice turned silent. You decide to search and hope to find out. You look around the external world but cannot get results. You did not realize the spirit that seems to speak to you is within. The spirit is waiting to connect with you, enthralled in bliss. A flash is illuminated in your soul. Your spiritual heart is wide open with joy and you know the way to connect with the spirit is through the activation of the power within. The connection you have been longing for is lying inside you. You embrace it with happiness and know your own soul. With joy and bliss you now know the love of your life is and always has been in you. You feel it stand by you. Your life shines upon by the spirit, through feeling its glorious orb through day and night. You see beauty everywhere; you see it through the spirit. You know thou art of God and God dwells in you, guides and empowers your life.

Your thoughts are now navigated by your own spirit. Since you are guarded by the spirit, you no longer travel in the lower vibrations, with anxiety and doubt and indecision. It eliminated the karmic effect that connects you and gets back to you. You no longer need to go through strange events and circumstances in strange and unusual ways that cause you pain and suffering and are based on certain experiences and past actions.

However, the karmic effects are not types of punishment for you, but they let you experience certain emotions to complete that part of your life and lesson in the best way through a change in your thought and that changes your fate.

When you think through the assistance given by your spirit, you can change chaotic events and the bad karma that might get back to you. You raise the vibration by using the high energy in your mind that changes your karmic debts to zero. You stop yourself from associating with negative karma: all this is expressed in a short period of time. The Karmic law will not bother you if you have higher vibrations in your thought and always dwell in the higher energy thought field.

The reason you no longer are bound by Karmic law is because you live in the spirit and have thoughts as the spirit. Hence, your thought always connects to the Divine one and to your real self. You are functioning in the higher consciousness world rather than when you are at a low frequency. When you are at a high vibration, you change your direction and with it change everything. You are absolutely free from karma and anything that you do not desire or no longer want to embrace. You live as a new you only when you connect your thoughts to the spirit that changes your life.

However, there are things you will never be able to transform; then it is better not to struggle with your thought energy to change them. You can choose to embrace them and cease from resistant thoughts. You will discover the day when you do not resist forceful changes in everything. Then, all things become more tolerable in that latent energy, which causes all change. You can make transformational changes through higher vibrations in your mind and a connection to the spirit. Spirit is the one influence that causes all changes in your life. So, if you want to change, meditate on the spirit and ask the spirit to help you to transform your life. Embrace your own spirit and every morning acknowledge you are doing fine, even though your current situation is not that amazing, but the spirit knows and will fix your life to become more durable and loveable. You must know that you change by changing your vibrations to the higher energy thought field and by asking that you be connected to the spirit and to your higher infinite self and also by always observing and obeying the law of nature. Do not force anything to happen: you will get frustrated. It is like trying to force summer to become winter: it is not going to happen. Observe everything that changes and the thing that causes change, which accomplishes all effects. Monitor the thoughts in your mind without wavering; stay still and silent. All negative thoughts will erode when you can emerge from the upheaval into stillness. If you transcend the negative with your positive thoughts, then, when it merges with peace, the negative energy might have diminished and so can no longer bother you. You must remember the spirit inside you will never change, even if you have done wrong in the external world. The reality is to set your mind to God and get closer to God and then you discover its essence.

The Divine is the absolute, the pure formless spirit from which creation and manifestation arise. The Divine was, is and will be the same yesterday, today and tomorrow. The Divine hates no one nor holds anyone dear. Those who worship God's spirit with devotion live in God and God lives in them.

Here is a simple question you may wish to contemplate: can you live without being influenced by your own thought? You will realize that you live thoughtlessly for a day, but this can also persist for a year, or even for your entire life, and you will not be affected by your own thoughts. At first you may find it impossible or difficult, but it is probable and possible.

Thoughts are powerful, but they are imaginary and make-believe. Your real self in you is genuine, absolute and pure. When you stop thinking, the mind cannot bring in any negative thoughts to fool you. If you really need to think, then allow your energy to move upwards towards the heart and to the center of your eyebrows. You will discover something that is pure in its nature. The purpose is to allow the purity and nature to flow without hindrance. Let the energy of your thought be determined by nature so it flows rather than being controlled and decided by its environment. For, it is unambiguous by the difficult situation you are in, your thoughts flow downwards and are misaligned with the spirit. So, it is associated with your conscious mind and body, and that is not really what you want.

Take a look at your daily activities: you are always connected with your environment, the places and the people with whom you make constant contact. They all have a profound influence on you and that makes you moody and sometimes you cannot do things right and follow your heart. The books that you read, the movies that you watch and the people you associate with all influence your thoughts and decision-making, even though you try to observe and monitor your thoughts. Yet you still cannot be objective: you might feel that you choose your thoughts but, in fact, you are using someone else's decisions and you just execute or struggle with them. You should choose your thoughts, but not associate yourself with them. Once you have your goal in the form of thoughts, then let it go and let nature take its course and manifest it for you. You then allow your energy to attract the right intentions and to seek an appropriate environment for your energy to help you to fulfill your desire's impulses.

Remember, do not let your mind wander, as that causes your energy to flow downwards. When your energy is pure and your mind is clear, your energy travels upwards towards the center of your heart. You are in alignment with your spirit. Your mind stops wandering and you have harnessed the mind to work with you. When your mind and heart is in alignment, you might have purity of mind and the energy can begin to go upwards and your mind can associate with your spirit: the thoughts left in the mind are purified and filtered and are now driven by the spirit. Your mind, thoughts and spirit are in alignment: hence, whatever you thought about will transform into reality. Your whole life will change and will not be subjected to external influences. You will feel a sense of calmness and completeness associated with your spirit. To get things right in your life, you simply allow your energy to flow upwards towards the spirit. Remember your physical weaknesses as you lean towards the ideal of the spirit's connection so that you create the conditions for increasing positive vibrations in the mind. As the vibration of your mind arises, your thought energy starts to change to yield all positive thoughts and echo back to you with no negative effects. The momentum of your thought begins to take form and be concrete and finally comes into the reality of your life. When this happens you know you live and you worry less and love constantly to connect your thoughts to the spirit. You are connected to God's spirit and always allow all your thoughts to travel upwards towards the Divine. Other things are secondary. You remind yourself of this when your energy is down and you steadfastly reverse back up towards the ideal of the Divine connection: you begin to feel your energy traveling upwards to the center of your heart and spirit. You must remain calm even in the midst of a crisis. Your thoughts will move away from things that attempt to influence them. You will feel joy arise from within. You can move your thought energy upwards to your heart through daily practice. You will attain all positive thoughts if your intention is pure and get results.

Our ability to carve an image in our minds in order to manifest what we want in the external world is a reality for everyone. Yet, as if it created reality for everyone, then why I am not creating my own reality? Before you can do that you are probably aware that, in our everyday activities, we have come across different realities and experiences. It is neither known nor unknown to us what might prevent us from translating our desires into actuality. These factors can occur during a day's activity: some days you have high energy levels, you did not get stuck in traffic and your boss praised you at work, then you feel peace and harmony with love inside. Some days, however, you feel low, with no energy and you have an argument with your significant other at night and you do not have a good dinner.

In fact, these obstacles can be created in the intellect through varied internal and external factors. For example, you constantly think something might happen to harm you; you believe the troublesome mountain of fear has surrendered and is next to you. Then you subconsciously align with those negative thoughts and feelings that tell you the pain can take place at any moment. You have forgotten what's true and you have distanced yourself from your actual reality. In fact, each moment you create is real if you believe... When you rush through any moment of life, you do so without thinking or being mindful that you might have inherited negative possibilities without seeing their true appearance. The only solution to this unreal reality is to awaken and to be at one with your higher consciousness. Return to your source and beginning that has and always will be there for you to assist you so that you can perceive better than all that you can see now.

Your ability to visualize images through the power of thought originated from the Universe Source. The thought enters you from the nothingness of the void. I know you will ask, "If the material world is enormous barrier, then why do we need it? Why cannot we just keep to the spirit world, as that would make matters easier for us, since we could think and be in control of the physical world without interruption?" You must be consciously aware that God created this material world to make life easier for us, not to complicate things. Everything creates a need to develop a common order before each object transforms into pure substance. Simply put, you cannot get a PhD without getting a Master of Arts, unless it is under special circumstances. It is so in the rest of nature: everything must understand the system before it can transform into a real equivalent. There is no obstacle walking on it. You see a picture in the mind's eye flowing through you that transcends to the Divine Universe. In the beginning, the image has no power unless it is directly aligned in vibrational harmony with the Source. You must continue to maintain that vision and see your image has transformed into a form from formlessness. The power that gives rise to your desire is the Divine, and you are connected together to manifest this impulse. It is the standard response to your thought that the Divine will make your order enter so your dream turns into reality, but the task is not completed until it has been manifested. Nothing can prevent you from getting your desires unless you derail, and change your mind. Then, the Universe did not know what to send you, and the result will be quite different from your original form.

Let's say the Universal Mind is the central point of production and branches out millions or trillions of sub-branches and divisions. You are one of the sub-branches: when trouble occurs you check your own branches first before looking further at the headquarters. The same principle applies to visualizing an image flowing through you. It transcends into the Universe and there is nothing unusual about it, since we all have known it. The problem is that you did not get what you wanted after projecting your item to the Universe for some time. You thought this Universal Law of Magnetic Energy should work, but it did not go well. You decide to investigate it in further detail. Firstly, you need to look into your own branch and find out what causes the problem. What is your original desire that you want to get? Did you think, "Meditate, and listen to your Inner Source to confirm what you need to accomplish from this creative goal?" Check if your goal applied to yourself alone. You cannot direct power at someone else or for someone unless they agree with what you do. Did you sit in a quiet room by yourself and were you undisturbed. Did you use breathing exercises and the complete relaxation of your whole body, so that you did not feel stressed? Did you envision a clear picture with an image, so you could understand what you would get? Did you add emotions to your visualized image? Did you spend time and practice with it every day? Did you carry on with the power of faith and maintain positive thoughts and feelings? When you experienced negative or not so happy thoughts, did you replace them with optimistic thoughts immediately? Keep an open-mind so that you know everything is OK. Did you express appreciation to the Universe for what you are going to receive? Did you change your thinking while you continued projecting the image to the Universe? After you have checked all the above, properly, you will know the reason why you did not get your desire. The Source grants you everything, and never fails you: but only if you ask, shall you receive.

Chapter Twenty-one

Living in the World of Illusion

What we know about the outside world has been conveyed to us by means of our five senses: what our eyes can see, our ears can hear, our nose can smell, our hands can touch and feel, and our tongue can taste. We are limited to these senses. Everything we hold, smell, listens to, and see in the outside world is merely an electrical signal in our minds; for example, we can see an eagle flying in the sky. In reality, this perception is not in the outside world but it is an electrical signal in our minds. However, if the sight nerve traveling to the brain is disconnected, we do not see the eagle again. It is an electrical signal translated by the brain.

The outside world is an illusion. Its existence is an image translated in our minds. When the electrical nerve signal is disconnected, then we cannot see it, and the outside world disappears from us. Our world is like a hologram: just exceptionally vivid and solid. This happens when we receive a signal in our brains that tells us that we see the material world. However, it would be ridiculous to say it is not real, or it is not there. Everything we hear is echoed back to us. It is a vibration from the empty void. The sound you hear is the electrical signal you get from the brain, it shifts into a sound wave so you can hear.

Similarly, anything you see as O.K. or inadequate, happy or sad, all such thoughts can evaporate into emptiness and leave no trail, so you retrieve a memory or you see a bird flying in the sky. For example, you are watching TV in a room: in fact, however, the room is in your brain. When electrical signals in the brain about the room are blocked, the room disappears. Therefore, all you see is a vivid desire and that seems to look real. It continues to be there and then suddenly it is not there. When the signal in the brain is reconnected again, then the image emerges again.

Let me explain that a lucid dream that emerges in young child's subconscious mind is actually real. In their world, they like to imagine things that are not so convincing to us, but true to them. However, they see these things to be as real as holding an object in their hands, and they can play by themselves by imagining things and have plenty of fun: they seem to exist in a different dimension and to be out of touch. It is all so solid and real for them. Then, all of a sudden, they stop it and fantasy ceases. It is just vivid imagination in the mind's experience of the external world, through the power of thought.

This is the way you experience and cultivate meditation: to relax so that the whole atmosphere of your relaxation just starts to come to you. However, how things are cannot be taught, as no one can give you that experience. You simply must undergo it and practice achieving it yourself. It is you who want to accomplish things and gain enlightenment, but you must try to practice yourself. For instance, you are in a boat and you need a push to cross the river to the other side. However, without that effort you will never get to solid ground. Enlightenment is the end of suffering. You need to be in the present and find it out for yourself. Your mind must be still in order to achieve this goal. Then, through meditation, you understand your own soul, and stay in that internal state of conscious realization that is enlightenment.

Remember all things are an enchantment in the external world. You recognize the difference between pleasant or unpleasant feelings in the mind, and are careful not to walk on their battleground. In fact, parts of ourselves are honest and parts are evil, and parts of ourselves are joyful and happy.

The reality is that, for millions of years, good and evil have been at war with each other. This fight will never cease and still exists in reality. They oppose each other. It is a sign that we observe with our eyes and mind until we cancel it, moving into a totally new dimension of experience, when we live in the world of illusion.

Living in the world of illusion helps you to understand that everything co-exists. All things that are right or wrong are in your mind as thoughts. You are taking in and transcending them out to the external world. When you train your mind to recognize this, it leads you realize that the opposite must admit of co-existence. They are fighting with each other. Everything consists of positive and negative so that things can continue to grow and evolve. If there is no negative, then the outside world will have problems and cease growing because no conscious creation is needed. Therefore, it is not necessary to remove the opposite, simply be vigilant and alert to its activity.

You must be aware that no matter how compassionate you are in your character, you will still find someone claiming otherwise. Imagine that you strive to eliminate certain things but, in a while, they come back again. You open your mind, accept and face them. The sooner you soften to everything and are open to accept whatever occurs, the sooner everything just gets better. You realize you do not need to fight anymore, and everything transforms into your impulses. You do not need to convert goodness or evil anymore: you let the world speak for itself. You start to take a fair look at the problem and become mindful, and your compassionate heart fills you with hope and expectation. You begin to see clearly, fearlessly and non-judgmentally. When this happens, the world we dwell in will translate by itself. You begin to enjoy the world you live in very much. You thought it was a tranquil peaceful place, and you were living in a world of illusion. You live now with more curiosity than fear. It is the way to enjoy living.

Chapter Twenty-two

The Pressure Today...

The pressure today is on how we can avoid any frustrating and irritating situations so that our objectives are consistent and fulfilled; however, we filter any emotional feelings that penetrate our minds. We keep alive the spirit of enthusiasm and embrace God's love. We should be vigilant not take the wrong path, and keep calm and be patient.

Patience means letting things develop at their own pace rather than jumping in with our own responses and conclusions, leading to fear or worry. Patience allows us to solve our problems in a peaceful and tranquil way, so that everything is easy and effortless. Patience will allow you to see clearly what you do, and learn to let you continue to explore whether an event is trustworthy: you have a choice to accept or reject it. Patience implies a desire to see the game as it unfolds, rather than trying to seek to validate it. You cannot perceive anything that has not yet happened, but do believe it is unfolding. However, you need to stay calm, and feel the silence within, and align with the power that guides you. You enjoy the stillness of the moment, take a deep breath, and ask yourself to resonate with the Source: you empty your mind, and experience that God is omnipresent. Stop yourself from thinking of anything and pay attention to what is emerging and happening. Feel the silence within and listen to the soul trying to tell you to be still, relax and connect to nature: separate yourself from all human conflicts, fears, indecision and the ridiculous assessment of psycho-talk about the end of the world.

I feel the spirit say, "Humans may have to face many catastrophes and adversities on Earth, but that is common. Many of these crises are for the purpose of learning lessons; however, the world is unlikely to end, rather it will continue to grow and develop and will enter into an Aquarian age. Do not let this rumor, or so-called "projection", disturbs you. Humans must stop casting their wishes on unpleasant events because a thought vibration has the power to transcend into the air, and when energy reflects it back, it will move into its physical counterpart as everyone's wish. Therefore, humans should always be careful what they wish for. Humans must live in consciousness now in the eternal present, in a state of thoughtlessness and they need continuously to establish a connection from within. They must want to live in consciousness now. Observe and monitor every human being, they will improve, and change, and experience the consciousness of God's presence. At any moment, they are conscious of each thought sent into the atmosphere with compassion and love.

"For individuals, as you begin to reach out for the spirit to take in your situation now, roll deeply into your inner soul and begin to recognize your own Inner Source, and return home to the void. Then you will know everything in the physical world is only temporary, as you resume your infinite self and surrender to God's spirit. You lived in the past, a life situation, and you live in the present, but look forward to the world. However, you are a different person to the one you were before. You will just continue to grow, and your soul will be everlasting and always-developing until it returns home to the Universal Source. On Earth, you are a bridge between the Inner Source, the spiritual realm, and God and the world. It is all a state of consciousness or awareness. Remember life on Earth is a continuum and there will be no ending unless God said so: until then, stay well and be well and receive many blessings on EARTH from God's omniscience."

Chapter Twenty-three

Thought and Willpower

Thought and willpower originated in the nothingness of the void. When your will is stronger than your mind, it helps you to generate positive thoughts. The thought-through words that you use are unambiguous, powerful, and encouraging: they show your talent and that you are ascendant. You align with the Source and you meet with the stillness and silence. Everything opens up for you, and you are being taken care of by the Universal Source. You feel its power, as though a spring were flowing through you. The flow of current traveling through your veins, your nerves, your muscles, and your whole physical body is strong and vibrant. It continues to cleanse your blood stream, purify your heart and mind, and yet no validations are necessary because you already know it is the power of the Authentic Self.

However, when your will becomes weakened, everything turns downwards. You have less control, no strength, your body feels fatigued, you are discouraged and you feel hopeless, weak and powerless. The mind terminates any interest you have and brings in negative emotions that might hurt you, and, at this point, you have difficulty defending yourself against the mind. Hence, you must awaken to consciousness now and harness the power of your mind by using your willpower to control your mind. Your choice is completely led by your spirit. When it functions correctly your entire body generates with reverberating energy that carries you whatever you wish to do at your command. Your willpower is exerted over the power of the mind and all things become possible.

In a relaxed and peaceful state, the brain gains inner strength. For example, you have the ability to influence others. You have achieved success in your field. You live well. You experience deep joy and tranquility. You have lucid thoughts and fear no evil. Your body is strong and whole, and that is reflected in your face. You are capable of controlling your desires. These are signs that you are making the right choices and maintaining your nerve, courage and willpower to carry on in your endeavors. Your life is full of energy and meaning, instead of being demanding, and you are in sync with your true nature. These points describe your happiness and joy regarding your job, relationships and the people around you. Furthermore, your life has more value and meekness and has a sense of being the full life that you came here to gain.

Do you maintain effective or negative influences over your mind? If you experience any adverse games against you, then you might have created an enormous amount of uncertainty in your mind and allowed the power of fear to capture you. You do not feel safe, and that, combined with uncertainty, becomes emotionally undesirable. It starts out extremely tiny, but it grows steadily and gradually expands into several branches and covers many areas instead of a single field. You should be aware that normally it takes one small thing to cause the opening of fear in your life. This excludes some hidden areas you may not be aware of or things that have not happened yet!

However, when your goal is well grounded, your fear will disappear. The mind is willing to cooperate with you. Therefore, your troubles dissolve by themselves, as you have given them no place: then fear fades. However, it can regroup before the mind agrees to house that fear, if you are not mindful of what you think and do.

The greatest fear has three categories: fear, worry and indecision. When these horrific emotions are hidden in your mind, your sure emotions are blocked, and you no longer have any interest in doing things. These three illusions of fear can come quietly without your awareness of their presence. You may not see them until your whole being is affected and attacked by them. However, you must be aware that nothing can be created without being conceived by you through your self-designed impulses. The sooner your negative and feared emotions blend together, the sooner the Law of Magnetic Energy will activate them. The subconscious mind will help the vibration to the conscious mind, and thoughts immediately begin to transform into a real chance of a horrifying experience: whether you are aware of those thoughts or are unconscious of them becomes irrelevant. Now, what did the oracle read about what your future holds in store for you? You do not need a crystal ball or psychic to tell you about your future. The past validated the present and the future is joined to your presence, which can be forwarded into the flux of the future. The past entered the present and the upcoming is reflected by the moment you are in, which can be forwarded into the coming event. So, you know what your future will be like.

Future events can be transformed at any time because they are still being conceived and are not written in stone. The answer is that everything you thought of must be in the moment and acted on in the now. Only the now can verify your current situation and bring you many wondrous things. The next minute you think about your future, it is already present, and the present becomes the past, so you must be mindful of your thoughts, and future you are holding in your hands.

For example, in your mind, after you pray, think that you will receive what you asked for, and you shall have it soon. That is, you can make up your mind to receive it. You should be consciously aware that only you can choose, and no one can do it for you, but you can make the formless into the formed.

When you deal with the three enemies, you must validate your standpoint so that these enemies go out of your mind and life. You must never compromise with them, but insist that they leave and remove themselves in the now.

Remember, if you continually let fear into your brain, you can never use your creativity to contribute to your greater convenience. You must remove these three enemies from your mind and then you open yourself up to being liberated, instead of being confined. You respond faster and enjoy a higher quality of thought-echoes in the brain and have tremendous courage to take on many challenges. You change and remove obstacles, in order to move on from those unfortunate memories again.

When you begin to see the most recent changes, you know that you have trained the mind to be still within you in order to hear the small voice speaking to you. You eradicated negative thoughts that knocked you down and eliminated the old habits of thinking fearful things in your mind. Fear opposes the key word "audacity". You have courage, so fear has disappeared, and no harm can come near you or hurt you.

When you remove things you wonder about, then your fear and doubt will soon end. They are no longer in your way. They have lost their values and vanished from your sight, and collapsed and dissolved by themselves automatically. Your assertion shows that you have determined to abandon them and transform your desires into undisturbed action. You keep yourself with profound hope and poise. Your positive attitude has drawn you to attract more positive things and events that came and emerged to you. You have generated joy in your heart and the world seems to change a bit.

Your courage and determination show that you have eliminated those uninvited guests in your mental house, and you have done everything possible towards the attainment of this. This triggered the Law of Magnetic Energy and the Law of Allowing and Abundance that brought all your desires to become absolute truth. The subconscious mind will trust and respect the vibration to the intellectual and transmute it into its substantial equivalent of wealth and success.

Now you eliminate fear and go on in the right direction in life. If you have a desire, and you want to succeed, you will be able to overcome all obstacles and even apparently inflexible barriers. With determination, you know even if you have to climb the mountain or dive deep under the ocean, you will get the answer you need. The means you achieve your challenge in life using willpower, desire, intention, faith and action and so change the life you do not like and find the one that is your ultimate reality.

You must always remember not to take on any fear, worry or indecision in the future. Let events unfold and take care of themselves as success is always waiting for you at your door ready to assist you. The reality is that the mass of things that you worry about will never end if you allow them to occur. However, when things occur, there are always people who will come along to help you to overcome your difficulties and confusion. You must accept that all things are possible and will lead you on by themselves. You need to cancel any negative and weak states, but do not try *not* to think about the problem. That does not work. Just remove it from your focus. You will stop worrying about tomorrow's events let it unfold by itself. You look out for the best, but prepare for the worst. You back benevolence and mercy and everything you look at changes.

When you were born in the physical world, you were a loveable baby and loved by everyone. Your mind was blank, and you never understood or experienced greed, hatred or jealousy. They had no place in you at this time in your life because your mind was blank. All you worried about was that you received care from your mom and dad and that they loved and fed you with good food. That met all your needs and excitements as a baby. Even the most evil man in the world was once a wise child as a toddler. Hence, it is politically incorrect to assume that a person could be dark when a soul who has just reached earth. However, as you steadily grew into adulthood, everything changed. You had your feelings, a personality, and features built up to meet with diversity in the world. Everything you did was just for the purpose of meeting your basic needs to stay in this whirlwind world. You worked hard to make a living so that you could live and stay in the state of beingness. Afterwards, you wanted to have a family, accumulate wealth, acquisitions, success, and gain political power. This is quite common, so you can make a positive journey on earth. Your soul and you are here to learn lessons and complete a spiritual journey.

Unfortunately, life might not be as you thought. You might have let yourself down either by personal tragedy or a family breakdown, debt, drugs, or failing college, and have lost your standard of reliability. You changed to follow an entirely different way: greed, hatred and resentment created a new you.

You use your ability to earn your living by cheating others of their assets in a harmful way. You hate seeing what other people have, you do not contain anything. You become a greedy and jealous person. You are jealous of others' possessions and think of harvesting them as your own. You spend all your effort, power and energy to scam others of their possessions without remorse and do it in a harmful way. You feel that this is the way to get rich quick by tricking innocent victims of their possessions so they are in your name. You achieve your short-term pleasure. Did you forget who you are? However, you do not seem to care. As the years pass, you can never attain peace within, but in your mind you only think of making more money by any means necessary. In reality, everything has a cause and effect; if you earn a living as a con man, you will get a lousy reputation and possibly suffer from long-term setbacks.

Time has passed: you regret what you did wrong. You think that living a con artist's life no longer has any value to you. You want to make changes and live a better life. You remove hate, jealousy and greed from yourself. Hence, you begin to meditate inwards and forgive yourself for what you did and open and light up your soul to do the honorable thing. You want to use the best of you to help others. You do not change the person you once were. You do not want to live in a lonely desert. You show real   results and repentance. You start to water your own soul and send love to others. This brings back who you are: a caring, loving person. You begin to understand love. Now you walk away from what you did and understand the value of your journey. You begin to see the quality of your life and the balance of the mind, body and spirit. You begin to know there is a soul-connection and are aware you want to do better in the now. You get more aware of your inward and outward journey and learn from it. You continue to do well and are aware of your purpose. You are now revealing yourself to the world as a warm, compassionate person who cares for and loves others.

You shine a light for your soul and start to affirm love. Everything happens for a reason and is a lesson from when you come here. This world also contains the positive and negative, light and dark. It also contains a place for joy, peace, happiness, success, and abundance. Now, use your willpower to create real meaning and design your life, until you expect the return trip back to the nothingness of the void and unite with the Source as one.

II. Energy

Everything surrounding us is manifested by energy. Mankind and other living things are created by Divine imagination and energy; by His expression of all things, Earth and the Universe are being created. Look around: everywhere, everything is surrendered. Next to you it all seems solid and concrete, but when you expand an object to its maximum point in a super-computer microscope, and you look at the object again, it will probably shock you. You see that it is made of multi-layered shells of invisible energy. However, that does not transform your perceptual belief that the item you have just seen is real and solid; you believe it and when you see the thing the right way, many possibilities open up to you and there are no limitations on what you can accomplish.

Thought is energy that has a profound impact on our day-to-day activities. When an idea flashes in your mind, apparently it has no solid character, so you lift it up. At that time, perhaps, you are not interested or you are preoccupied by something else; so, you mark it down. For a while you defy it, but that does not mean you do not desire it. When you desire something you need to feel enthusiastic and an emotional attachment to it; so, if an idea keeps coming back to you, then it draws your attention, as surely you do not want to discharge it. When an idea connects through your mind, it creates an electric nerve impulse that travels through your whole body to activate every organ, nerve, blood cell and your heart beats so you know that you want something and it is at that instant that you manifest the thing you constantly desire as your actuality.

Now you can relax knowing that all beautiful things are created through your innermost thought impulses, even though you do not know yet what you are going to manifest in your consciousness in the here and now. You harness your conscious mind and apply your intuition and are aware of which force to manipulate and how: just by feeling something, you will sense the energy moving around your whole body, and you will develop an instinctive feel and understand the whole of what you need to do with it. The energy we use constantly comes into our lives automatically without striving so that we can advance and continue to grow and develop. We all can influence matters through thought-energy. It is a matter of knowing how to manipulate it correctly and rightfully and use it to benefit all humanity and living things and give you a deeper understanding of how you want a problem solved.

Chapter Twenty-four

Meditation

Through meditation you can relax and silence the mind to stillness to attain the joy and happiness you want to obtain. You ultimately reconnect with the Source, the Mind of God. It helps you focus on what you really want to manifest in your life. This means that no matter what you focus on, it becomes magically magnetized into the energy field that surrounds you. Sooner or later, it transforms and manifests into your physical reality. This is why it is so profoundly important to stop your mind from wondering about what you don't want, instead of focusing on what you actually do want, in your life. Meditation helps you stop the mind from wandering along the wrong path. When you can fix your attention on what you desire, you can instantly stop thinking about what you do not want and remain concentrated on what your impulses desire.

You can practice meditation at any time and in any place. You do not need to limit the areas in which you do meditation. You can meditate while you are walking, showering, cooking, sitting, waiting in line, or when doing anything you can think of: just by doing it. You simply sit still and silence your mind by emptying or clearing it for a moment, so you can reconnect with your Source. When your mind is empty, it cannot bring in anything to hurt or upset you. You begin to feel as though you were set free. You are not being controlled or forced to do something you do not want to do. You are connected to the original source of who you are as an Infinite Being. As an Infinite Being, you are free to do everything, yet you do not carry any earthly things with you. You are absolutely free from any earthly bounds and expectations.

You have nothing to worry about because you are nothing but

an empty soul in the Universe. You are a free spirit. You originated as an Infinite Being that dwells in a human body to walk a spiritual journey on Earth.

When you have a moment, sit or lie down quietly on a couch with no disturbances or people around you. If you desire to do so, light candles and play soothing sounds to assist your concentration on inward meditation. The purpose of this meditation is to relax your mind so you can refocus afterwards. Now take three deep breaths and quiet the mind. In the beginning, you notice that your mind still wanders around and thinks of the many things you had done earlier. You do not need to worry, though. Bring your mind back to the focal point of your origination and purpose. After 10 minutes, you notice that your mind begins to settle, and many unreal thoughts start to recede. Your real expectations can now be obtained from your inner state of mind, which is different from the external world of desire and happiness. You begin to hear your inner spirit speak to you. You realize the thoughts and ideas coming to you are more lucid, and they support and strengthen each other side-by-side rather than being separate. The more time you spend in meditation, the more you realize the progress of your spiritual efforts. Eventually, your personal will and the Source will start to flow harmoniously as one and become oneness.

Meditation will help you forget the world that is full of jealousy, hatred, and the unloved. If you can live without attachments and impulses, the world completely changes for the better. The transition is like sleeping in a brand new place. At first, you have trouble falling asleep. Once you get used to the place, however, you sleep very well.

In the same way, in the beginning it will be difficult to perform inward meditation. But over time, you will learn to do it more easily.

If you can control the desires of your vulnerable mind, you can immediately relate this control of your daily activities. It may surprise you to learn that we can control the activities of our wandering minds, and we can already recognize our capacity to remember our desires. We can control the way we desire things. Once you manage the ability to control your desires, which enhances your self-awareness, you will perceive the way to inner harmony.

After a prolonged period of practicing inward meditation, you will notice that your impatience and anger are banished. This occurs when you connect to God's love through your inner connection with the Divine Source and will lead you gladly to share this love with others. Your life transforms into a self-motivated relationship with the Divine. You become the person God means for you to be: you become more like the Divine, behaving like God, by showing kindness and compassion. You join with Him to achieve the joy and happiness you really want to accomplish on earth.

You begin to comprehend more in life; you begin to deal with the fear and resentment you have accumulated over the years. Your past resentment towards people, places, and things has isolated you in a world of your own and restricted you from living in the present moment. Resentment is the fallout from hiding the upsetting events that have discolored your life. Resentment encourages anger, frustration, and depression, all of which suppress you. When you don't deal with your resentment, it causes mental and physical illness. However, love is the only atonement that can repair the hurt you've received over the years. You should meditate on forgiveness for those mistakes over the year that you have done; you do not want to resist it; with little practice gradually, love will work miracles in you.

Chapter Twenty-five

Meditation II

A student asked, "How does one meditate, teacher?" The teacher replied, "Be alert, enter a spacious calm, and feel the moment of peace in your mind."

Meditation involves bringing the mind into connection with the Divine. Meditation is achieved through the practice of mindfulness. Meditation helps to undo or remove any harmful thoughts in you. It transcends everyday life to reveal the goodness and kindness that are your real nature. It is like the sun shining on beautiful flowers, showing their true nature. It will enable you to honor other hearts with your own gladness.

The practice of mindfulness will ease complex situations and reduce your negative energy and emotional pain, which may have been with you through many lifetimes. You need to perceive, rather than withdraw from, those emotions and treat them openly, consciously and with acceptance and openhandedness. This applies to whatever emerges to help you with your thoughts.

Meditation is the development of mindfulness and the application of being one with the Divine. You do not have to sit to meditate. You can meditate while you are walking: simply listen to the silence in your mind and empty your thoughts.

Meditation builds one's attention and awareness to a level of strength that will remain unmoved even in the chaos of life around you. Life is full of challenges and decisions, and participating in meditation will help you to construct a holistic life.

Calm and auspicious conditions are created during meditation. Before you have complete control over your mind, you will need to be aware of your environment.

During meditation you perceive that the candle flame of your mind is unstable. It swings and moves in the violent winds of your thoughts and emotions. The flame will burn constantly once you calm your thoughts around it.

Then, with a glimpse inside, you become aware of the mind in a state of rest. Slowly, your thoughts, emotions, and the instability of the landscape fade out. The moment that you calm your mind, and you have the ability to concentrate and focus at will, you reach mindfulness. You wake up from a state of unconsciousness.

The most significant aspect of the meditation posture is to keep the back straight. The inner energy will then flow through the subtle channels of the body, and your mind will truly rest. Do not force anything. You should be relaxed.

Sit with your legs crossed. In addition, disregard duality, and instead visualizes oneness. Rest your hands comfortably over your knees. If you prefer to sit on a chair, keep your legs relaxed, and be sure always to keep your back straight.

When you meditate, you do not always need to use a specific method. You simply empty your mind with thoughtlessness, and you will find, especially when you are inspired, that you can bring your mind to this state and relax instantly.

You do not need to worry about whether you are in the "correct" state. As you relax in a moment of rich understanding and wakefulness, an unshakable certainty will emerge. With your mind quiescent, and entering into the emptiness, your meditation will be successful.

A study lead by a university researcher suggests that meditation can have positive biological effects on the capacity of the body to fight infection and disease. Additionally, the group that meditated exhibited an increase in the activity in the left hemisphere of the frontal part of the brain, indicating lower levels of anxiety and a positive emotional state of being.

You feel contented and at peace, as you have released yourself from the anxiety of problems, and this will bring both peace and joyfulness into your life.

Chapter Twenty-six

Spiritual Blessings

Deep inside every heart, in our being, we are longing to receive spiritual blessings from our God-Source. Even though each of us our desires for God's blessings varies, it cannot be denied that it is latent deep within our Source's being. It is implanted in our DNA, and in every living soul.

Why is this so? Because God designed us that we should seek His blessing whatever we do, then by His power and with love, all things are allowed in our destiny.

However, God does not intend each individual to manifest anything without His blessing. In Genesis 1:28 God blessed them and said to them, "Be fruitful and increase in number; fill the earth and subdue it. Rule over the fish in the sea and the birds in the sky and over every living creature that moves on the ground." Thereafter, humans were able to fulfill their destiny to overpower and oversee all living things on Earth, and its inhabitants. It was a free gift from God. You can see this is not something that we have to earn, but is granted to us temporarily as a gatekeeper by God. It is a gift granted to each of us to live freely, happily and to govern the Earth effectively and fearlessly.

Spoken blessings to an individual enable them to fulfill their life's purpose. For example, when parents send blessings to their children before they leave home for college or for work, they are able to make outstanding progress and move forwards and gain tremendous success. This is because there is a place within for them and only them, always. Giving a blessing is like giving permission to your children to proceed in whatever direction is right for them and to go with confidence. Hence, a parent's blessing will have profound impacts on their children's lives.

Words of blessing carry the weight of the power from Heaven. We know it is a blessing from God's spirit that is authentic and powerful. Their impact on which we are, on our hopes and change the way we think about ourselves.

How do you give blessings to your son or daughter? You simply lay your hands on your children's foreheads and say, "May God's spirit bless you and shine His light on you, acknowledge and empower you always. Amen." With blessings for your children, they have access to everything they want to accomplish in order to thrive. Your children will prosper despite their aptitudes.

On the contrary, we will note the lack of this power when a parent's blessing is withheld or missing. Your children's hearts will feel the void, though they cannot define why.

When you enter an agreement with your parents' blessing, you will hear yourself thinking thoughts of absolute knowledge and feel empowered always. You feel self-confidence and high self-esteem. You feel confident in your own words in front of a crowd. You speak with great attention and people listen and trust you. You do not compare yourself with others, because you are full of talent and worth. You are recognized and you easily receive compliments from others and say 'thank you' when someone praises you. You are a genuine person and humble yourself before others and make no demands for personal attention.

However, a person who lacks blessings develops a pattern of being rejected by others. They may develop the behaviors of self-rejection, are aggressive, have lower self-esteem, feel a lack of love and tend to acquire the approval of others. When they receive criticism or rejection, they speak aggressively towards others.

The truth is you cannot get rid of criticism with a critical attitude. Likewise, you cannot break a spell by cursing others. Rather, you bless those who curse you; then you will break the curse with blessings. You have inner peace and are blessed by the Universe. Nevertheless, any bad behavior or angry aggressive attitude you should have must not be kept, because it produces bad fruit in a person's character and personality.

The best way of blessing is no striving and live life with joy and happiness and then everything comes easily and effectively. People who lack blessings constantly need to achieve more and work harder to impress others. They do that because they want to fill the void in their souls until they feel pressure within and exhibit the signs of negative emotional stillness.

A person continues to live in the Land-of-Never-Enough. Aggressive behavior will develop and motivate a person to climb higher to succeed, but this is connected to emotional pain from the past. The old pain in a person is fuel and energy so he can produce outstanding achievements and earn his fame and fortune.

A person can overcome anything to live well, even a diagnosis of cancer. Because you accept you cannot change, when a blessing comes to you from God's spirit, you are so thankful that ultimately you are healed. You no longer need to carry the disease you never deserved, so you get on with your life. That is because you are a part of God's creation; hence, you should be blessed.

God designed you to be blessed at every stage of your journey on Earth, so be prepared and accept it with gratitude. When you show your gratitude to the power that created you, you show your appreciation and trust in God's spirit so that He can continue giving you blessings: whatever you do will thrive.

By being connected to the deep energy in your core, your Source energy spreads through a blessing-reaction to your entire body and mind. The moment you get in touch with this energy, a deep wave of joy arises and penetrates your body. You know you are blessed by the Divine. You know truly how powerful this Divine blessing is and how powerful your body and mind are, as they can be inspired by God's spirit. You are fully embraced with Divine blessings throughout your journey. Follow every breath you take for your consciousness to abide. It is the path to find the deeper peace and highest spiritual connections and blessings.

Chapter Twenty-seven

Infinite is Your Inner Strength

We cannot change who we are or remove the Inner Being from ourselves while we undertake our journey here. It is just one means by which we see ourselves on Earth. There is no other person the same as you, because everyone is an original, and your DNA can prove that you are different from all others. What is it inside you that make you so different from others? It is your unique personality, temperament, behavior, likes and dislikes, your color preferences, the way you chat and respond, your lifestyle, your beliefs, faith, religion, memories, philosophies, and thoughts. The attributes described and represented as "who you are" distinguish you from every person around you, near and far. You introduce yourself to the world, as "I am..."

Where do you come from? Perhaps you think you come from your parents. It is as if an apple were to come from apple seeds. Think again! You are not what you think you are. I suggest that you came originally from the void, the Universal Source, the Mind of God. You lived in many life-forms before you were born to your parents, and they were freely selected by you. Hence, you are clearly a spirit; you are a supernatural, spiritual being with a provincial, human experience. This is your true nature. This is where you come from.

There are two sides to you: the finite and infinite, but they are not the only ones. You cannot perceive any difference with your naked eyes. Even if a doctor orders a CAT scan on your brain, there is still no sign to show that you have a spirit dwelling within you: but it is there. You understand you cannot remove the unembodied from you. The invisible side of you has existed for years, and has no beginnings or endings. The reality seems clearly that our soul is infinite: only the body has limitations and will expire when its energy becomes thinner and less dense. Death will end every aspect of one's presence on Earth. Since we only use a particular body once, if we choose to reborn, then we will have to select a different physical body and attributes. What we call birth and death are indivisible: they are like nighttime and daytime, or the two sides of a coin. You own it all.

From where do we originate? We start asking this proper question loudly since the beginning of time, but we are unable to find a perfect answer. For more than a decade, we still are searching and work on to get an answer. Why are there many different races on Earth? The diversity of life is evident in the enormous number of different species, plants and animals that live on Earth.

The physical body is present in the "I," but the body is never divine. It is the short-term sanctuary for the soul. The physical aspect has a mind that operates seemingly independent from the subconscious mind, but can blend with it in writing. The soul depends on the energy and nutrients from the physical body. Therefore, need to for the body to keep up its strength and health.

Although we have a powerful subliminal mind, our mind likes to think independently and work differently. It loves to exercise the freedom to make choices that cause our links to the Universal Source to become misaligned and disconnected. It makes the soul inactive. Consequently, instead of training our minds inward, we turn God down and create an egoistic life, clinging to accomplishments and ambitions that expand out, ignoring the fact that they are moving us toward the emptiness. The absolute loyalty to God eroded.

Again, God permits you to fulfill your desires; He made you righteous in the bargain. God answered your prayers; you are free to choose all you desire.

"You think God exists? Doctors heal your diseases. God does not heal you. When you get sick, He cannot do anything to stop it. Which one is the God you choose to accept and believe?" Said the voice.

"I do not want to make any choice."

"Reality is reality, you know. You just keep on fooling yourself."

On one level, the voice is right. Realistic and difficult arguments against God are not particularly strong based on the facts, but they disappear once you look deeper than the material world.

A little girl asked God why he had created this world. God whispered back to her, "Well, you want to know why your Lord God created this world? Love, my dear, love is my intention for creating you, the oceans, the animals, the plants and all other organisms. I show this to you because of love, so you can understand it. Allow me to lift you up so you can see where the cosmos is, little one." Soon she was lying in the palm of God's hand.

Although we have distanced ourselves from the sacred, surely we can see the journey to the transitional zone as an experience closer to God continues to exist. I see everything in front of me without judgment. I see the stars and the moon passing in and out of my consciousness like flying clouds. It is complete and exclusive. I could never forget this uplifting experience and quantum journey. We do not have different mechanisms that cause it; nonetheless, feeling close to God happens at all ages, among all people.

We are all capable of going beyond these material bounds, yet we fail to recognize this ability. Anything subjective must trigger the mind before we can feel God's presence. An event must be taking place inside the mind to cause a response that gives rise to the honest creation of beliefs. They bridge your finite world to an infinite realm where material dissolves and spirit emerges.

For example, the spirit within that triggers your mind enables you to survive in the face of danger. It is the spirit within who wants to protect you. You turn to your Inner Source because you need to meet your goals and desires. The spirit brings you peace, so you can rest. It helps you find peace even in the midst of external chaos and turmoil, so you can meet calmness and tranquility. The spirit can also confirm your positive emotions so that your inner world is blissful. You call the spirit to inspire you. Your creative abilities arrive from nowhere—the spirit gives you all upon request.

Your subliminal mind can connect directly with the Universal Source to get whatever you want, good or bad, if you believe in it with your whole body, mind and spirit: you can experience it all. This could bring bewilderment in the beginning, since it has no roots in the substantive world. Your mind can imagine the power your Source-Being has possessed. The Source-Mind gives you healing and miracles. It proves to you that miracles do happen, but it asks you wait a little longer with patience, so you receive the best. Creation starts in your mind, in your thought. Imagine that, without the alignment with God's spirit, our lives would have no form and it would be difficult to overcome our problems in the present. We would be so much happier, so much more productive and so much more alive by making a conscious connection with the Source, our creator.

The reality comes through imagination in your mind and matches with your own Source of being. Each person projects a different view of reality, matching the Universal Source: that is, God. However, God is invisible still within everything; you need to shift your thinking to allow in His presence. Nevertheless, do not label God with a term or form. He has no form or shape. He is the Divine and worshiped: we address Him as, "God, the Father". Our visions of God cover the vast range of human experience and transform from moment to moment. Even atheists need their God, who is absent from them, but believers need their God's omnipresence, His peace, love and light. The subconscious mind will manifest and deliver whatever images of God you imagine through thought. God's reality is real, even though you cannot perceive it. You care by means of a force that transcends time and space, an invisible force that exists forever and loves you unconditionally.

The seed of God dwells in the central code of everybody's hearts. In fact, what you see in the mirror is the genuine reflection of who you are. For example, imagine you see yourself in a state of fear and worry; that is the image of God you see reflected back at you. Imagine you see yourself as capable of accomplishments; then you see power, ambition, and completeness. Imagine you see and feel calmness and tranquility inside; then you see peace within you. You see a peaceful God in you. Your inward conversations determine what your outer world looks like.

If you believe you can become a lawyer, a politician, or an author. You can have any attributes you have seen or imagined. Any negative attribute can be produced in the same way and become your reality, you only need to imagine and want it.

Your mind can create and organize unlimited thoughts. According to scientific research, thoughts manifest in our minds at a rate of two every six seconds. However, it is true that not all thoughts can be validated, or are useful, or of help to you. Thus, with your imagination, you see the world within, and ultimately transcend it to the Universe, and so you later meet with your goals and desires. However, you need to be constantly aligned with the Inner Being, still, in the silence that brings the vibration into harmony and be aligned with the Universal Source to achieve superior results.

When you call upon God, He will receive and answer your desires; however, you must point to the correct answer so that God will come to aid you. God will be extremely glad to accelerate the process if you decide what you must have. God will then act as per your request. For example, if you need help, then God will act as your counsel. If you need protection, then your God will act as a protector, as a father protects his child. If you want peace of mind, God will bring peace unto you as a peacemaker. If you lack wisdom and knowledge, at that moment your God will make you understand and give you the ability to get your work done. If you want miracles, your God will create miracles for you. If your life is in jeopardy, your God will move you from harm's way so that you will not get hurt. If you want to lend a hand, then God will bless you and broaden your sphere. This will help you to find a way to call upon God's service and receive blessings. God will help you use your imagination and make a pilgrimage to the fifth dimension/transition zone where miracles happen. You will experience God. Your thought cooperates and prepares for such a trip. No doubt! The transition zone is where formlessness is transmuted into matter. Everything there is beyond the mind's knowledge and beyond time-space. All things come from zero consciousness. It is the beginning of the Universe and miracles happen here.

Your body transforms to lightweight from heaviness. You realize this as you climb upward and you feel it. Next, your breath becomes lighter, and you feel an energy flow through your whole body; then you think there is an increase in sensitive sensitivity of all your senses; color and sound are clearer. You are going into the light. These changes seem to ordinary people like me; this is not limited to saints. It is a change of joy and happiness. This is described as if it is a constant moment of timelessness. It is the inner-peace that gives us the impression that we arrive home to the Divine, through inner and external experience. When this wondrous moment passes, you must return to the material world. You cannot stay long on a cosmic journey, as material fact keeps pulling you back to the current world. To stay in the transition zone is extremely difficult. However, you can visit there any moment you want to; there are no regulations preventing you from revisiting.

Our mind is always happy and ready for God's omnipresence. He is the invisible power above, below, and within us. God in us is not invented or optional but is real and dynamic. We are always hunting for God, desiring God, and wanting to see, feel, touch, and receive our Almighty God. Until you believe and trust in God, you will not know who you are. Your opinion does not lead you to the spirit; seeking is always needed. Some people believe that God is omnipresent and within reach or simply that God is within our hearts. Looking at the sky, you have seen God, and the spirit is always revealed through intuition, inspiration, signs, or symbols. Even clouds, birds, trees, and nature help us feel the love of God surrounding us through the conscious, infinite present.

In order to be consciously aware of the unwavering omnipresence of God, we need to end our old beliefs that are no longer valid and replace them with new notions and trust and faith, and go to wherever the spirit leads us. The material world is a place of learning, but the ether-world can bring more drama into our lifeless lives and beyond.

Your subliminal mind possesses the power of infinite intelligence. To have love, health, achievement, and abundance in life, a latent part of this intelligence must be applied and used. Our minds can respond to the Source-Mind, so we transform them by taking action.

There are different stages in your life as it continues to unfold. You are doing this by asking, by seeking the sacred: so, knock and receive.

You build balanced family relationships, have a sense of belonging to the community, and are filled with material gratification and contentment. You fulfill your life by achieving high political power, status, influence, and other ambitious goals in the illusionary world. You enhance your current conditions through inner peace and contentment. You feel bliss, tranquility within, and self-acceptance. You work inside so that you change outside. The invisible Source will only point the way. You dissolve all problems within you. You trust the Universal flow so that it is possible to make sense of the point that what may be considered unthinkable becomes probable. You fulfill your life through forgiveness, tolerance, gentleness, empathy, and insight. You fulfill your life through innovation and creativity via research: you raise awareness of science and art. You fulfill your life through the power of love, kindness, thoughtfulness, and service to humanity. You fulfill your life through alignment with wholeness and nutritional health. Each of these aspects can be accomplished and divided into different stages of completion, proving that the hidden omnipresence of the Source is behind us at every level.

You understand and acknowledge that each stage of your ability is guided and supported by the Spirit. As each process begins to unfold, there is an established approach that will enhance your involvement. You may be unaware of this, but it is sound and the ideas are true, even though you might not notice the "Spirit." You may not want to look at the internal reference, for it reveals truths of the self to you, but still, the idea appeals to you. You only have to believe in it; there is no need to be dissatisfied. You enter into that part of the holy place called "the silence", and you let the Source guide and lead you to meet your heart's desire. "Without further ado, join it" makes sense to you.

When you see your realization in the external world of people, it is reasonable to see the different roles God plays in it. God the protector, He protects you from fear and anxiety. In the physical world, it is through government and the law or courts that God keeps you fearless. He is God the Supreme in a world of power struggles and challenges, where competition reigns in business, power struggles consume the executive body, and only one winner takes it all. The God of Forgiveness has attained the supreme and foremost source of the good, as God. God the Scientist and Inventor guides and encourages you to evolve and grow. God the Spirit sees a world full of insight and benefits all. People contemplate the omnipresence and consciousness of God, and they find spiritual support and comfort. The God of Pure Infinite Being raises many seers and prophets, such as the world-famous sixteenth century French prophet, Nostradamus, and the American sleeping prophet, Edgar Cayce.

This fits into who we are as spiritual beings. The world has no boundaries and is full of possibilities.

It is difficult to know what or who God is until the day you meet Him face to face in His divine kingdom; then you know who you are—a spiritual being. Currently, our possibilities of seeing God could be possible, but can you see God in the third dimension world? The problem is in the multidimensional transition region, which can produce different visions of God and make your reality. You believe in, and experience, what you want to see, so you can relate to it. This can be as simple as seeing your own self-reflection. Your imagination creates a sensation and a divine image that you can understand. We welcome that God is living in humans. He dwells in everyone's mind. "And let them make Me a sanctuary, that I may dwell among them" (Ex.25:8 NKJV). Seek ye the kingdom of heaven within.

It is true that meditating for a period in silence will trigger your Inner Source. Your head becomes empty of thought, and you become aware of your active soul; regardless of what you are, you mix with it. Your inward awareness blossoms, and finally, you meet your inner-bliss and tranquility. Meditation helps you change how you view yourself, the circumstances surrounding you, and the opportunity closest to you. During meditation, you can repeat the word "OM" to aid in silencing the vulnerable and unharnessed mind. The word "OM" helps you connect with the inner world more easily and quickly than you thought possible by slowing down your breathing. Chanting helps you to ignore the five senses, and to make direct connections with the inner soul. It helps you to quiet the mind, so you can experience mind contact. This allows the brain's activities to be contained, to become immobile and refined, until finally, you experience complete silence. Another reason for chanting "OM" is that it forms a response ring; it is as if the brain produces the vibration, listens in, and then responds to a deeper level of consciousness. At this point, your subconscious mind has taken over, and your thoughts have crossed into the spirit realm of the ether-world where they learn by implement their own laws.

The purpose behind meditation is to aid you in achieving peacefulness and tranquility. The great majority of people in the world are aware that God is in the sky somewhere, but He is outside our illusory world. During your waking hours the mind is so logical; everything must be seen to be believed. Hence, in order to meet Him, you must work on your inner self. This applies also to Angels and Archangels and other entities that you want to make contact with through your inner consciousness, otherwise nothing can happen in the sweetness of your affection. The connection is always made from within—a direct connection to the spirit. The connection within must continue. However, if you are blessed enough, you can win a response from the unknowing cloud somewhere, and this will get you closer to God. It is one step closer to God than just thinking about Him and His magnificent creation. Naturally, we still rely on the illusion of the material world for a solution. You need a God you can imagine, talk to, and see instantaneously. The personal relationship is perfect for one reason: it is the best way to feel the love of God.

To achieve restful awareness, you must meditate on the peace and calmness inside, so you do not experience emptiness within or without. Eventually, you will realize that you are conscious of God, of yourself, and of His willingness to help you. You will feel God's presence. When the mind has attained absence of thought that produces attentiveness, the chemistry makes transformational changes in the entire physical body. The breath is less rapid, the heart pump slows, and there is reduced oxygen consumption. You tap into a new portal of the fifth dimension—the constant consciousness of the spirit realm activated. You feel relaxed and calm; joy replaces the mind's chaotic life; inner darkness ceases. "Be still and know that I am God" (Psalm 46:10a, NIV). Only when you realize that peace lies within, will you handle the spirit of God through the complete implementation of meditation. You will find a happiness and peace that cannot be found in any part of the world. You will be well pleased when communicating with God in the silent place called your own inner world.

Thirteen years ago, I wrote some words to express the spiritual and mental pains and sufferings that had troubled me. "In the dark night, gaze through the eye of the window, I cannot see nobody on the street. It is completely dark and silent outside. I see the light, gaining more peace and stillness despite the constant endurance of pains and sadness suppressed within. I hurt and distress, but the love of God lifted me up and desired me. At last, I felt safe in the comfort of my dwelling."

Let me share some details. It was a terrible, cold, friendless night, but my soul escaped from the pain to meet happiness and peace. I was lying on a bed and communing with the stillness. My brain suffered severe pains, but gradually I regained my senses and dexterity. Finally, through the love of God, I was in the safety of my home. Certainly, the pain detached from my physical body and was replaced with ease and calmness. I started to think I was immune to pain. I no longer worried whether the pain existed. I endured pain, and God offered support and relief. My mind quieted down, and I felt the silence within. The God of Peace continues to be felt in my consciousness now. The steadfast omnipresence of God had given me wholeness and vibrant health. I felt I was at one with Him through meditation. The peace of God always rises from within, at the most proper time and in the right place every time you or I or others struggle. He will come and help us in silence.

The body can endure pain, depending on the message you send to the physical body. You and the mind can manage your physical response fully. You are the decision maker, and pain can be stopped by meditating within. You make peace and harmony with your soul when it gets caught in the turmoil.

Last night I visited the transition zone. I saw a white light speaking to me. I asked the Light, "May I know who you are?" The voice replied:

I am your Lord God. I convey this message to you, so after you return to Earth [you may] accurately understand how to call on me for help. I love human beings. However, humans must call on my real name and [with right] details. I will look for a purpose. I know in the real world, humanity has many names for me, but when humans need healing and miracles, they do not call me directly. So I look but do not know what their needs are. Now, when you need help, you should have a goal in mind, consciously aware of what you want. Then you should send your request, and I will respond promptly. When you fear for your life, you should ask your God of Protection and Comfort to move you from immediate danger. When you need healing, ask your God of Healing, and I will bring transformation of healing and miracles for your specific physical condition. When you lack knowledge and wisdom, or when you want to create a new language, ask your God of Intelligence to enhance your aptitudes, skills and talents. When you want to make goals and to have much, ask your God of Authority to give you a governing authority and power, so that you can succeed in the activity you want to pursue. These are the examples I give you, so you can use them to suit your needs. I shall publish and explore more about them later when we meet again someday.

Upon receiving this message and returning to the physical world during my waking hours, I felt the idea was just.

I think my physical body needs healing, so I call upon God, the Healer who delivers and heals my body; now I remain intact and nutritionally healthy. I believe a miracle has occurred. I felt my physical body being uplifted and strengthened. I feel my body has changed tremendously.

God the Healer heals the world. The God of Peace brings a state of tranquility, quiet, and harmony. He created our world with inner calmness and peacefulness, so we can live in joy and happiness. While you think, what do you show on? The spiritual realm seems to have a feeling that we all know extremely well. It records and stores our memories, thoughts, desires, and wants. If you focus on these events, they turn your flight back to the past. The spiritual world is not a secret; it is just complicated to understand, and it takes time to realize it because our thoughts are fragmented, coming from many places. The mind though filled with thoughts is not an enigma.

God assures you that you can always find a center place, always located at the center of yourself so you may take refuge and comfort there, saving you from fear and confusion. The world is filled with violence, so if you tap into your own inner peace, then the issue of violence is solved, at least for you personally. If you can connect with the core of yourself, you can connect to the heart of the whole cosmos. That still consciousness might keep the place lit for you, from which you can track every move surrounding you, and any action you deem within the silence is the soundless witness. You are not affected by your environmental surroundings; yet you are within the situation and realize that you stay connected by the sustained activity going on around you.

You are at the core of everything and see everything as just, reliable, and valid.

In the physical world, everything is imagined, and progress can change from moment to moment in the timeless present. We need to attach a tag to everything so that we know what it represents. For example, your college professor likes to assign a grade to your paper so that you know how you are progressing. However, all these labels are the short-term because, when we try to explain things, we let them become established in the external world. By recognizing them, we want them and let them play in our lives. We have a strong desire that allows the results to be available; that is, we prepare to receive it into our world. Now think of something you want or desire. What is the difference between something you want and wanting a thing? For example, compare wanting to love with loving. Loving is allowing "want" to be received, and finally it does happen. Desire is the author, and loving is the combination that allows it to happen; they are different yet alike. Loving involves the emotions; you are already loving something.

Pay attention to a time when you tried to do something; think of your body's response. For example, compare trying to play a piano with playing a piano. They are different feelings and sensations. Doing and allowing show you are certainly doing it. To try without physical force it leads to motionlessness and ineffectiveness. When you practice doing and allowing things to occur naturally, you will become aware of an effortless sensation. You must accept what you do when talking about, thinking about, and wanting it to happen. It involves being guided by the Spirit in the ether-world.

Consciously recognize and seek the invisible to help you does not mean put yourself in harm's way; it means that you let things flow through you with the help of the Spirit. This allows all to freely unfold, so you can see both sides of the coin emerge at the same time. All things originated from the unseen realm before they came to the material world. Indeed, the Spirit is among and within everything. You do not need to try so hard to make it happen; you just let it happen.

If something you think is irritating you, change your attention to becoming more flexible. Let it run through you and continue to believe things will change and improve. Relax, let go of the unthought-of problem, and know that all things are occurring the way they must, just sooner than expected. Now, enjoy the blissfulness center and be ready for the incredible things that are emerging and awaiting you. Allow yourself to work with the inner spirit in the enchanting world of the concealed, uncertain, and bewildered that you experience.

Relax for a moment. Then, recall an upset incident with another person that angered or frustrated you. Now, clear your mind, be calm, take long, deep breaths in and out from your solar plexus, and continue to show in. Let the anger disappear from your awareness, and let everything be easy, the way it should be. Feel your innermost thoughts and let them drift through your whole body quickly. Observe the moment, and continue to allow yourself to experience it. Now, give your attention in and notice how your feelings manifest themselves, but do not think. Notice that cruel and undesired feelings start to fade and disappear. Continue to watch this with your loving heart, and accept whatever comes.

Meet the experience within, without tagging or explaining. It is subtle at first, but you must take personal responsibility for identifying it. You can make your life experience living in the unknown Universe. The change in you becomes a valued experience, and many deeper spiritual levels unfold inside the mind. Connection with God is clearly the way to meet calmness and peace.

Jesus wants his disciples to be "in the world but not of it." He wants them to be separate and disengaged from worldly ways; wises in the knowledge that no-one can overcome their souls, and engaged in the sense that they stay motivated to live a decent life. It is a balance working in one's life if one can handle it. Accept things as they are and get ready to detach from them when necessary. If you continue to meditate stillness, in the silence within, even though nothing happens, you will still feel the peace and will miss nothing. People, events, and places can change, but never give up on your beliefs or the courage within you. It would be better to choose to keep both the internal and the external. Your inner world is the secret to yourself, while the exterior must keep going. Hence, the balancing act Jesus referred to is, "in the world, but not of it."

If going inward is the most important process, then detachment is the next important one. When you disconnect from everything and anything, the external government is unable to represent you; it cannot keep you, because the separation has rendered those in power ineffective. The Universe does not discriminate against anything you do or explain how best to give from your wealth, success, and prosperity. You continue to keep up that the idea is just. Then you will begin to see improvements in your life and be able to continue to make them. As your life progresses, there a measure of tuning required as you begin to resonate with the heavenly world, which is so different from everyday life.

The words "going inwards" mean something different from "inner silence." Inwards means that which is within, to find something within, or the center of something. "Going inwards" implies an ability to apply prayer, meditation, chanting, and thinking so that you can finally arrive at a place where you can reach that inner silence. Inner silence is the ability to support activity within spiritual consciousness, and the authority to do whatever you want to carry out. It is trying to meet the goal of blissfulness and peace. When you go into inner silence everything blossoms, all problems can melt away, and you can become wiser there. You gain insight, and secure world peace so that your fears will end. It brings your experience back to zero, to a state of purity and void, where your true spirit can return to the Universal Source, the mind of God.

Now you will want to get peacefulness and everything that lies beyond silence is wisdom. There are two stages. In the first stage, you do everything according to what you feel with your five senses; you are aware that you could make a mistake but have no qualms. The second level of consciousness is quite different; here, you trust your intuition so that it guides you in what you do. You blend with your innermost thoughts, but you should not cling to them just because it would be easier; you must work with the spirit. You understand the required standards and see everything from a deeper perspective. This second stage is the true reality. You just have to be aware of the world within and understand how it functions and constantly use and benefit from it.

Insight and intuition combine to lay out a solution for you; therefore, you cannot fail. A part of you recognized in advance what would happen. This is when you make peace and harmony with the Spirit; you let the Spirit guides you. When you do, you open up possibilities for receiving life's bounty.

Your intuition is a gut feeling like lightening; it shows through intelligence, transmitting with it a sense of the righteous that defies explanation. Where does your intuition come from? Intuition could come from the conscious and subconscious mind combining to bring you a sense of unlearned knowledge. The sooner you start identifying the source of intuition that is a part of yourself, and was given by the Universal Source, the sooner you can assume that God is omniscient.

Are the people who do evil things unaware of their wrong beliefs or actions? I strongly believe people are undoubtedly aware of what they do, but just want to make it clear that they are dissimilar from the rest of humanity. The main purpose of evil actions is destruction. These people destroy everything around a person or harm other people. Their erroneous beliefs are a bunch of facts or dogmas. They stay in their own reality, and they continue to commit destructive acts so their negative energy merges with evil.

The basis of our journey on Earth is to experience life here. While on Earth, everything is uncertain, so we must find out what needs to be done to live freely and fearlessly. Understand that there is a resounding success plan for everything; however, we must also realize there is an opposite side to life. Perhaps it always existed in essence—a novel awareness of evil on Earth. It is probably the manifestation of the negative side of our hidden characters and the true nature of antimatter that bounces around, surrounding the Universe. We are certainly aware of and accept this very action has consequences.

Sometimes, when your guilt is too small and is not worth recording, you just have to leave your guilty conscience behind and acknowledge that the situation was beyond your control. You engage in constructive activities, and prepare yourself for a new start. Perhaps you will see a whole new day dawning for you. If you cannot do that, just keep fighting off the gaffes until you do. You may think you made unforgivable mistakes, but now you need to move on and discard that which chains you down. In time, it will all turn out right. Your soul is ready to move forward, and it is up to you to stop those external events. There is no wrong or complete solution here because the result is one you impose on yourself for an unforeseen event that is beyond your power. For example, a man's journey home was delayed beyond his control, and he was unable to be with his dying father. He felt guilty. He had the insight that his true love should not change his obvious outer shell. As soon as he understood that, everything was all right; he returned to a state of innocence. In the eyes of God, all souls are pure and can be forgiven. The same article tells us that we are misled if we keep holding onto our past blunders. They cannot create a feeling of blissfulness; all guilty consciences and anxiety may, in time, be forgiven and banished.

Occasionally, it is difficult for us to decide what is the right or the wrong view. However, there is a secret place you can go to seek advice: will you be willing to answer your guide there?

On one side of your mind, you may feel emotionally that you want to push ahead and make it to this still, silent sacred place. However, despite how much you want to, going inward does not happen. The old belief system refuses to cooperate, and the real cost of trying has not been successful. The embedded guilty conscience recorded from memories is still intact in the subconscious mind, and you need more than part of your emotional desires to avoid ideas of right and wrong. You can neither force nor deny your intuitive senses. However, with persistence, it is possible every moment, and you can even choose your terms. You hope that you can remove the old beliefs permanently so that you can hear the sound of your inner soul singing to you. There is a lot of work to be done through extensive meditation and self-reflection to stabilize and sustain the mind. Nature is a great healer. Be still with the trees and mountains: you are able, in your still, quiet moment, to feel the Oneness of the Source. Awareness comes from the heart. When you really know something, you feel it deeply. You have to mark your awareness and understand the Universal law as it hints to you. Every step forward is an indication of your interest to persist until success is felt and achieved and you reach the desired goal. All you have to do is the best you can with what you have. Whatever your goal, you must accept self-acceptance totally: do not depend on others, you can test yourself and you are your own best teacher. You are a life-time student and never stop learning. When you realize that you are right, you never need to worry about that mistake again. You recognize that you made the right decision, and at no time did you do anything wrong. Liberation returns the spirit to the sense of morality that was always there. The whole process involves being true to yourself and experiencing ecstatic consciousness. The feelings of duality fall away, and when that happens, you should feel a strong sense of tranquility and a silence that is released in your whole self.

After the New Year, I began worrying that something was a problem. It had bothered me for some time, and I needed help to solve it. I had no clue and wondered who I could call on for help. I thought about it but didn't do anything about it. Then one morning I went out to take care of some business. While I was crossing the street, I heard someone calling, "Herman!" I looked. It was someone I knew, but I had lost touch with him for two years. Later that afternoon we met, and I mentioned that I had cried out for help because I was going to have surgery and needed someone to pick me up. Anesthetic would be given, and my thoughts and physical activity could be affected for a few hours. He agreed to pick me up.

As soon as he said he would help, I felt so relaxed. I thought that I was surrounded by more than just synchronicity since this was not just a chance meeting; it was significant. Did the invisible have a hand in this arrangement? I had never thought this game plan had already been made. Only when the intensity in the spirit world connected me with that person did I become aware that the game had already occurred in the black space of the Universe. I did not realize that until the day has dawned and clear everything in the material world, it remained hidden from view. This happened until I exhausted all notions of what to do. Instead, I claimed responsibility and looked for help but failed to find any. The remote job, guided by the hidden power and no longer controlled by my thoughts, indirectly and silently helped me achieve my desire. When I deferred to the Universe, a new portal opened and provided help.

The Universal Source was aware of my urgency and was ready to share the relationship with His creation. His love follows from His receptive nature. Our God is infinite. The mind must depend on the Divine Source to deliver miracles, and the soul must blend with God's spirit to achieve His unconditional love, goodness, and peace.

God chooses and is willing to share His original right with you and listen to prayers from all humans. Your troubles will be taken care of if you consciously align with the Source-Mind. However, you must confirm your part of the bargain, which involves some spectacular beliefs: You are responsible for your own thoughts and every issue. If you listen carefully you hear the quiet voice speaking to you, letting you know that every thought and word have consequences, even minor, insignificant still have the potential powers that can damage and hurt the reputation of others. You must know whatever you imagine already exist and not just your own life experiences that take place in your limited physical space. You should make an effort to use it wisely and not overlook the power of thought, use them properly; it helps to remind you to remember the Oneness and validate your gift and aptitude.

Can you confirm any of the above beliefs? In my spiritual practice, I think these beliefs are reasonable and justifiable. It is true that every intention has powers and works closely with your true intentions. Hence, one must be consciously aware that an object has its own merit and virtue. It can fundamentally change to suit one's absolute truth. Therefore, you must make the effort to have unambiguous thoughts, and God will assist you to reinforce whatever you need to construct in order to reap the benefits. Your pasts, presents and futures are all ideas in your mind while you are still human.

Perceptibly, you cannot have a beautiful relationship with a woman you do not love. Similarly, if you do not believe in God, you close every portal and stop yourself from creating a loving relationship with the Divine. What you do not know is that you missed all the goodness that flow to you and through you. Life is a flowing river when the river is blocked every portal closed, and your life end. Open that portal and allow the river of your life continue to flow, evolve and develop. You do not need to see what to believe, but just believe what you see; you will see the beautiful and peaceful things occur to you; you should be shared with others. Never allow fear and doubt in your consciousness. All things change.

You just do not think God fits in, so you shut down the most remarkable things and miracles that could possibly occur in your life; you reject them. However, if you know God and let things happen, the window of opportunity opens to you. When you enable this abundance, it helps reduce your rebelliousness. In stillness, in your mind's eye, you can perceive people doing things haphazardly, tending to shut themselves down unless they fix their troubles. It is unlikely that they do not want to be happy; they just have no idea where they can get help from. If you want to reach out to them in such a situation, you may meet resistance.

Conversely, when you have something that you can hold onto, you are living a decent and supported life. You want to communicate with people. You feel love within; you respect others, and feel that the people around you also respect you. You have experienced love in a meaningful, inspiring, and caring manner. You no longer exist in the field of self-destruction that full of thorns but are noticeably living in the Land of Promised, full of wealth that you can share with others. You know this is true in your heart; you know we all are connected in consciousness. Everything is connected to everything even animals, the earth, trees, and mountains.

"Following your heart" means that you do what is right in compassion and kindness. It is the love of God that inspires you to do righteous things for others. When you think God is within, you think of the loveable warmth shielded around you, knowing it will bring peace and prosperity to you. God will not tell you what to do; but He is within you, and you are made from the image of God. Hence, there is no difference between the love of God and the love of your own loving kindness. Since you are overjoyed by knowing that God shares His love with you, your life is full of hope and expectation. You are always aware that God dwells within you. In response, you stop thinking, still, in silence; you perceive God is always as close to you as you thought. Think of God now and you are in touch with Him instantly.

Relinquishing to the Divine flow is the natural way to create and restore your loving relationship with God; God knows the way, and He guides you with His unconditional love and might. He recognizes all your needs and realizes how to make your life easier, happier, and less painful. You desire a closer relationship with God now to reap the benefits, internally and externally.

Love surrounds you and holds your world together, but you must genuinely desire it. If you have no intention to align with the Divine, then true love is difficult. At least, nothing worthwhile will happen. If you have not candidly surrendered yourself to the love of God, then linking is unlikely. If you continue to focus on the negative and disallow love from coming down your path, your problems will never be fixed. It looks as though you do not see it, therefore nothing will occur to you. Furthermore, you closed the channel and you lost your awareness and God cannot guide you to where you want to be. Deep within you is the power always to connect with God. When you are frustrated or puzzled, find a quiet place you can sit and talk with God. He has always been and always will be with you. Connect with Him now. He is right here with you this endless moment. Feel Him with you now! Love needs care. Love is kindness. You cannot expect care if you have not surrendered. It is difficult to show a close relationship when you do not believe the spirit within guides and assists you. If you genuinely want love to come to you, surrender to ALL-THAT-IS, because love is useless without surrender. Love is the link to the Spirit of loyalty and obedience.

God has no form or shape. He has no desires or preferences. He allows everything, so whatever you ask shall happen. God is infinite bright, white light for all living creatures. He is alive and omniscient. He is a wide-ranging God who perceives every man from the same perspective with no differences or opinions. The deepest secret is that God never changes, but our approach changes.

God is not, in your lifetime, to be met in person, but the system is available through reflection upon the power within. He is in different dimensions from us. That is one reason why you never see Him in the external world. You are not here just to get what you want or to fulfill the Ego's control. You crafted your own life, and you keep the horizontal and vertical sides of your destiny. Before being crafted, you encounter obstacles and limitations and feel powerless in a way that causes confusion and complexity about what you should contain your thoughts, how you are designed, and how to be. Disappointedly, you have not yet realized your innermost desire. Your life seems to be in turmoil and despair and is often controlled by external circumstances and conditions. However, when you decided to regain control and ownership, your life began to change within. The change took place almost instinctively, and you never felt uncertainty. No matter what has happened to you, every event has a great chance, a place, and an explanation. Then you begin to see that everything in your spiritual journey starts to make sense. From the time you wake up in the morning, you begin to understand that everything is prearranged by an invisible power, so you have no idea how it will unfold. Although it is unclear yet, the day appears to confirm you are capable of dealing with it without difficulty. The ability is available to you inside.

For example, a person submitted a query to the Inner Source: "Why am I surrounded by an evil human soul from the past?" He was surprised to receive an immediate response: "You invited that wicked soul's presence." He was shocked to discover how accurate the answer was. He regretted what had happened but gladly accepted the past and kept going. From this point, he persistently followed his spiritual path and listened to the innate voice inside. Based on his current belief system in real-time, he submits to no outside assistance but continues to meet the sensation so powerfully that his intuition grows by itself. He follows it to find his own happiness. Now he begins to see all his wishes granted because he is by the forces of God.

When a thought occurs to you with a pure purpose, you can change it into reality. Certainly, your opinion is paramount, and you stick with what you think. However, a lot of groundwork needs to be done before you win this fabulous accomplishment. For example, your thoughts must be centered on the now and disconnect from the past or the unknowable future. You must stay alert and respond quickly to correct your errors. You must pay attention to signals, signs, and symbols for references and clues. Your whole body, mind, and spirit must be consciously in alignment. You must patiently wait for the product information to come to you. As long as you are in harmony with the forces of God, then you will see all your wishes and desires come true, but you must follow through to meet true happiness. You have nothing to lose when you give your request to God. Your entire request will come true someday.

If you meditate on the above patterns and qualities through inner silence, then you have a genuine desire to materialize your passion.

An efficient way to transform your passion into truth is and always has been to craft a beautiful image in the latent mind. Creating a picture in your mind can transform your wish quicker than you thought. When an image flashes into your mind, everything remains there, containing no external effect until you transcend your intention to the Universe. Your passion and outcome has unchanged. All thoughts remain illusory and invisible as far as you can see.

Now consider the idea that you want to reach out, such as creating a trip to Australia. This wish is manifested in your mind only; it is not yet an external reality. To move from a first concept of fulfilling it requires plenty of fieldwork. The image is acquired internally and shot out to the outside surroundings. It relies upon the inspired image in the mind. The whole visualized image is about vacation preparations, trip planning, updating your passport, booking an airline ticket, changing money, and making accommodation arrangements in your destination country. All of these activities are visualized in the mind and then transcended into action externally. In all these preparations, your mind aids and harmonizes with the invisible. All events take place initially in the mind and then turn to outer manifestation. You can see how things are going to be because you do it with the Universe. Past events and conditions do not influence this process because all circumstances and conditions are considered separately and are not origin-related. You just do it. You know it will work out perfectly. Now, through creative visualization, you beat your journey into reality and enjoy the trip. You have manifested your dream; you are in charge of everything now.

The Universe supports what is best for you by not judging.

As the event unfolds, you are not a passive rider but instead a dynamic passenger on the flight. Your business is to stay active until the trip has been completed. You stay alert and keep as much information as possible. The turning point in life starts as a small signal initially and only transfers when you decide to let it. Being vigilant in all the things you do is a significant part of spiritual evolution. God always assists and speaks to you in silence, but you have to pay attention and listen well to what comes to you. In this way, everything can be accomplished.

A healthy and relaxed approach to life and taking care to avoid extremes is an ideal training method in one's daily activities. It is necessary in every aspect of our lives. For instance, when planting a crop, one should care for its development with great thought, gentleness, and skill. Too much or too little water will destroy it, and too much sunlight will not increase the harvest. What it needs is a safe environment where it can grow healthily. In another instance, if a person is physically overweight or underweight, this can be dangerous. It will cause undesired effects. You depend on reliable and practical knowledge to help you take care of yourself to meet excellent mental, emotional, and spiritual health and development. If you thought your self-importance was based on your consciousness, which is Egoistic, it should be avoided. Rather, pay attention to the pain that occur as an unsatisfactory aspect of existence. This will remove your heightened Ego-self down to zero. On the other hand, if you focus too much on human suffering and misery, you may become discouraged; once more there is then an imbalance.

In that circumstance, you need to look at the whole situation and decide the lack of equity. However, perhaps it is necessary for you to meet your senses by reflecting on your successes. Hence, you stabilize your mind and inspire a change from that low or negative state of mind to healthy living.

A solution to stabilize and balance your mental capacity is the best thing you can do for your well-being and spirit so as to experience a full and joyful life with no regret. By the time you make the return trip home to the void of emptiness, you have nothing, and with a smile, you go back to where you originated in amorphousness and liberty.

The balancing approach is relevant to your mental and emotional health, but it is essential to your spiritual growth as well. There are different ways in which you can check your spiritual needs. However, you can use the connection integration of academic learning and meditation for your spiritual growth. This is vital, so there will not be any unevenness between theoretical knowledge and effective implementation. Doing this gives you a break, and it provides a secure and reliable source of power.

Perhaps you are thinking that if you allow yourself to "go for the crown" in one activity, such as a sport, you will make your highest ambitions and be satisfied. This may be better than living in a quiet, relaxing atmosphere. You aim for the top of the mountain; otherwise, life might become dull and unsatisfying. This may be valid from one point of view, but you need to understand the origin of secondary behavior. For example, clothing, food, shelter, and transportation are basic needs for survival. However, neglect of these needs can become a complication in our continued existence. It becomes more difficult to hold and enjoy the right to life.

If one has to worry about constantly running around to earn one's daily bread and live comfortably, this can become extremely difficult to meet. Conversely, if a person has real assets, he will not have this same problem. His goal is to try to maximize his potential to acquire more assets to satisfy the Ego that drives him to "**DO MORE**." The very essence of acquiring more is a matter of privilege to someone who believes that to do otherwise would result in a sense of discontentment or omission. This aspect of seeking more and more is an attempt to fulfill the Ego's demand. This is the reason we need to consider suffering and misery, however irrational it may seem, which will lead us beyond the state of hyperbolic behavior. Ultimately, the idea of going to extremes means that you will eventually become spoiled. Therefore, we should seek balance in everything and deliberately broaden our outlooks. Then we can solve our crazy thinking that leads to self-destruction, negative discontentment, and serious consequences.

When you intentionally think and live with the compassionate heart within, you make conscious, significant efforts to be vigilant of your own thoughts and attitudes. This leads you to adapt positive vibes from negative thoughts and block out harmful messages to others. When your inner heart feels resentment instead of ecstasy, then you should stop and find out what went wrong. You must redeem any mistakes and cause no harm to others. Your center heart feels elated. You want is to love and respect all living things, as clearly observed by the invisible, compassionate heart. Hence, you assume full responsibility for every thought, word, and deed that you produce.

Within your consciousness you will find true peace, safety, and happiness.

Perhaps you want a piece of classical music, a deluxe dinner in a thriving, excellent restaurant, and skiing on a snowy mountain; obviously, it is the most motivating and welcoming of activities for you. However, problems could occur when such activities become your primary concern in life. To seek external events too much could easily create an imbalance in your existence, leading to setbacks and discontentment. These external pleasures could invisibly affect you so that you chase after more annoying things, such as drugs and alcohol, an addiction to unrestrained events, and do things that are beyond your scope and abilities. Regrettably, the more you chase after vanity, than the deeper you put yourself in the danger zone where it will negatively impact you. What you want so strongly has become your own sense of detention and unfortunate result, trapping you into believing that it will help you find joy and everlasting glory. But, you can dream about; it will not happen because external pleasures will only tell you to become attached to them, and they give you no choice other than to automatically cause you to want more. It is like when you dine in a deluxe restaurant; it encourages you to go back again. It becomes your greatest wish. You lose sight of all other pleasures. Immediately you feel frustrated and hurt that you will never get enough of what you covet. You must stop doing these things so they cannot overwhelm you. However, when you know who you are, then sensual pleasure becomes irrelevant. You win real peace, happiness, and confidence. You realize that dining in an excellent restaurant does not give you joy and happiness. You know food is what you enjoy, but your identity does not come from eating an excellent dinner. You eat your food now with even more enjoyment than you had in the past because you are inspired and happy within your consciousness.

You know that you cannot see, touch, or taste the invisible spirit of the Universal Source in the physical world, but you can feel the infinite incredible power of the Spirit that fills the air, the power that is giving you eternal bliss and happiness. That means you think it is always available to you, as is the longed-for joy transcending the material fault of your body into everlasting and ever-growing eternal life. To connect consciously within is the only way to meet and verify that thirst for joy and happiness.

You stop asking for more than you need. It is like starting to learn that you must be satisfied and happy with what you are before anything can happen to you. However, you are certainly in no way capable of drawing near the speed of the external events you want to pursue. You think you are always late and challenged to run faster, but you keep trying to have just enough speed to support a shift shape balance with the fast-track world. Now you claim you do not need more because you never used up what you had attained; hence, you stop demanding to be provided with more than needed to keep up a proper balance. You experience inner peace and tranquility because you have transformed the way you learn about things, continually adjusting to your new realities. You just have to realize that the unexpected event can never bring you success. You realize that only going inward and meditating on the idea can return sheer joy and happiness. Open yourself to the infinite love and resources available to you. Your experiences started to change because you saw the power within, where you before only noticed that your child cognitive Ego-self needed outside enjoyment. Now, changing your intellectual beliefs to the emotions and physical forces that are always with you will unveil ecstasy, serenity, and tranquility. Notice the difference between the joy and happiness attained from within compared with external happiness. You get it!

Consider that there are two stages of being in consciousness in the now:

The first stage involves dealing with your surroundings to transform them into calmness and stillness. You contemplate both peacefulness and stillness. Then you connect with them, so that they become one with you. Soon you are relaxed, continuously and intentionally allowing silence and motionlessness to surround you, resulting in significant lucidity.

In the second stage, you are aware of everything you think, and you realize that your thoughts have been softened, which allows you to continue to stay in stillness yet coherently remaining cautious and vigilant about any imminent danger. Thus you keep your motionlessness; there is no rushing or hurrying, and you are fully aware of your inner consciousness.

Stay in your real place at zero, from which all creation emerges. Zero represents the mind as emptied, without thoughts. Your mind needed to cooperate with you. Life is, and always has been, unfolding; you just have to stay alert and attentive to everything surrounding you, yet remain optimistic and balanced, in the same way that water makes waves. Besides you need to wait for water to return so that it can blend with everything. Just patiently wait. There is no need to hurry. This cannot be rushed, and ultimately, your destiny will be fulfilled. The things that you need to do will take place in their own time and sequence. All things are unfolding according to the Divine pleasure. All that you need will be sent to you at the right season and place, save you from hurry. Relinquish your control, be relaxed within, and trust in the unfolding power of the Universal Source. Be in a state of gratitude and align with this Source. Trust that everything will be taken care of. Let nature take care of everything for you. Relax, join in the fold of life, keep up the state of nature, and know that all is well. When you practice staying in stillness, it will become a regular part of your daily life. Allow yourself to fall into it gently. You do not want to make the process difficult. It is through the slow unfolding that you master the power of continued existence and see the unseen intelligence that flows through you, making for a life that is easy, relaxed, and that lets life change so unhurriedly that you can enjoy it forever.

In the conservative world, when we need advice, help, and support, we obviously look outside for counsel because some others seem to possess the ability to read minds effectively and are more able to offer their help to resolve others' problems. In order to master other minds, naturally we need inner power at the same time as we have mastery over ourselves, then we can understand the mind of others. If you think you hold power and knowledge, then you are truly the master of your life and omniscient. However, you may consider changing the way you look at these two notions of knowledge and power. You are invited to assess your level of mastery by going inward to see the inner world; you will be amazed and see from a new perspective. It gives you an opportunity to understand and focus your life and not on the behavior of others. You gaze inward, thinking of your own welfare and self-mastery with no concern about others. Then you change all situations and conditions to shift and place them inwardly. Before, you thought about power over others; now, you have replaced that with an inner strength that harnesses the power within you. This allows you to conduct yourself with wisdom that is also generated and stored within you.

As you begin to change the duration of your thinking, your

existing surroundings will go through rigorous transformations. For example, you will awake and realize that you are responsible for every one of your thoughts, and every one of your efforts has the potential to influence others. You realize the responsibility for your reactions and that others may stop to apply power over you. Rather than act irritated, you manage to harness the power within, and you support calmness and stillness.

You change from reacting, an emotional response, to applying mental energy to examining and exploring the situation with patience directed towards yourself. By seeking to understand your thoughts from within and to understand the behavior of other people, you regain personal control over your own awareness. Other people do not have any idea how to respond to this, but that is not your concern. Your soul remains calm and still.

The weight of your thoughts is suffused with silence, with the harmony of the Inner Source internally and infinitely flowing through you. Because of this, you should always look inward for the wisdom and knowledge of the Inner Source, for information and details that align with life. Stop looking outward for control, power, strength, and information over others; rather, move towards having control over your own review and approval processes. In this way you send your profile to the Universal Source and to eternity.

You should always keep your serenity despite what you may see or think about those things that you should support and that are taking place around you. True peace and calmness rest in the heart of your own knowledge and the loving kindness within. Reliance on external force is unnecessary. Instead of relying on others to help you in your upheavals, you should deal with your own anxious feelings. Although you are living in a world that likes to blame others for mistakes and deeds, the key issue is your own business, and your emotional state is in your own mind. The truth always requires you to remove negative energy. When you call on the delicate Authentic Self, even in the center of the crisis or turmoil, you can still arise from the ashes and transform pain, painful conditions, and suffering into cheerful and tranquil feelings.

Consequently, you change and get self-mastery over your life. You erase the list of adverse conditions and life improves tremendously. Ultimately, you are enlightened in consciousness in the here and now.

When caught in a "Catch 22," most of us do not know where to go. The best way to solve our problems is to turn inwards, pray, and reflect on God. However, when things did not change for us in the past, we often stepped away from this inner-relationship and returned to obtaining wisdom from external forces. As paraphrased from Jesus' words in the Bible, "They have willingly closed their eyes to the truth." (Is. 44:18, NIV) We have placed our views on barren grounds and are hoping for supporting spiritual roots and development. However, we did not expect that it could cause unperceived self-distraction that brings us hurtful, painful experiences. Only by focusing on God's Spirit do we create a bountiful harvest, fruitfulness, and greatness. The only way that you can align with God is unconditional surrender to Him. This allows you to change using the authentic power inside you. It requires knowledge, understanding and wisdom that come from the Universal Source. We must respond to the Source as we learn from Him on a new road of change, as we wage war against the age-old battle of unbelief. We listen to our inner-thoughts every day, and we continue to check our old habits that might continue to hold us captive. When we consciously align with the Source, we know now, clearly and effortlessly.

The inner-wisdom alerts you that you have a choice.

Do you want to live in confusion or have an emotional calmness that results from a tranquil interior view? It is your choice! Keep this insight—do not allow external events to disturb you or to be a source of disquieting energy, as that will never allow you to do what you need to do. Self-awareness and self-knowledge will flourish when you practice tolerance and responsibility for your emotions, deeds, and actions. You are responsible for your own feelings and for your right to go through life without allowing people and your surroundings to overpower you without your consent.

Do you find yourself affected by economic upheavals and negative situations that you blame happening resting on the world's changing economic model? Perhaps you place the blame on a series of events that has taken place around you? If so, then you have lost touch with your Authentic Self. If you continue to do so, you allow yourself to be swamped and changed according to the blowing winds of circumstance.

The solution for a disturbed environment is to tap into stillness and silence. When you enter the holy, secret place of the inner silence, you can change any defect in the domain of problems and troubles. Silence is the ideal solution to turbulence, conflict, adversity, imbalance, pain, and suffering. You have a say in every moment; you are either connected to God which brings you eternal peace, or you are a prisoner to your Ego. As a prisoner, your disturbances or disorders keep you from living in a world in peace.

Listening to the Ego is not necessary; it will just confuse you. You must stay calm and steadfast and find a quiet center for yourself. Be quiet for a moment; stop thinking regarding what is going to happen or what is surrounding you now. Instead, take a few deep breaths and plan on cleaning and emptying your thoughts. Then you will begin to see yourself returning to zero and you will unexpectedly feel calm, filled with joy and happiness. Intentionally stay in stillness even with your questions still pending, your answer is to stay still. It is the best way to solve all your heart's troubles. You will be in harmony and peace with the inner power, which is your ultimate reality.

We all have the hidden inherent capacity to arouse immense

transformations that will grant us the calmness, tranquility, peace, and knowledge that are our heritage. You are neither harnessed, nor have you been at any time, and you never will be. You have to let go of any idea you have about controlling anyone or anything, including yourself. Your life is under the direction and supervision of the Universal Laws of Nature, and this sacred temple of Heaven does not need advice from you.

However, you are a part of creation. Hence, you are and always have been involved in, and participated in, everything that has happened around you. You helped to bring into being all that you have seen in person and all that has transpired. You have the knowledge that upcoming events, whether you agree or disagree with them, love or hate every minute of them, are beyond the conscious mind's ability. They are all unfolding according to the Law of Nature. The Law causes the seasons to change, as it causes the moon and the sun to rise and set daily.

The nature of weather is a cycle, and so it turns to rain, to storms, to snow, or to a sunny day. When wintertime comes, trees lose their leaves and birds fly south to escape the cold weather. However, when you look at your life at this moment, you cannot see this invisible Law and its patterns; you only begin to see it as events occur.

Although invisible Laws are the governing energy used to control the horizontal and the vertical, they do not misrepresent or abuse their power over your life or the activities of any organisms. They love to see, strengthen, and improve your business, as well as the life of all organisms living on Earth. The truth is that their vital energy flows through you and continues to increase your strength, health, and dynamic areas, and they quietly change you via the power of the Universal Source. They are consciously aware of everything that is above, below, around, following, and close to you. They remind you with signs and symbols and let you think you are cared for, protected, guided, and completed. However, they are not the same as the Ego that takes pleasure in admiration, awe, shock, winning, and commanding all things. The force of nature allows all living things to show themselves at the right moment and the perfect place. It has never commanded you; rather, it sustains and guides you all the way to being virtuous, so you can live serenely and unafraid.

Anytime your zest is in alignment with the Universal Source, you will begin to recognize you are actually dwelling in both positive and negative of the duality world. By doing so, you will change from being judgmental, disrespectful, and ungrateful for being capable of feeling both tired and relaxed, both brave and frightened, and taken care of.   The Universal Laws of Nature affect the occurrence of these events.

Your negative thoughts express themselves and insist that you can learn to remove the undesired pain from your life without having first blended with the Universe. However, the Inner Source within requires that you use harmonized approaches in perfect alignment with the Source. The Inner Source urges you to avoid excessive use energy, knowing that everything is unfolding as it should; you know your innermost thoughts agree with this. Gloomy thoughts will fade in time, and they will be replaced by a review and determination that will appear at the right time.

Now, begin a conscious, psychiatric process for yourself: learn to relinquish every natural desire to the invisible Source. At the same time, allow others the freedom to be themselves and to practice their own designs. This involves talking to yourself so that you learn not to judge anything or feel frustrated; rather, sit back and relax. Allow events to unfold as they should, because they give a spiritual response for the feelings you are judging. (You must constantly remind yourself that everything on Earth is dynamic, even though you do not see it or feel it.) Invite the Divine's determination into you by accepting whatever action you are experiencing. Then, you move forward without criticism or restraint; thus, you shift to the core. Now, release the system that allows the Source to flow freely through your life. Be vigilant about the ego-mind that may always be scheming and leading you in the wrong direction by insisting that you should stop. It urges you to reject the Source, which represents the best unfolding of everything.

It is important that you must also awaken your mind to the entity you should see: the author's mind, or the Universal Source.

The belief that the Ego can manage your zest is a state of illusion and a complete rejection of true reality your own Authentic Self. You must be vigilant and not let the Ego-self make you believe it. The most dangerous times are when your mind is not alert or when you feel distressed and tired. Meditate inwardly on the belief that problems on Earth can be taken care of by a calm and tranquil nature. By putting aside our pride and differences, we should be able to help each other. At the same time, we realize chaotic events are unpreventable, but, by maintaining unwavering attention when upheaval and catastrophes occur, we know how to manage these situations more easily without causing more problems than we can take on. When we can see all, it will help to keep us from the Ego's control. We will no longer feel frustrated and displeased, stressed or anxious. Rather, we will replace these feelings with ease. Then, when we are rested, we will feel the emotional help of love and peace that will have emerged at the right time. Furthermore, you are reminded that it is not what you see surrounding you that makes you feel immediate comfort. It is the key events that transpire through you, connect you always with joy, and align you with the Divine unity and peace. They encourage you to do what you do. The eye of the needle cannot walk you through everything: the Law of Magnetic Energy is all.

Are you following your kindness within to guide you in walking the great way, fearlessly, and without worrying that anything will go astray or lead to deadly consequences? Can you accept being received with tremendous honor and respect by others? The best strategy is doing right, avoiding division and corruption.

The unique way you see comes from within you. You see that the oceans, the lands, the animals, and all organic life forms are connected via the Source. From that perspective, you see what would change your life dramatically. The world and your life on earth are just one mega-powerful life force with many bodies. Earth is one giant collective consciousness of vital life force. This unity creates a point of enormous strength, which has more horsepower than the entire world's computers connected together. Everything is essential, every living organism, including those both seen and unseen on Earth. Unfortunately, we continue to distance ourselves from this collective consciousness, going our separate ways and choosing to distinguish ourselves from the oneness.

The world is part of you; it has never been separated from you. Understand that you can survive even if you do not see it as part of you, but surely the oceans, the air you breathe, the water, the plants, the animals, and everyone else on Earth are part of you. Think about it; when the world gets polluted, you may be affected by it. When the animals and plants are deficient, you are influenced by that too. When you see people with no food, living in poverty, and striving to survive, your heart hurts with love and compassion; you recognize their pains and feel it within you. By seeing yourself in others, you will find the kindheartedness, generosity, and commitment to change your choices and have confidence in your individuality and differences. You have every reason for feeling the need to use your natural ability to help them. You should not see things from the Ego's interpretation: neglect, lack of interest in others, and thinking you cannot do anything about it. You can use this for your zest by adding compassion, kindness, and warmth to your personal belief system and changing it from within. You will change as you switch to align with the Source and start living honorably, healthily, and peacefully.

One of the most powerful things in life is healthy living. To avoid complacency, one must have already experienced illness to prevent it from happening again. However, there are various reasons your heart can become tired. When your body feels sick, it means that some area in your heart is not in accord agreement with God's spirit. For example, fever, fatigue, shortness of breath, and coughing are proof of illness' presence. The general equivalent of such symptoms in our mind might be fear, worry, anxiety, indifference, anger, hatred, stress, or impatience. Different activities in our minds show that our thoughts are out of alignment with the Source. Our true Authentic Self should show compassion, purity, kindness, genuineness, tolerance, truthfulness, and patience. Many of the palpable senses might describe our complete qualities and unique features. If you are compromised by negative energy, your head could feel tired. That could explain why you are thinking pessimistically. You want to redirect your mind back to your chosen, original, positive emotional state. When the thoughts in your mind wander, that creates imbalance and malfunction. These expressions can be explained as your emotional self experiencing fear, illusions, worry, and indifference, which are signs of detachment from the Source. These negative energies could alter your physical mind and body completely, which could explain why you are experiencing anxiety, fatigue, and shortness of breath, pain, and sorrow. These negative energies begin with the negative ego's craving.

The ego's power will be in your thoughts, and leads you to take part in these negative activities, whether you are doing so intentionally or unwillingly. The dark shadows will weaken you. It will get worse if you let these toxic ingredients abide in you; it will hurt you big time.

Now, sit quietly and breathe deeply, in and out. Meditate on the current troubles that you have, confirm that you relinquish all unwanted desires, and gently lower your body to be healed by the power of God the Healer.

Listen to what your Inner Voice says to you about your current situation and then continue to meditate inward to improve your life. You try to discern the positive and negative sides of your problems and perceive which deep thoughts are leading and affecting you, then begin to remove the imbalanced thoughts in the mind's eye. Ensure that you are tired of living in negativity and negative situations; you can stop and remove them. Then, go ahead and remove them from your consciousness. Change begins to emerge; you continue to support the continual development of healing, you experience the Divine Light within, and all your troubles fade away. You are no longer in bondage with the dark gloominess.

Then, say to yourself in consciousness, "Although I am suffering with my bodily pain and illness, I command all negative poisons to flow out of my physical body permanently. By the Power of Divine Light presence, I persistently invite healing and miracles to heal my sick body. I cast out all fears, worries, and confusions. I understand that I do not have any remedies other than intentionally aligning with the Divine Light Power. Therefore, I am not suffering from pain because I am not. I understand my body is the refuge for my soul; I intentionally move forward, casting out all sicknesses, and replacing them with purity, good health, and positive energy.

I am consciously aware that sickness and pain are part of the healing transformation, and I accept this. I intend to meet and resonate with people who bring only peace and tranquility, and no harm will come near me. This allows me, constantly and forever, to connect with joy and bliss ignited by the power of God's spirit within." When your thoughts are satisfied, you should be physically healthy and no virus can penetrate your body. Any illness is refused entry at the door and bounces back to where it originated. This happens when your mind is complete, without any gloomy, negative thoughts or emotions. Your wish is granted, so no negative energy can come near you.

Your body can communicate with any negative message, so if you focus on negative thoughts you will become tired, then disappointed, almost instantly. Any message can communicate and respond to your body's gestures so that you feel confident or negative in your consciousness. Your body reacts according to your current feelings and the emotional state of your mind. If your mind is willing but you are physically tired, your body can still heal itself and return to its original state of well-being. Hence, you own a blissful state of mind, and your body will cooperate with you. It will work with you, continuously striving for vibrant health.

Imagine seeing yourself abiding in a world filled with joy and happiness, blessing you with miracles of peace and harmony with no differences or disagreement. You see the Divine energy flowing through everything and everywhere. Even a thunderstorm can transform into a miracle, like sparks of fireworks, so everybody can enjoy it. You just enjoy your life with your body, mind, soul, and everything surrounding you. It makes you think so calmly and joyfully.

When you look at the sky, you see visions, and the invisible seems to talk with you. Birds are flying freely everywhere. They do not want to change what they are but certainly accept all the freedom of flying high and being in perfect harmony with the environment without fear or worry. Fair or evil situations do not apply to them, nor do they alter the way they fly freely in the blue sky that the Divine created for them. Nothing can change who they are, and we humans should do the same; we should live nonviolently and without fear. In order to live peacefully and fearlessly, we must trust ourselves as part of each other. We should love each other, share in each other's happiness and sorrow, and send out sympathy and compassion, so miracles can change everyone's life. It is within reach: caring for all, light for all, and peace for all, in command of the Divine Light-Power.

Visualize a world where you continue to receive the Divine energy flowing to you, with no puzzlement and bewilderment, you only see the peace, joy, and love, and the same source of Infinite

Being. Beyond that, there is and always has been the Divine Light that protects, hints, and helps us to make plans to improve the high quality of our lives; it knows all our needs.

Imagine a world in which everything you see is blended together with trust, love, peace, and harmony. It is a place that does not recognize words such as "conflict," "hatred," "envy," "greed," and "war." All humans are willing to share every success and satisfaction with each other honestly, truthfully, tolerantly, and with patience at every moment. Indeed, we are the people; we are the people originating from the Source, the Mind of God.

I certainly think we all need to live in peace in a relaxed world with no warfare, no cultural differences, no greed, and no envy. We need to do this with calmness and peace—anything is possible, even more so than ever before. It could be a difficult and uphill battle, but it needs to be accomplished so this world's peace initiative can someday become reality. There are many good-hearted people, like former U.S. President Bill Clinton. His clear vision for attaining peace is excellent. Mr. Clinton is a kind humanitarian with a passion for world order for the benefit of all humanity. In the timeless present, Mr. Clinton is, and always will be, blessed by the Divine. His actions come from the heart, producing work that is worthy; this is greatness. God leads him and supplies all that he needs to work for peace, and he will someday make success. He is in the Divine; in perfect harmony with heaven's way: He is a major division of that perfect order.

Humanity is under the umbrella of heaven. Heaven knows the way to overcome everything in a peaceful and silent state. We can never beat nature, so we must choose to embrace all it has to offer us. Indeed, we benefit from what nature has offered us, such as the four seasons, the rain that helps crops to grow, the sun that keeps us warm, the oceans with their separate waters, and the mainland. This all occurred without our effort through the Divine, hence, we can relax and enjoy the benefits sent from Heaven.

We do not need to ask for anything because Heaven knows and supplies us automatically and infinitely with what we need. The supply is endless, providing for everything; there is never a shortage. There is more than enough for everyone under the care and vigilance of Heaven. However, you must be satisfied and show respect for all you have received, and then you shall receive more. As soon as you give your order, all will come to pass. Everything is arriving in the flow of Divine time. It is similar to your destiny being guided by the invisible hand of the Source. You do not need to order it or ask for a reservation; all will appear when you want it most.

When you call 1-800-777-Heaven or send an email to heaven@ heaven.div.hn to place your order, then it will come to pass.   You must patiently wait for it to appear though; do not push it, to prevent side effects. Heaven does not want to be pushed, and it cannot be hurried. However, it completes everything at the right time to meet your needs. Visualize an image: you ask Heaven to stop the rain. The rain cannot just stop as per your request, but it will do so by Divine timing. However, your request is noted. You must be patient and wait; Heaven will do everything exactly as it should be. Heaven will never disappoint you, but it works according to Heaven's schedule. Perhaps you think you are running out of time, but, in fact, Heaven always delivers just in time and not a minute late.

By creating an enduring relationship, you constantly connect with the Universal Source. Then, when you make a shift and trust God, your creator who created you, the process starts to work immediately. When this occurs, nothing can break your relationship with God. Furthermore, this allows you to use your internal instinct that guides your daily life, and not trusting potentially confusing and painful plans that come from someone else. Perhaps you have experienced fraud from someone you trust; you probably trusted that person too much. Now is the time for you to make the steadfast decision to remodel your past choices. It is time for you to make conscious connection with a source of Divine choice, and turn back to the desire that is right for you. Then, everything will be manufactured exactly as expected and all confusion will end to exist. Why not build trust and respect for yourself and let your Authentic Self navigate your life instead of acquiring an external agency's help that produces no benefits? You want to honor yourself and all others around you as your coach or trainer; nevertheless, you will eventually be a better person by depending on your Authentic Self.

Nothing on Earth lasts, not even a deluge of rain that will stop after a day or so. All things will return to their original condition of nothingness, from which all things originated. Everything on Earth is short-term; it was not intended to be long-term. However, infinite souls are ever-lasting, ever-evolving, ever-changing, and ever-recycling as part of the basic principle of the Universal Laws of Nature. The Invisible Source that governs Heaven and the Universe is set up this way to allow you to perceive things clearly. Therefore, we see, obey, and follow this command, and through this understanding we strengthen and lucid our minds and thus allow the Universal flow of life to continue. We live with all things in peace with love. When the loving force continues every living thing persists without resistance and the Tree of Life flow ceaselessly. .

Nature will never force us to do anything against our will, and it knows nothing lasts forever. In fact, once everything is created then it is already packed and on its way to respond to nothingness. You, as an individual, should follow the way nature works and select your best option to resonate with the Universal Laws. For example, if some sticky, burned bread clings to a frying pan and you need to get it out all at once, you know it will not be an easy task. However, when you let go of your resistance, that sticky, black, burned bread inside the frying pan will slowly erode. This is because you have consciously chosen to be part of the recurring law of nature.

You are reminded that even Heaven cannot force an effort to occur. All things must be allowed to happen naturally and freely. Therefore, all matters, large or small, must agree to occur naturally.

If you want to meet peace in both the inside and outside worlds, your priority is to stay calm and allow all thoughts to arise from within. Ultimately, your every desire and initiative will be revealed to you effortlessly. You will achieve your aims. If the answer has not yet come, you might have to wait patiently for it to pop into your mind. It is as if a storm is brewing, and you must simply wait for it. Currently, you have no ability or power. When you reach out quietly and gently to Mother Nature in every moment, confirming that you want to live in peace and harmony, a previously unknown peace will make its dwelling in you. You have chosen not to be the host of the ego but to be humble before God. You make peace and maintain inner calm wherever you go. God Most High loves you; you are His ears and eyes. He hears and sees and answers every request. God will help you realize that you must surrender everything to Him to meet everything in this world. Therefore, you must seek God and begin to see everything in God, without end.

Seek the calmest emotional response in the context of your life, even in the midst of economic crisis, in an argument, or in a traffic jam. You can always find the calm center of yourself and then tap into the stillness and peace or just be. Take a long, deep breath in and breathe out serenity and peacefulness. Continue to clear your thoughts, and do not make judgments on anything. Stay out of violent situations or fights with others, so that you do not force others into madness. Limit yourself in any situation and circumstance, even in the most troublesome times or those which have never happened before. React to stillness and stay until the chaos returns to the normal state of calmness and tranquility. You must be consciously aware that fighting never solves anything. Rather, it creates a more annoying and uncontainable situation, and making peace becomes more difficult to meet.

You have the divine ability to stay still and centered with your Authentic Self when you reply to the circumstance and conditions of your life. Therefore, you are able to influence chaotic events, regardless of how difficult they may seem. You have the ability to break the iceberg and shatter it into pieces, so that the crisis vanishes into the thin air. All things return to a state of peacefulness and tranquility. You can put this into practice should a corresponding problem ever recur.

There will be no winning when weapons are used to end war or conflict. Violence cannot melt down any inconvenience or disruption, and it should be used only as a last resort. Weapons are the tools of torture, destroying and wrecking life. Weapons serve the purpose of evil, are used to promote violence, and should be avoided. We should live life according to the principles of the Universal Laws of Nature.

The Universal Source inspires the life-force, while weapons of mass destruction only destroy. Unfortunately, we humans have failed to learn to restrain ourselves from sharing negative energy, craving profit and wealth, and feeling jealousy. People who think of using weapons to do things to others or take from them will never succeed. All humans, regardless of their geographic location, race, or beliefs, should align with God's Spirit to promote harmony and tranquility and not ambitions that only come from the false Self-Ego and, often, the chaos events. The source of such ambitions is the evil eye, which is what happens when we look with judgment, envy, and hatred upon what someone else has.

If we kill each other by using lethal weapons, we will stop the fluid energy continue to evolve and develop and flow freely through the spirit inside us. The evil force will then celebrate victory as it creates problems and a time of grief. Taking pleasure in winning a war aligned with the dark cabal's intent to kill is absurd: It shall never prevail. Similarly, a person thinking of winning a war is in a state of denial and is confused, and delusional. It is a negative sign when his or her wicked nature comes forth without understanding the consequences. Conversely, the Source embraces peace, and all things connected to the Source will succeed in abundance. The higher promise is peace; the one goal is to love. These will always win a victory over all.

In the physical world, we express our true nature through the Authentic Self connecting to the Universal Source, the Mind of God. However, when we engage with the evil force in killing others because we listen to the Egoistic mind, we resonate with the conditions that cause pain and suffering. This leads to separation from God; we chase the business to prove our superiority and feel extremely powerful, and we only want to show we are above all things. This turns ambitions into the aimless pleasures and aims at destroying all humans to the point we forget we are here to seek the spirituality harmonized to all humans. History has shown that from the simplicity of bows and arrows that end at a short distance, we have advanced to using the most advanced, powerful weapons of mass destruction (WMD) that could end the world remotely by a nuclear blast, with just one push of a button.

Weapons allow evil to flourish and harm life; they are the evil servant of the dark force. With them, we have the capacity and the ability to destroy the Earth. Luckily thus far, no one who possesses WMD has used them. Let us hope that we avoid our own destruction and the role of hatred will stop; this will allow us to awaken to our true nature of infinite wisdom with love and peace, through the perspective of God's love, and share in Divine fullness. The being who shares in it increases in greatness by all that comes into existence within so that the great abundance of God's gift is received. His grace is available to everyone, replacing the destructive force as the global superpower on Earth.

Those solid mass destruction weapons are against God's will; however, violent words, negative inner-most thoughts or bodily gestures, and aggressive behavior are just as strong, and they can also threaten human life. For example, if someone says, "If you dare to come one step nearer, I will use my sword to kill you." The person's words amount to a threat to life in tort. (Tort is a civil remedy: a wrongful act for which damages may be claimed by the injured party.)

Those violent attributes are not part of our real identity or higher consciousness soul. The true nature of humanity is non-violent, kindhearted, loving, and caring, and will receive God's unconditional love and eternal peace, which is available to all of us. Hence, with every moment you live in the timeless present, you must expect peace and God's love and be consciously aware of His omnipresence. When you are aware of God and His presence, you can feel the harmony surrounding you, and all pains, hatred, and feelings of isolation and insensitivity fade.

Start today: Be nice to all your fellow humans, and refuse to use threatening language; cancel hatred, jealousy, and envy from your mind and your daily activities; and, more importantly, never use deadly weapons of any kind against others. Never promote violence or hatred, and never respond in a negative way to your children. Instead, educate them with love and peace and live in the Great Way. Listen to your intuition and it will help to encourage and aid you to act honorably as your day unfolds. Clean away every gloomy idea that feeds your mind so that when you receive an inspirational message, your account will consciously change and feel fabulous, and you will be inspired to do practical things.

Bear this in mind: All creation comes from one Source. In a moment, all of God's creations return to the zero; this means all things go back to the Universal Mind of the Universal Creative Life Force to make one change—the Source.

We all know God has no form or shape or gender but is pure, void, and hallowed, a white light of unstructured energy, dwelling perfectly within all creation, and relevant to all. Although this invisible white light energy is hidden, it is full of enthusiasm, is vast, and is never weakened. It is always available to us: above, below, surrounding, and all-pervading. It is the leading real-life activity within every creäture on Earth.

Now that you are aware of the Infinite life energy living within you, you must ask, command, and verify its existence so that it will connect with you in the consciousness now. You need to trigger and expand its existence so it can easily move to help you. Because it is free will, you always have the choice to activate or deactivate it. Only you can decide if you want to associate with the inner light to get power. You must do it; the Universal Source cannot do it for you. When you decide to activate this Authentic Self, you allow it to aid you so it can go with you during your journey on Earth. When you connect with the Light, you can always feel inner peace and calmness. You will love the inner light and never forget it. It is part of your everlasting power from Heaven to support your journey on Earth. When you use the Inner Light everywhere you choose, you will only attract positive events, and others with the same beliefs will be drawn to you.

You watch and listen to your first question that originates from your own Inner dialogue. When such a thought arises in your mind, simply listen to what it says without questioning; let it tell you what it wants. You may get some negative notions speaking to you, but do not worry; allow them to speak, and you will find that what they want is to feel good. Give them the life they want and an opportunity for discussion, and they will be happy and slowly erode. Enabling the negative dialogue in the infinite now may help you to select the current position if it is favorable to you. At the same time, this enables you to remove the greater illusion of fear and anxiety, so you shed no evil judgments.

Transmute the way you always think by tapping into the Inner Source. It will change the real reality of your life, and you will begin to live more positively and fearlessly.

When we talk about your body as a haven for your gentle spirit, we refer to your origin. You came from nothingness: the void. You are the Authentic Self, the boundless energy manifested by the same Source that created everything, including every living creäture on Earth. Therefore you align with your own Source's ability to attract capital and people, and they will make your life easier. The key events you predict will happen, and even your negative economic situation will diminish. The light will make sure you have everything you need to succeed easily and accurately. You are the people, and you are the primary source, loveliness, and greatness. Indeed, you are the vast importance connected to the Mind of God, the Universal Creative Life Force, which is never-ending and no beginning. God is "the Alpha and the Omega, the First and the Last, the Beginning and the End" (Revelation 22:13, NIV).

If you want all your desires to register, you must change your inner belief from "It will possibly never happen for me" to "It is emerging." Then, look for signs and symbols that show your appeal is on its way. When you pray and ask for what you want, keep in mind that when you believe you will receive, then you shall have it someday. Thus whatever you think about will be what you receive, with the help of the Inner Source, which transpires everything into reality. What you think now to be totally impossible will become entirely possible.

Up to now, while writing these words, my mind had been so relaxed; then, suddenly, the word enemy flashed across my mind. "Enemy," I thought. "Why did this information come to me?" Then, silent for a second, I concentrated on and contemplated the question: Can I live without an enemy? It seemed that if I always thought about my enemy then I would compromise my health; in other words, I would hurt myself.

It is clear that when I contemplate a person I dislike, my blood pressure instantly lifted, my heart beats faster than usual, all negative thoughts about that person emerge, and emotionally, I become disheartened; my whole day explodes just by thinking about the person I dislike. In addition, a past event about that dreadful relationship, recorded in my subconscious mind, resurfaces to disturb me. I take responsibility for my well-being. I must stop perceiving and revisiting an age-old conflict, which only distresses my awareness. I deliberately choose to erase those memories from my subconscious and concentrate and meditate on perceiving the peace, love, and forgiveness that is the basic essence of my being. I choose to forgive those who have before wronged me and have closed that part of my life forever. Now, my thoughts are clear; I will not have enemies, and my heart will experience more joy and happiness. I love being, but not-being with hindrances, frights, and struggles. I am free from hatred and fear; I am liberated.

The void is emptiness, which hollows out of the core of a hub, to which everything connects and then branches out.

You should live from the center of the void that is the core of your being; everything extends from a vessel, the center of your beingness (the important element of existing or coming into being). You have the hidden part of you that is the center, and you have the obvious component—a physical body that refuges your spirit, so when both mixes, that becomes you. The hollow invisible space is the center of your every movement. Your thoughts, blood vessels, cells, heartbeat, five senses, organs, lung, liver, colon— your whole body—and all your energy flow to the external world from the hollow. All your inspired thoughts come from the center; they then enter your mind, going in and out, just like your breathing. Without the void, you cannot assemble your thoughts as yours. When you are disassembled, you might have returned to nonexistence or nonbeing, even though your body is still here. Once you were here, and then you are not. It all depends on the usefulness of what is the truth and what is not possible. However, the reality is that you are a spiritual being; that will never change. It is always true that only a genuine expression can blend with the truth.

You cannot view or eradicate your inner self, but you can meditate within and experience the true nature of the vibrating, loving energy of your own inner spirit. You can always find the loophole that allows you to enter the silence, sacred space that is absolute, void, and perfect; it allows the invisible flow of love through your physical body. The more energy you send to yourself, the healthier you will be and the more you will be in harmony with your Source being. As you continue to send this loving energy to every organ and cell of your body, your body and mind experiences a dramatic shift in your energy field. You will feel energized and want to continue what you do to get more of this optimistic energy. You can meet this holistic journey through inward, self-loving meditation, which helps you reconnect with that silent and sacred place inside yourself. The purpose of meditation is to obtain silence, so you can give your soul to manifest itself and to allow you to stay in the nothingness void.

When we depend on the vivid colors of the external world, obviously, these bright colors blinds our eyes; we cannot clearly see the actual image created and observed from the inner realm. Our attention is mainly drawn to earthly pleasures and material needs. Everything created in the fantasy world looks perfect, but it is actually full of illusions. All things are provisional and never permanent. Since everything is just coming and going, life in the material world is limited to a brief and passing existence. While our eyes can only see the colors that suit us, we continue to investigate and seek unwise things that lie behind the world of manifestations. We spend energy to acquire material things; hence, we neglect our creator. At the same time, we lose our awareness that God is behind all creativity.

If you believe you can use the five senses to experience everything from the external environment, then you have to think critically about what these intellectual senses can do for you. You may think you need more money and power, but you can never get enough. Neither one can ever fully satisfy you. You continually look for more in your everyday life and think you can gain it all. Your whole life is based on getting more than you need. Consequently, you never feel inner peace and tranquility. You seek out more and more unusual things and continue to pursue the "impossible." Your life becomes an obsessive drive for new items, resulting in a waste of energy. This paralyzes your spiritual growth, distances you from your ideal life and sends you down a shaky path towards the material Ego.

Why do you impatiently hunt for substance and constantly seek out more power? It sometimes seems that with every breath, humans want more material possessions to satisfy their harsh external needs. Some people think this can free us from pain, suffering, scarcity and poverty. It defines the world's belief system: those with more money in their pockets have more profound experiences than those without. In truth, though, money may or may not serve the purpose of joy and happiness amidst external world experiences of gratification and contentment. Instead, money may show a weak connection with our Source being and unconsciously enter into an illusory agreement with the mind.

Intelligent people will never look for material wealth and power; instead, they want to watch the world and name exclusively with what is clear and true. You can be consciously observing this world while at the same time fully present. Inward meditation is a place where you can imagine and design a life of fulfillment. In the silent, nameless void content, you find fearlessness and joy, creating a luminous sea of infinity not found in the mortal world. From the inner perspective, life is divinely full and illuminable. It never ccases. When you meet the Divine you will continue to grow, evolving into a spiritual reality that is truly all you need. The search for more money is Ego based madness and reflects the expectations built around the Ego's concepts and beliefs. The true value of yourself is found when you detach from the gloomy Ego and to certain degrees meet liberation from the self.

When you are consciously aware of your true nature, you realize that all substances in the world are transitory, including your current physical body that hosts your infinite soul. The Sage recognizes earthly appearances and avoids and overcome the Ego temptation of accumulating more wealth and power. You should use your aptitude to learn more than just what is visible. Go beyond your usual sensory experiences, and you will see that a red rose is more than just a common flower. It has many features, such as a pleasant fragrance and soft flower petals. Use this understanding you can tap into the creative, power of an invisible force that brings tremendous and seemingly impossible miracles. These miracles come out of your deepest hidden desires, not to have treasures, but to be possessed Divine contentment in the here and now.

Where do the seeds come from? They come from nothingness or nowhere. They naturally arise from the formless ether-world, created by the designer who makes these seeds available in the now so that you can enjoy them. When you realize that all things come from the spirit realm, you will connect with it. You will want to go into your inner consciousness to experience your true nature within the invisible nothingness that connects us with the Universal Source. The sooner you learn that the inner world is your own choice, the sooner you will know that you can have the inner strength to aid you in the mortal world. When you can relax and focus, you will find that everything you ever wanted is always there and that going inward is your only solution.

You simply have to get back to that childlike, innocent Divine connection again. As a child, you believe you have that innermost connection with the light of all things, and you feel that you have had inexpressible joy and fun. Unfortunately, growing up has changed every one of your experiences; but you simply remember the memories of childhood and reignite that internal fire again to consciously reconnect with God's spirit. Cultivate support and appreciate all that you have received. Meditate on gratefulness, but never on accumulating more acquisitions, wealth, and power.

Your mind should be detached from any of your conscious thoughts and impulses; they bring no joy or happiness. Instead, you should pay attention to inspirational thoughts inspired from

God's command. When God sees that you have strong trust in Him, He will emerge and make His dwelling in you and with you. You always sought and searched for God but, unknown of yourself, the Kingdom of God is invisible living within your heart. You only need to meditate inwardly and in a silent, sacred place you shall see God. Then, all your confusions will vanish because you know that God has always been within; as you focus inward, all that will be clear. You know the latent illumination of God is always dwelling within, and the butterfly is the caterpillar from which it emerges that bestows all your needs in the mortal world.

When your mind is silent and has thoughtlessness because you are silent in your innermost center, you make a shift and begin to see beauty omnipresent, hear the sound of the mantra that uplifts your spirit, experience the taste of watermelon as gourmet food, and in the inmost center discover that the kernel of truth will only cultivate within your awakened consciousness and that the illuminate light actually has lightened the inner realm where everything is contained. Learn to become the master yourself; choose to live within. From there, everything that is born will come with possibilities that change the external world in which we are acquainted.

Always live without attachments; resist the urge to want to keep them. You want to detach yourself from everything and be able to let all things go without a second thought. You will get everything in your life, and wellness will be yours. You will be surrounded by the still power within, and the precious seed that you have will also be contained within. Relax, enjoy, be well, and benefit from every moment with your own reality, which is eternal peace at work from the creator, the Universal Creative Life Force of the Mind of God.

Although you can connect with people's minds via collective consciousness, you think independently of all other people. It is imperative that you keep self-determination of both your negative and explicit opinions of other people and never let others decide for you. You should not let their assessments be more prominent than your own determination, regardless of how much they love, help and support, or dislike you. If you think their evaluation is more accurate than your own, you will be profoundly disturbed and afflicted.

You should not try to seek the favor of others; instead, trust your own internal intuition. This will continue to allow the natural flow of the Divine to sparkle through to your creative thoughts.

However, when you are dealing with a significant legal issue, such as, a living will, allow your Inner Being alerts you to consult an attorney as if applicable. It is this belief that nourishes your unique thoughts, because you are granted the distinct abilities to do your job of fulfilling your purpose and meaning of being here. It is essential in your journey to seek within to seek out. What hides underneath are the gems of your innermost Source being. Are you willing to bear, share and discover your Inner Being, the ever-ceasing creation of the Divine? It may seem difficult to believe at first, but this is definitely significant for your infinite existence in this life and the next.

Your Inner Self is the invisible seed for your spiritual reality. Although it is unseen, it is not unreal. With this truth in mind, open your spiritual ears to hear and open your eyes to the light to see the unseen and welcome new hope in things that have been concealed into your life. You cannot have these feelings without first drawing your attention to them. Then you must persist to try to see until you feel an inner connection with the world above that the Divine is seeking you as so you sought Him. It is the undeniable truth that both parties are longing and seeking each other because of love. Through the internal awakening, you are now reconnected back to the source of your creator. He has helped you to realize and perceive who you really are and all things to which you are drawn. Believe that God has drawn you close to Him, like a magnet attracts to another. The Divine is calling, so you must answer His call. Would you like to respond to seek out for Him and invite God's spirit into your life? It is your call; you should do it.

The Inner Source does not organize or interfere with things; instead, it lets them do in their own way to produce clear, visible results. Whatever agreement satisfies your journey's goal will occur naturally, produce effects, and be in perfect alignment. Even if it turns out that you receive only criticism, this is also part of this arrangement. Pushing for results is what you should not do; they should always occur naturally, regardless of the ending. Never decide the last outcome; let it flow freely through your mind. Step outside your body and mind. Being outside of your mind means there is no chance for the Ego to change your decision or cause you distress. Wherever the Ego is favored problems can arise, but your true nature will change the major implementation of external favors with the consciousness. Then, what others think of you will neither surprised nor bother you.

Your thoughts agree that your life is in harmony with your own Inner Being. Your own private notions are all you need. However, if you begin to feel insecure and disagree with others, you may try to trust in other's opinions instead of your own; this is unacceptable and will cause misalignment with your own Authentic Self.

Allow yourself to remember that you are a Spiritual Being. Letting other people's opinions governing their own self and what you should or should not be tended to threaten your real, eternal self. Those other people do not realize that their physical consciousness is aligned with the Ego mind; thus, seeking their approval doubles the jeopardy that your physical mind will become focused on power. Your real body is not a main collection of physical attributes; your Infinite Being is you are communicating to your physical self.

Your inner spiritual consciousness is where you receive your creativity through your latent mind. Honor your intuition and your true nature; be passionate about your thoughts, for these are constantly aligned with the Universal Source and with the loving essence of the Mind of God.

You connect to everyone and everything whose origin is the Mind of God through your latent spiritual mind. By living through the Higher Infinite Soul, you can also reach the spiritual guides and guardians of others who might help you. Your temporary material body is the host for the Authentic Self in this provisional illusory world. We rely solely on the outside world, and our primary focus continues to be on acquiring assets for ourselves more than sharing freely with others. World peace will continue to be a fantasy as we strive for personal wealth and worldly goods, and struggle to engage in life. Change will take place only when we learn to enjoy sharing our wealth and love with each other. Unfortunately, our potential to create a positive future is uncertain, at least for now, because we disregard all indications and recognitions of the truth: Your Infinite Self has the most inherent potential to continually transform you, so you can live fully. Let us work together to engage in a new transformation and prepare for the quantum leap! We seek and have sought God and world peace. We claim that we wish for peace, but we must be willing to seriously undertake the work that is required to have our wish granted through the lucid inspiration of the Source, the Mind of God.

Now contemplate the lucid notion of the eternal, which has never transformed; it continues and has no beginning or end. It is endless, lasting forever. Since the eternal has no type or format, it cannot be seen, heard, or touched, but it is useful; you know it is and that it always has been.

The spirit world is invisible, inaudible, and intangible, but when you go inward via your spirit, by intuition you can see it, hear it, and touch it. Your spirit and intuition then merge with the unseen, unheard, and untouched; they blend to become one. To see without eyes, to hear without ears, and to touch without hands, is living formlessly. You need awareness to resonate with the spirit world and observe the principle of the Universal Laws of Nature, which create and govern all life.

Tapping into the unseen spirit world enables you to see the unseen, hear the unheard, and touch the untouchable, formless force that allows you to attain inner harmony and peace and ultimately, meet your goal: To give eternal peace and tranquility and to live an authentic, spiritual life. To have a true spiritual life, you must renounce the Egoistic concept that identifies with material things, acquisitions, abundance, wealth, gaining higher clout, titles and fame, and achievements. (I recognize this song sung and written by John Lennon entitled, "Imagine." Imagine there's no Heaven It's easy if you try No hell below us Above us only sky Imagine all the people Living for today Imagine there's no countries It isn't hard to do Nothing to kill or die for And no religion to Imagine all the people Living life in peace You may say that I'm a dreamer But I'm not the only one I hope someday you'll join us And the world will be as one.)

Was John Lennon just a dreamer, or can his dream transforms into reality? I believe one day we will share his vision and turn it into profound reality. Every vision begins with a dream; all changes through our inner consciousness and later transform into our true external reality. This is a vision that is our true spiritual growth, true experience and true fulfillment of our reason for the Source being, which turns formless into one inner connection through one Source, the Mind of God. Then, you re-enter the zero from which you and all life forms originated. By doing so, you are restored to the absolute realm of Infinite Being, and you live in a world that is formless.

Now, look up into the distant sky—see a cloud, a star, the mountains, and everything you possibly can, and then turn your attention away by gazing at an unmoving tree outside your window. Continue this vigilant observation. When the wind blows, track the progress of every leaf, and then see as it returns to quiet. The leaf reenters peacefulness and harmony with nature and has no complaints. This is a principle of the Laws of Nature at work; everything should cooperate with everything else, with no risks or challenges, but by simply accepting what is and what is not. All things remain unchanged and live happily together with ease, blissfulness, and calmness. The sooner all things happen, the sooner the silence returns, and all things stay calm. Hence every occurrence must be allowed to happen as it transpires; we must willingly accept and realize that we cannot change the state of nature because we have limitations of power. We cannot transform nature's forces.

Acceptance makes it easier for everything to occur naturally and simply, without effort, especially when we are consciously aware of our limited condition in the world. Only when we look into the silence can we change things remotely or hear an audio recording from afar and link it to the things that moved it, without touching it. Then, we want to live life within the spirit, so we join forces within and connect to the Inner Source, echoing its peace and transcending what we see within to the outer world.

This becomes our reality, which we have filled with love, health, wealth, success and tranquility.

One of the most rewarding things in life is living in absolute inner peace with your being. Empty your thoughts demanded by the Ego, your false self. When your inner consciousness is at peace, your heart beats easily and naturally; every organ, blood cell, and formed part agrees and cooperates with you for your nutritional health and wholeness, because they always listen to the messages vibrating through your mind. When you send a stressful message via your Ego-based mind, your body becomes stressed and angry. However, when you subdue your nerves, the impact on your body during the day and night becomes more gentle and subtle, and you feel the joy. Your body appreciates that you do not worry it so much, so it responds without fear or restraint and lets you experience a full and abundant healthy life. Your inner realm and projection to the external world are synchronized and allow you to live in peace with the Mother Nature of all living things.

Life is a continuum, a cycle; it comes, and then it goes. At any one point, there is life, lifelessness, life, and we are a part of it. All things have a lifespan, including our computers, televisions, or any other living things, large or small; there is no exception. Life can result in any form, and when life becomes thinner, it expires. This means that all things created on Earth have a committed time frame with a closing phase. Some live shorter lives, while others may decide to spend a bit longer on Earth than other people; at the end, though, we all return to zero (the place from whence we came). Although all living things will manifest differently with unknown expiration dates, the last rebirth, rebuilding, and resurrection are consistent, because life never ceases.

When we willingly accept this life's cyclical changes, we always triumph.

Endings may cause pain and sorrow, but they signify new beginnings: a vibrant life. There are many reasons to feel sorrow and pain, whether it is on completion of a project, the end of a relationship, a completed retirement, or even the end of life. In fact, you should understand that after things have flourished into being, they prepare to return to their roots. Your soul will return to zero and integrate with the Universal Source, becoming one. The end allows you to return to your origin, a placeless place, back to your roots with your creator—to what is—and to be a free spirit again.

The final place for achieving peace and enlightenment are in this void of emptiness, the null void of your origin. You have a sense of peace when your time is up, and more sense of inner peace comes as you return to the Source, where all cycles end and begin. This is the final fulfillment of your own destiny—what you have been here to discover all along during your personal, spiritual journey.

Your soul will walk along this journey with you until the end, and then you will return to the void of nothingness. You have lived in many life forms and have been in and out of many different relationships. Life is still coming and going, and you live despite the transitions from beginnings into endings, back into beginnings. You are created in the physical body, but your spirit consciously connects with the oneness of the Universal Source. You know everything is eternal; you can always start again. When your loved one leaves you, let go: do not feel guilty or hope to reconcile. You must believe all things happen for a reason if it does not happen you have never omitted anything yet you still, in silence, you find calmness, peace, and the contentment inside.

Doing so will obstruct the constant flow of your Life Spirit and cause hardships for you; you do not want that to happen. Let the relationship go. This applies to business ventures that fail as well; do not feel guilty. Let it be part of the natural flow of life. Do not get stuck in worldly events with their comings and goings. You must allow for continuity, where endings become beginnings. When you start to change, all things will run smoothly, and you will accept this with gratitude.

Remind yourself that your Source has always worked through every event; then try to add to your Source through your innermost thoughts. Your problems can always be resolved, and you are not judged. The Source never abandons or disappoints you; it is always helpful. When you feel emotional pain, you are not judged or punished. Rather you are, in all stages, free from judgment, and you experience steadiness. Always tell your thoughts to be consistent, flowing like liquid silver. The Source is the author of all things, the Mind of God; it is ideal. You can depend on it. It brings new relationships, quiet, and happiness. It brings joy and blissfulness; it brings nutritional health; it brings everything and anything. What you believe, you shall receive.

The Universal Source is the author of all life; it is formless, limitless, and infinite. The Source is beyond time and space. When you look at life with the infinite perspective, you will appreciate the idea that the Source Being is the only connection you have where you thrive. In your totality, you have a powerful spirit within and a substantial body as a host for your soul. The soul is never exhaustible as it is unstructured and has always been there ready to tell you.

The more we live within, the closer we get to the Source. The Source's energy never expires, and the more you use it, the more dynamic you become. We must not keep it to ourselves but share its wealth with everyone. The Source has always included us all: No one is significant or better than anyone else. The Source treats everyone equally and impartially. Hence you should stay in harmony with the impartial nature of your Source, and you should be inclusive of everyone in all your thoughts and behavior.

The Source offers care and peace to the entirety of nature without judgment. Eliminate your tendency to judge anyone in your thoughts. The best way to do this is to make sure you respect everyone. You must realize that others share with you the same logical extension from the Source. Seeing those you do not like and commenting on their behavior is like disagreeing with and criticizing the Source. Thus gain the respect of everyone, without discrimination: Then you will be at peace within your Authentic Self, and all of your conflicts and problems will easily dissolve. Do not consider yourself to be all-knowing when you think of others and compare yourself to them. There should be no comparison: We are all divisions and expansions of the Divine.

Extend your generosity to anyone and everyone through your close relationship with your own Inner Source. It is in this way that you can individually and directly extend your inner energy and loving heart to others. Giving and sharing your money to help the neediest shows that you understand the significant benefit of sharing your wealth—you are fulfilling your living time well, as the Source desires for you. The Source is your truth and dwells within you. Quietly, your own soul recognizes you have made the right choice for humanity.

Now, keep an open mind when you get into any difficult situation or circumstance: Always seek the Source within to guide you to solve your problems without casting judgment, but in those moments be fair and just.

The everlasting and ever-giving spirit lives within us and cannot be extinguished: These energies are our consciousness, functioning whether you are aware of their existence or not. By working with these two energies, we will be lead to wholeness: our ultimate goal on Earth. The Source is everlasting and persistent, formless energy: By blending with the Source, you will help create your own perfection. Triggering your internal energy is the way to live with oneness, accomplishment, calmness, and a new approach to understanding your entire physical life. Through the practice of meditation, you will feel you are in a tranquil state of contentment. You will think you have entered a real country where everything is pleasant yet motionless. Within the landscape, you hear the faint sound of a waterfall flowing down to the river; the birds are in tune with nature while the flowers are beaming and welcoming you. The air is refreshing with no pollution; your whole body, mind, and spirit are completely relaxed. You toss out all your daily stresses and the age-old thoughts caught in your mind. Your brain has no thoughts and is at ease, and you continue feeling the silence entirely within your being. You breathe out the loving, compassionate, transcendent spirit, stirring it into the air and the Universe: It returns with peacefulness and aid, flowing toward the four corners of the Earth. With no interference, you simply love that things happen peacefully.

You are not confused about what is happening, but allow for it discreetly within you.

There is a core of mega-talent, dimensions and details that are guiding you toward your vision, and it wants you to be aware of the endless peace and happiness that you can see from within, always flowing smoothly and evenly. The invisible formlessness wants you to realize you are from the omniscience of the Divine and its effective and creative energy—the Universal Mind of the Universal Creative Life Force.

You track your creative energy, doing what you are inspired to do. Trust your Inner Source as it guides you to change your judgment and as it utilizes and releases your natural talents. You can do anything when you apply yourself steadfastly without doubt and fear. Consider that you are guided by the Inner Being, which makes you shine and display precision through uncertain times. It is a creative energy that is above, beyond, and below everything—the company that brings you your true strength. It is an essential life force by itself. It is always connected to love and to God; it is never separated from them.

Think about this before you believe that making acquisitions is particularly useful. Think again now; can you separate your identity from your acquisitions? Maybe this is a difficult thing to do because you associate your self-worth with your financial resources, even if you do not have much. It is understood that living an inspired life does not mean you need to be free from everything while you are still alive and well. However, it means that you can stop the Ego's influence and make a move away from it. Then, you can choose to let go of the idea that you want to learn more. You want to honor the harmonizing power within you that is guiding you to get a full connection with your original power. Perhaps you do not want to attract more now, but you still need to know how your zest is, so you can enjoy it more and keep everything simple.

You experience life; you do not just live for your own opinion; instead, you think of yourself last. Struggle to survive is not necessary in time all good things with get better but you must keep on, keeping on living creatively. Balance in everything is essential as it enables you to live happily, be relaxed, continue to support the Light, and just be.

Heaven is eternal. The Source of Heaven and Earth is always connected. Earth is the shift from the uniqueness of the Source's Expression. The energy of Heaven tolerates Earth while, in turn, Earth resonates with Heaven. Earth is the perfect extension of the Source. However, our responses to this right of Heaven's contract are such that we must go to the core of the Source and not to our finite Egoistic center. Since both the infinite and the finite can abide together, they will continue to grow and develop infinitely.

While living on Earth, it is easy to forget that our core network is connected to the Source. Here, accumulating acquisitions and achieving higher power becomes our ultimate goal and desire. In fact, the Ego believes that we need all these worldly achievements to prevent the belief that we are somehow lacking. The Ego concept demands that we do more so that our success and energy expand in the external world. If we accept the false Ego-self, we are convinced that accumulating more things makes us feel better than everyone else, that we will stand out become more brilliant and successful than others. The Ego also requires us to reject the notion that we are part of the oneness of everything in the illusory world. We must decide the false, Ego-self to be wrong, and whatever the Ego believes; these are not our primary goals and aims. Don't believe that the bigger the plans and goals are from the Ego-self, the more we are missing. These plans always turn out to be incomplete or unattainable. Only our true self knows what our plans are and sees what we need to be happy and satisfied.

The general belief is that everyone wants to live comfortably, and that is easily understood. It should not be a problem because the benevolent Universe has a wealth of everything for everybody to share; it is a never-exhaustible, limitless resource. However, the Ego cares for itself exclusively. The Ego-self does not want to share anything with anyone and is never satisfied. It thinks about, and wants to accumulate, continually more wealth, power, fame, and possessions. The Ego considers these the elements as necessities for living a life of significance. The false self is only concerned about its own interests and benefits; there are no others who matter. Other people are challengers or enemies; they are not worth considering and should be defied or ignored. Rivals are a threat to the false mind and must be vanquished or eliminated immediately and unconditionally to avoid complications. Furthermore, the Ego likes to fight to show its strength; it takes vengeance for everything it can and does whatever it takes to win. That is not inspiring.

We should reject those Egoistic notions and deliberately choose self-worth—a concept that keeps our place in the Universe in perspective and honors the Source from which we came. We should not look at negative in this way; rather, we must change our thoughts in order to transform our lives in the Great Way that will bring an end to the disputes that keep us constantly discontented. In addition, we should give to people wholeheartedly and ask for nothing in return. When you do so, you can attract many unexpected, positive things to your door and open up the infinite possibility of fulfilling your goals. The Universal Source connects with you when you allow others to reach their goals first and receive yours later. Consequently, energy flows freely across the world and continuously aligns with your charitable events as joy and happiness arise from within you.

At any moment, you should refuse the Ego's need to acquire more wealth and instead think of giving meaning to your existence. Then, you can feel more connected to your current situation, and you will quickly become more gratified than when you are dwelling on your personal circumstances. With this in mind, can you grow and develop? Visualize what it would be like to deny the Ego's power over you. Now, visualize in your mind's eye this conversation with your Ego. You are in a place that is calm and beautiful. You do not feel angry, but rather full of love and understanding. You say in a tranquil voice, "I cannot take your suggestions anymore, as I feel exhausted when I try to do everything you tell me I should do.

I cannot be your follower any longer, as you have turned my life upside down. I respect that you are a part of me, and I do not hate you for who you are; I simply cannot continue to make you my priority. I now ask you to leave me alone." In this moment, imagine that you push the Ego out of your consciousness. Without waiting for a response from the Ego, picture all the negative energies being forced out of your mortal body. You renew and restore your energy flow. Align with the Source energy by picturing a bright white light, charged and entering into your crown chakra and moving through every part of your body—through blood vessels, lungs, heart, kidney, colon, veins and down to the sole of your foot—and outwards to shield your external body.

Now resolve to cast out all negative emotions related to unfortunate events and to put your own life in order. You may discover your weakness is a lack of self-confidence. Concentrate on your thoughts daily for 30 minutes; your task is to think of the person you want to be, creating a clear picture in your mind. Complete faith will transform this into outward action and, ultimately, transmogrify into physical reality. In addition, make sure that you devote 10 minutes every day to practice the ever develop of your self-confidence. Your disadvantage can be overcome, and fearfulness can be translated into boldness with the help of creative visualization and inward meditation. This can be as simple as writing down your positive thoughts until they become part of the working equipment of your subconscious mind.

Your imagination may become weak through lack of action. However, it can be revived and made alert though active use. Center yourself in your deep life desires; you will use this force often in the process of converting desire into what you want to have, to be, and to do. If it is money you desire, you can bring it to you by imagining a large sum flowing into your bank account "The blessing of the Lord, it makes rich and He add no sorrow of it." Proverbs 10:22; if it is superb health you want, continue imagining yourself translating your current status into the tangible reality of good health. You must follow what you perceive and with the aid of imagination turn your current life into a new and fulfilling reality.

Begin today to take decisive action to serve others first through selfless action. Be vigilant, and your inner joy and vibrant health will be what matters most to you. Try to live without desires and let life happen to you, noticing the positive energy that is flowing from you to the four corners of the world.

Try to live without desires, and let life happen to you. Observe the positive energy flowing across the globe and returning to you, becoming your own blessings. You are actively receiving because the Source is constantly giving out everything you need. Stop demanding and start receiving. All things will come to you, thanks to the great generosity of the Universal Mind of God. Let go now and heed the Divine. Arrange to meet everything you want to fulfill your destiny and be completed, and ask your God to make sure that this will indeed come to pass. You win when you are more like God and less like the Ego and when you are continuously connecting with God to make peace. By defying the Ego's preferences and demands at every moment, you will feel gratified and fulfilled. You will continue to explore and experience the deepest parts of your Inner Self. You know that you are not alone and that the living God is always dwelling in you. Now you open your eyes to see, hear with your ears, and understand with your heart. When you are confused or in doubt, a thousand books are inadequate to explain everything, but, when you have realized and understood God's spirit lives within you, a few words are plenty for you to understand. You are happy that you have found God, and you offer your genuine heart to serve Him in the Great Way.

Living in harmony with the Source is when you know when to stop—enough is enough. Then you begin to understand the reality of life. The pursuit of more power, more money, and more possessions is like sharpening a knife too much—its cutting edge will soon be lost.

Overdoing anything, and that includes over-eating, is dangerous and will cause harm to your health, especially when you do nothing to control your behavior. You will just accumulate more negative energy, uneasiness, and anxiety.

Hence, we must be satisfied with continuing to cultivate compassionate living. If wealth and power is your thing, then you must recognize when it is time to retire. This is the process of heaven, as opposed to the material world that we live in, where we are addicted to always wanting more so that no one has the sense to know when is the right time to sacrifice his or her own rights and offer an opportunity for other people. The Ego wants you to gain more of everything for yourself because it makes you believe that more means better. When you know that enough means enough then you will be in conscious alignment with the precise perfection of the Universal Source. The aim is to harness the mind so it knows that too much of everything will not bring triumph, but rather it will bring a certain degree of disorder and weakness. Your silent prayer to God to strengthen you will be answered, and you will be richly blessed for your meekness before Him.

If you have always appreciated everything you have done, and you have not been looking for credit badges for your efforts, you will retire when the work is completed. You will only want to live comfortably in the world. This is important to your heart and soul, which form the optimal alignment with Heaven. It brings deep inner peace and blissfulness to your daily actions. You will understand the Laws of Nature and let go of the idea that you must reap rewards for your services. You will seek tranquility and contentment in what you are doing, and not in how it might eventually help you.

Although you are now living in the material world, you are not of it. This is the way heaven wants you to be: disconnected from everything yet still living in the world. If anything bad should happen to you, at least heaven can catch you when you fall.

In today's fast-track life, can we live in spirit, without allowing the negative Ego to dominate, while continuing to meet with success and comfort? You have probably learned that "No servant can serve two masters" (Luke 16:13, NIV). If the darkness takes control of your daily activities, the only way you can escape from the Ego's control is to be aligned with the Source. Then you will stop seeking new material things and instead see everything from a new perspective. It might be difficult, but when you put your trust in the greatest work then all other works are just plans. When you consider yourself connected to the invisible spirit, all things will be completed and manifested through you. This happens when you relinquish everything to God's spirit and do not attempt to control your destiny. You simply let go and let God take over. Without forcing yourself to obtain more, you will be in a place to do more, and you will ultimately feel more significance in your life. Then you will begin to need and consume less. Your Source being will urge you to do less, and more will be done for you, through you.

Stop having judgmental thoughts about those you think are not acceptable or not related; instead, consider and include them. Think of them as if they are extensions of you. This will cut your self-importance and arrogance.

Letting go of your Egoistic thoughts allows you to connect with the oneness that shares your joy with others.

Thus, you give yourself a chance to become a part of the all-encompassing Universal Source. Now, imagine yourself in someone else's shoes, and feel the pain and sorrow that emerges in you. By envisioning yourself as one of them and knowing how painful it would be in such confusing, hateful and upsetting conditions, you will not exclude anyone, and you will need and want to be there for them.

Now, start cleaning out your repressed memories; you need to cancel out—memories involving people, events, places and things so an inspiring message can help you write your thoughts. You must let go of all traumatic events that you have experienced; seek the Source to end those negative thoughts and help them leave you. Those people, places and events, as well as their energies, might still be attached to you even though they are long gone; nevertheless, you must continuously clean them from your memories so you are released from them. Soon, you will remove all those past events and return to your natural state. Then, you can call the Source to charge you with the pure Light. When your life is in equilibrium, everything starts to run smoothly and continues to grow and evolve. The cleaning process restores your true nature, and afterward you can work on others.

The greatest reliance is and always has been on the sacred place in the heart of your being. Within you, hide a piece of God that is instinctively aware of what to do and how to be. You should always appreciate and follow the Inner Source that guides you. When you practice in a powerful way that clearly works, the Source will lead you to the high quality of life that aligns you with the Universe; this will allow you to begin the shift to aspire with Divine consciousness in a way that you never would have imagined. You will do well because the Divinity inside you will direct you. However, you must let go of evaluating yourself and stop putting a dollar tag on yourself. You are not merchandise; you must stop putting a price on all you do. Let go of need: Intentionally share your bread with others. You will feel happier because you no longer will need to verify that you are someone, or worthy, or that you need luck to endure life.

You know that true happiness cannot be measured by the token of money, but instead must be experienced via the tranquility inside the real you. When you generously share what you have and are in harmony with everyone, then there is no doubt that you will make everything effortlessly. This is because you have activated your Source being and allowed the stream of energy to flow and grow endlessly. When energy returns to everyone around you, you will receive and benefit. You give up the Egoistic assumption that we are what we do, and instead strive to live in accordance with your most Authentic Self. Then, you live in the Great Way. Eliminate self-importance and ambition, replace them with selflessness and meaning, and live truly with your real nature—a divine being. When you align peacefully with Divine oneness, you switch from relying on external knowledge to internal wisdom. You become confident that the kernel of the Authentic Self will guide your energy and echo meaning. In fact, you need do nothing but simply allow thought energy to come to you and show you the truth within you, helping you make victory in your life. After this, you will be willing to help others with joy. Thus, you will live in wholeness and fullness and continue to let yourself be. When you trail your own shadow to make success at all costs, you carry out more than you imagine. You choose to travel in the Divine direction of life. You are aware that you do not need to struggle to be still more seductively transformed. The desire to strive for more is strong, but you decide to let what flow to you naturally. You breathe through the Source and vibrate at a higher frequency than when you were fueled by the Ego. You begin to question aspects of the Ego that rule you before. You know that life is not about what you do and have. You begin shifting your attention to your Source, and you come under its care. You begin to shun the spotlight and feel more grateful for all that you have received and shall receive. All of this will flow from the reliable omniscience of Divine oneness.

We know that living naturally and walking on a peaceful journey is the process of being here, but for years, Ego has convinced us to focus on reputation and be an important person. Ambition is fine; however, you should conquer without striving. Creating your own intention and desire is acceptable; you simply relinquish your attachment to the result. Detachment does not mean you stop desiring and creating; you just surrender your desire to get closer to the Divine oneness. When you can transcend into the truth of who you are; you are able to transcend your dreams, open your mind and raise your energy vibration accurately draw the desires you deserve.

The Ego's perspective is more work, less pleasure, treat every rival as an enemy and beat them all. Ego concepts thrive on the approval and opinion of others. Since you have changed your belief system to unity from separation and diminished your self-important qualities, you transform to become independent from the accept opinion of others. Imagine the tough time the Ego has when you arise, leaving everything to the Divine and practicing radical meekness.

Nature does not control or make anyone does thing unwillingly; all things will last for short time and then disappear. All things will end. Thunderstorms, forest fires and earthquakes will end, and everything will return to stillness. However, these natural occurrences must agree to pass, despite the fact that we do not yet have the power and technology to prevent natural events from happening. Although we may be able to predict these incidents, we still cannot stop them from occurring.

Nature's howling power is omnipotent and awesome. We can never win over nature's force; however, we can choose to live harmoniously and resonate with it. Relinquish the desire to pressure anyone or anything, and choose instead to be the recurring parts and peacefulness of nature. You are reminded that any desire must be fulfilled naturally and willingly, and even God cannot overrule an involuntary action. On the other hand, if the collective force of the conscious mind controls events, then an individual attention has no option but to accept what another has agreed with.

For example, if a strata council of the apartment building where you live decides to increase the monthly strata fees and you did not have a choice in the matter, then you must endure the collective mind's decisions—joint minds made the major decision. However, you should pause for a moment to connect with your Authentic Self and regain serenity and peace in the present. Do not let the Ego pressure you. You still have a clear choice to create steadiness in your mind instead of showing your temper or unhappiness. You should function in a calm, serene way. Soon, you can connect with reality and live with ease because you will no longer be in conflict with the occurring event. All negative energies shift and move closer to your Source being. You know what it is, and its power travels through you. What flows around and through you is the truth. You get your responses, and they are aligned with nature. Ultimately, your actions are intended to connect with the vibrations of Heaven. You feel inner peace and tranquility.

You remove all clutter of personal preference and importance. In fact, every material possession you now own is from Heaven, and none were obtained by you alone. Everything you have received is a gift from the Divine. Therefore, you should share your incredible gifts with the needy and end your Ego's selfish notion of want to do extra; instead, you should be grateful that you are living in a stress-free environment. You put your true essence on the generous path of giving by becoming like God, who is always ready to offer more without expecting anything in return. Heaven certainly treasures you; change your obsession to compassion. Thanks to your faith and determination to live with your truest power, the Source, you are in a condition to receive unlimited blessings from the Divine oneness.

The natural flow of the Source operates with no bias, so it asks you for nothing but continues to offer you and everyone with food, shelter, clothing, transportation, sunshine, air, and water. The sun and the moon were created for the benefit of all people to enjoy their warmth. The sun lights up the whole world daily, and we appreciate its energy. It has not at any time demanded payment or requested respect; it may never expire and is always free of charge. Imagine if the sun would only glow when it received payment for its life-giving energy. Soon most of the world would be transformed into total darkness. Fortunately, nature is fair to everyone, and the sun is more than happy to give the entire planet with excellent, full-time illumination without bias, conditions, or terms. Showing off your assets and status does not give you wisdom. It is better to give by providing for others, expecting to gain nothing, and aligning yourself with the Universal Source.

Follow your desires, and make sure that you do not persist for your own benefit or advantage, but rather for the highest good of others. Walk the path of the Source, and distance yourself from your Egoistic desires to recognize the need for effective spiritual accomplishments.

The journey of your life will change when you give thanks for all that you are, all that you achieved, and all that you received. Say this gently: "I thank 'You' for walking with me during my sleeping hours and waking hours." You can replace the "You" with anything that is guiding you during the day and at night. Indeed, you can improve your thankfulness to the sun, the sky, the stars, the rain, and, then again, you can practice giving thanks daily, which helps your spiritual growth and development. Your gratitude and attitude training helps you focus on the Source of All-That-Is and let go of everything and detach from the Ego's control. There are no limits to showing your appreciation, so continue to practice it. Certainly, it will transform your life to reach a completely new level; if you continue to show respect for others and everything that is around and next to you, the world will turn the spark, ignite the fire, and acknowledge your goodness, and you will no longer be enslaved but will become completely free in creativity and humanity. Do not limit your reverence to humans; your generosity can extend to anything and everything on Earth. You will see the excesses of self-importance and recognize the importance within everyone, which is the ability of the Source.

The Source does not ignore anyone but accepts all that is. There is no special rightness, carelessness, or priority. The essential aspect of living, which is living by the Source, treats everything equally and impartially.

The moment that you think you are right is when you open

up new principles of fair versus imperfect, which causes you to be misaligned with the Source. Then, you introduce new things repeatedly. You do not know whom you should follow. You must follow the Source: oneness. God's spirit does not remove or reject things, but just is. There is nothing for you to get; there is no standard, no right or wrong, fair or unfair. If it seems as if it is doing nothing, it has already done all things. This is the key aspect of nature. You must go with your true nature. It encourages you to think in your essential style. Let go of what the Ego tells you. Do not thirst for recognition of the excellence that you desperately need to find in yourself to avoid gaffes and dissatisfaction. You should instead create and experience in the Source-being of your own uniqueness and oneness. You do not want to prioritize morality; feel your integrity and inmost love and discard any need for control as described by the Ego's belief focus. You support the value of your life even when you experience a fall. Without falls or misfortunes, good fortune cannot follow. When good fortune comes, you might only think of the joy and forget all the bad times. Hence, the hurricane of your life is unavoidable and unprecedented, but you can allow it to grow and raise you to the highest frequency of consciousness to protect yourself against falls. You sign up for life with the Divine and live life with a compassionate heart. You are here to do a spiritual goal, and you must not be surprised when you meet challenges, difficulties, and tough times. In fact, challenges are opportunities for development and advancement to a higher spiritual level where gratefulness replaces regret.

We traditionally think that wholeness has everything that has been completed and occupied. It indicates that all things have arisen from the oneness. The sky, the water, the sun, the moon, the stars, Earth, all living forms and ideas are integral parts of the whole. Thus, when you start to live to fulfill a strong sense of purpose, your whole life will begin to change by the Universal Source in real kindness, and your life will never be filled with obstacles. You will never worry about how you are perceived by others; humbling yourself is a better way to the oneness Source than the deepest search for ambition and reputation.

Since the Universe is within the whole, and you are in the whole, you begin to see and feel the interconnectedness of everything. For example, for you, as an individual, your red and white blood cells keep you existing and living healthily. However, if one tiny cell refuses to cooperate with all the other cells, the virus will affect the rest of the cells in your body, and as a result, you will become seriously ill. Nevertheless, unless one of the damaged cells is gobbled up, if left unchecked, illness will eventually destroy your body's system (the whole). This is because the damaged cell is not related to the whole. The damaged cells work alone as they end the vessel (host) upon which they depend for their own survival. Our bodies' systems are a wide diversity of separate living organisms that work together for us in a shared relationship. When you are depressed emotionally, your body's immune system can fail in response because you are not living in harmony with your Authentic Self. Thus, your body becomes imbalanced.

Subsequently, the normal red blood cells are not able to carry oxygen and nutrients nor repair wounds. Your body becomes imbalanced and is not able to defend itself against viruses. Consequently, all your normal blood cells are infected by the damaged cells, and ultimately your body's functions are fully weakened and endangered by the virus. The virus modifies its destructive nature to take on the whole of the body, and much of your body will slowly fade. However, white blood cells have a total different functionality than the red cells in your physical body. The white blood cells analyze the virus before they decide to protect it. The white cells seem to have a memory of former attacks by similar viruses. They are able to pass on the information or data so that it may apply to the whole someday.

Not all the cells are responsive to your body's system. Some cells are more effective than others. Earth has the equal strength that can affect all living things within the whole. The white blood cells differentiate; they have a great responsibility to keep the whole body healthy. However, viruses sometimes overcome the body with disease, and you become ill. This happens when the white blood cells in your body fail to protect the whole. Thus, you must stay vigilant and activate your Source. You can protect and serve the Earth like a white blood cell. You, as an individual, can support and respect the environment in every way by fostering greatness in an Earth-friendly system as part of its oneness.

We are a part of the wholeness, but division of wholeness is potentially dangerous if it does not extend to growth and success. Your lifestyle needs to have a relationship with the whole and serve love through a bond with humanity. In other words, wholeness and mortality agree to become one, so you must think they are both parts of your life and make peace with the whole. Wholeness means maintaining a sense of balance with the kind and compassionate Universal Source. In humanity, you are able to detect your role in the play orchestrated by your Source. You have an Inner Strength guiding you within to be the best you can be, so you continue to live a purposeful life full of meaning.

We have the ability to fill our lives with possibilities just by observing the principles of the Universal Laws of Nature. Through the true authority within, we can accomplish divine actions to protect—instead of endanger—the environment of planet Earth. With the inner expert assisting us, we will thrive when we act benevolently and selflessly, and we will not allow the Ego to cause us to lose ourselves on the wrong path.

As you begin to live in wholeness, you now see that you connect dynamically with everyone rather than partner with the separateness, as your Ego prefers. Seeing that you are within everyone's consciousness makes you want to live peacefully with every creature on Earth, regardless of ethnic and cultural differences. The more you want to practice living in wholeness, the more you want to merge with it and slowly release the Ego, your false identity, and change your old belief system. Then, as you begin to see and feel the difference that happiness reflects from within, it encourages you to continue to merge with the whole and transform yourself to become a lifetime lover of oneness, and you begin to grow and love it. The whole Universe is the expression of the Source's oneness of love. It simplifies that God's spirit is love. Our nonbeing state is an eternal purity and incredible bliss created for the purpose of being here on planet Earth and the reason for the art of creation to transpire.

For example, you stand in front of a mirror, and you perceive a blissful image of yourself. It reflects joy and contentment on your face, making you realize that you are no longer caught up with stress and worry that defines the old you. By being content, you will never be upset or dissatisfied. You are the author and crafter of your own life. A crafter craves a state of art and needs to practice his expertise before becoming an expert in his art. Living a spiritual life needs long-term practice; then, someday you will see your life has transformed from copper to gold, and you will always check your inner self with God in your heart.

In order to live a genuine infinite life, you have to wait until the time you must return to the spirit realm that is your original nature. You take a return flight to the nothingness. "You were created like God, so you must please Him and be truly holy (Ephesians 4:24)." This is an invitation for us all to return to the loving, kind, compassionate, purified, void, and empty place where God resides and join Him.

When you change your thoughts about life, you allow your true self to unfold and know that you are in the arm of the Divine, and the people you look at begin to change. You begin to see that their being knows precisely what they want to do. Feel the connection to everything, and practice nonjudgmental love, beginning with yourself. You know that one day we shall return to oneness with the Source. Now, direct your attention toward the Divine, and feel His presence in your heart, body, and soul. Redirect your attention from internal to external circumstances; take a long breath in and send out love, peace, and light energy that is part of you and flows through to all life.

Ask yourself if you are taking every step in the right direction or entrusting life with true essence from your intentions—including your career, your relationships and your health. You are unbounded, unlimited, pure energy; you can create anything you want and be surrounded by the Universe and ask with a firm certainty for that which you desire. The Universe will soon answer your request and return to you with your desired outcome.

One important thing when you speak out loud to the Universe is that your vibrational words should contain energy, which activates the center code of your heart and body and triggers the mind to cooperate with you. Words are very powerful, especially when you speak with certainty; they catch the attention triggers the entire Universe through your spirit and echo back to you to confirm your intentions. You proclaim who you are to the entire Universe and invite the Universe to help and grant your heartfelt desires. Your vibrational energy echoes to the Universe and shows you are no longer separated from it. You ask the Universe with firmness and boldness, and the Universe answers your prayer and returns a positive outcome to your impulsive desires.

You probably know that when you choose to live an infinite life and walk on a spiritual path, that field is where all things originated. When you align with the Source and get close to God, you feel inner bliss and stillness. This is a step towards spiritual healthy living and wholeness in which you take care of your well-being and live happily and fearlessly. You are guided by your Authentic Self within. You are living in a different stage of your life, which is navigated by the internal spirit, and you choose to let the spirit take charge.

God loves you and always wants to be with you and serve you; discard your servant Ego, remove your veil, and your conscious thought will allow your optimal energy to flow through within, so you will be conscious of His Divine presence. God always patiently waits for us to be connected and aligned with His vibrational energies and lights. Your self-realization is a spirit, which allows you to make a conscious connection with the All-Power-High to attain oneness and unity with God.

All of this awareness comes from within you, with the power of intention of moving in the right direction of the Source and back to your origin as a spirit. The best way to do this is through yielding or relinquishing everything, making you free of worry. It is impossible not to accumulate material possessions when living on Earth, but if you can get less, you will be worry free. As a person committed to spiritual practice, I attempt to live a simple life; however, this does not mean that I stop wanting and desiring. I relinquish to the Source, which decides for me. It works for me, and so far, I have not complained and have received and obtained everything from the Universal Source.

Recognize that my little Ego mind does nothing and that the Source creates everything, including you and me. As I continue to write on the LCD monitor screen, I know I do not own this piece of writing, but God does. The spirit guides my hands and grants me the creative talent and ability to write this book and others. In fact, I surrendered to God's presence a long time ago. Everything comes from God's spirit and is manifested in the spirit realm before making itself apparent in the physical world.

Nothing would ever be harvested without the aid of the spirit allowing it to happen and then thrive.

I think that even my achievements are a trademark coming from the Source. In fact, without the grand magnificence of God's spirit, there would be no buildings, no computers, no roads, and no railway bridges at all. Now, at any moment before I begin to write, I call the spirit to direct my thoughts and turn me into an instant listener. The more I surrender each day, the more I like and am in tune with the peace and love of God's omniscient spirit.

You harmonize with the Source by changing your thoughts. In the beginning, your new way of appealing to the being will perhaps be overclouded by the Ego belief system. You experience times of uncertainty, but you can get information by looking inward. In addition, when you think that your life has taken a step backwards, look again. Things might have changed instantaneously; you just did not realize it. The Source is always there to help you, but you must be aware. When life looks deceiving and confusing, you should stop what you are doing to clear and remove all negative thoughts. You realign with the Source, stay still, and let your Inner Being take control. You must work with it if you want to make the next leap. It might look difficult to prove externally, but you must keep a state of calmness. Look around you, take a deep breath, relax, and become consciously aware of all things so that you can begin to rebuild. Know and recognize that all things take place in Heaven before they are broadcast to the external world. Once you know this, fears and worries become pointless. You think all is well.

You may realize that you cannot change the outside world, but you can change your desires to a higher plane. You believe all things are looked after by the inexorable spirit of God. You gain more by detaching from all that you have and making sacrifices to all that is needed to help others. In your individual pleasure and bondage, you turn your inner spark into a blaze to be merged with and verified with the powerful fire, which triggers the other stimulus.

When you trust that the all-creative life energy will never disappoint you, you must keep going and never surrender. Believe that you will reach your goal, regardless of your impulses; you will satisfy and fulfill them someday.

People who have connected with the Source tend to view external events differently; they realize that inner peace is essential to life. Powering up one's internal channel takes less energy and allows for more work to be done. You guide yourself by the endlessness of God's beliefs and not by setting goals, desires or incentives to be affirmed by other people's standards.

Now, acknowledge that the Source's omnipotent and invisible power over the Universe can do something for you, and accept that you can take advantage of this. God will never find fault in what He does, but He will continuously offer His consent and help; the God of Almighty often heals and performs miracles. Despite that external conditions may seem to be in complete disarray, the Source within reminds you that all is well and that abundant goodwill is clearly present. The Authentic Self is hidden, but you must simply call upon it. Do not feel disheartened; instead, continuously believe that you will see the truth and fulfill your own spiritual needs. Then, suddenly, do you realize that God offers His hand to you.

God's mind has never changed, but your perspective has. God has always seen what needs to be done before you ask. You need love; He sends more love to you before you even ask. When you need knowledge and wisdom to complete a project, He grants you the aptitudes and silently assists you in getting your work accomplished.

Let go of the habit of seeking authentication from the physical world before transforming something to suit your own reality. The invisible nature of the Universe will always be encoded, strange and unknown, so if you think that this story could lead to the Divine host, then immerse yourself in it. You are not going to do this in the material world until other events unfold.

So, do not waste your time trying to figure it out; just be content with recognizing and accepting it. Even if you were to try, you would miss or lose it. Do not bother resisting the need to see or experience before you can trust something. By transmuting the way you look at the world, you will change the way you see things with doubt, uncertainty, and defects, along with the reverence for life and death. You will certainly find entry into the profound enjoyment of future success and better observances.

All things are considered positive or negative, named or nameless; however, it is difficult to see both sides of the coin at the same time. The Eastern point of view is different; people there have yin and yang. Indeed, all things in this Universe hold two sides: the light and the dark. However, it is inevitable that we do not see the opposite; instead, we consider them to be strange and contradictory to each other. We need to consider only the natural or anticipated materials; hence we choose not to accept different ideas.

God's presence is an invisible white light—an unknown mystery where everything originates; at the same time, the white light is within everything. When we look at the unseen, we want to see this invisible, strange thing from the mysterious realm. Afterwards, we tend to translate it into our own terms and forms so that we can understand it in the physical world. In fact, we feel disappointed because the results do not meet our expectations. However, the sooner we surrender, the sooner we can realize that the invisible ether-world allows us to see the mystery. Simple explanations could work, such as thinking by desiring or wanting and then changing our thoughts to not want those items. This allows things to occur naturally. Then the invisible opens its realm to us through inner spiritual contemplation.

We unite with the inner realm through the inner spirit's union, but we cannot do so directly via physical form. Connecting to the spirit's realm during our waking hours is almost impossible, but it is easier to make contact through meditation, thus creating a conscious connection with the ether-world. Once you see such manifestation and do not strongly desire, you are able to see the mysterious world. You simply observe the Laws of Allowing and let things manifest for you. For example, when you plant tomatoes in your garden, you must allow them to grow, and then they transform from the seeds. Let the world unfold without attempting to configure it. Just let everything be instead of looking for explanations and reasons. Do not attempt to make things work; instead, simply allow them to happen, and then they will happen. Relax, surrender, and allow things to take their natural course; recognize that some of your desires will emerge in how you think your world should exist and not how it exists at this moment.

This means that whatever you think the result will be, it will be.

In the physical realm, the concept of something or someone being beautiful has created an almost instinctive record in our subconscious mind concerning the idea of living in a vast duality. This way of thinking has happened quite clearly and has been accepted by just about every culture and society in the outer world. However, by shifting our judgmental thoughts to a nonjudgmental state, we might genuinely live in the bliss of oneness.

Have you ever recalled a beautiful woman in your mind's eye? In other words, your mind's eye interprets the attractive woman you saw as a goddess. This shows how beauty is in the eye of the beholder, regardless of what the universal standards of society say.

Therefore, the idea of gorgeousness must be held in our intellect, and we also have a clear sense of the nonbeauty idea. Now, think of how many concepts in the twofold (dual) belief system depend on opposites. However, when you remove your experience from the untruth that you know, you may find that truth to be correct. You may then have to change your way of thinking. This is remarkably similar to how our ideas of death could not exist without birth or rebirth. A window of opportunity will always open and never close. In other words, when one door closes, another possibility will present itself almost instantaneously; everything that happens in the outside world is, and always has been, tossed from two sides of the coin. It gives us a taste of what the other side of the coin is like, even though the two sides can never match. As a result, this allows all things to exist and coexist, ever developing and ever evolving.

The concepts of the twofold belief system let us experience freely, so we know and are aware but do not judge. The choice offers you similar experiences either with or without risk. Needless to say, the concept of opposites occurs only in the human world; it would be ridiculous in the animal kingdom, because animals do not have intellect. The animal kingdom, the trees, and the flowers have no practical vision of what is acceptable; they simply exist, living in harmony with the whole and without judgment. We human beings should seek God to help us through difficult times so we can handle change, emotional stress, and pain.

When you cast judgment on an event or on someone, your mind determines that event or person does not meet your ideal. However, what causes you to make such a judgment about a person or event? Obviously, you must be experiencing both an internal and external conflict. It is likely that your soul is not resonating with the person. All things that happen do so not by coincidence but on purpose so that you experience the binary part of your journey. If you can, consider that no two instances are the same, and even events are similar regardless of what has happened in the past. However, it will be better when you accept the situation without creating an opinion about it, and continue. Living without prejudice and in true alignment with the Source is the way to live life with joy and happiness. It suggests that you utilize your openness to determine the opposites and spend a joyous and peaceful life with the oneness. The perfection of the Universal Source allows this duality while you perceive the unity that is truth.

Consider that life and death are identical and that they are parallel to each other.

We seem to possess no choices, but we know what they are.

Accept that the existence of both is unified and true to the life that is living within the Source. Then, ultimately, we return to the void at the end of our lives like we are the water that makes the waves move in and out and then realize that they are the waves that combine with the water into one.

You may consider allowing yourself to live in duality within your belief system and possess different thoughts without cancelling them. Similarly, you are finite and infinite at the same point. Therefore, you have the ability to transform your surroundings and at the same time maintain the advice given by the powerful Authentic Self in you.

Realize that demons and angels are two parts of a whole. They exist and always have existed to balance the energy of the Universe. Accept the duality of the system in the fast-track material world while understanding the connection with the wholeness of the eternal Universal Source.

Live in the world with consciousness and forget the need to sort out everything as day or night, evil or angels, positive or negative. All things have a twofold appearance; we welcome them with gratitude, and we are consciously aware that we cannot change this reality. This is a part of our consciousness that is always attached to the material world, not to the Source.

Now, meditate on the word "dual" in your mind's eye. People apparently still look alike and show no differences from each other. It is difficult to determine outwardly whether a person contains a duality of good and evil or possesses solidity on only one part of the coin. However, this can be reflected through conversation and direct contact with that individual.

Then, the personality of that person starts to reveal his or her true character and who he or she is within. In other words, his or her true identity is powerless to hide. Knowing the truth, however, is not always pleasant. Seeing into the truthful inner soul of a person is all we need to do, and it will set you at ease.

When you are vigilant with your thoughts and aware of your surroundings and circumstances, you are coherently aligned with the Universal Source. Ultimately, you will know where you want to be and will understand how your needs relate to your current situation. Now, assume that you are a frog living in a pond; you love where you are in the area and are aligned with the Universe since you can certainly move around openly, freely and fearlessly.

You just love your own soul; perhaps you certainly love that you are a spiritual being. You move freely through the water or on the land, moving peacefully, playfully and courageously. When it is time, you need to return to the void; if this is the case, you do so willingly and eagerly. You always want to return to the wholeness of the Source. You see that your time on Earth is only temporary, and your final destination is to be returned to the nothingness of the void. You also know that when the time comes, you need to complete your flight home to the Source.

You have always aligned yourself with the Source. You prepare yourself to move easily and quietly, and you see what leads you without fear of reprisal. Once you have attempted this, there is no risk, and trying again would produce the same results.

However, you will know that at least you have tried, so there is no possibility. Other things become irrelevant, and everything is accomplished. For instance, how were the steaks you had at that diner last week? I want to eat there. Now I have tried their steaks, and they are soft and delicious. Now, you have eaten at that diner. Eating or having eaten at that diner is the same thing, and it remains true forever.

You should arrange your priorities to ensure contentment at any time. Do not overwhelm yourself with everything; this is irrelevant and unnecessary, and it allows the outside world to rule over you. External factors could offer some serious temptations, but you must be vigilant over your desires; do not seek the extremes, and be content with life. More possessions and accomplishments that are directed or checked by our Ego's minds should be avoided. The false self wants us to work harder and see more than is necessary, whether it is money, acquisitions, power, status, or other things.

You should always be vigilant, and do not go by those inviting attributes that lead to resentment, insecurity, corruption, and chaos. Instead of getting more of what you have already gotten in the conscious now, you practice gratitude and pursue happiness, simplicity, positivity thoughts and emotions, love, courage, and a wholesome life. When you continue to seek good things, you shall see tremendous good things coming to you with no resistance; you will be able to turn any task into a pleasant experience and an interesting adventure. Whatever you do, put everything into it and give it your all.

Another way of practicing tranquility and contentment is to meditate on the question "How may I help or better serve others?" By casting this image in your mind, you will begin to see changes in your life. You want to submit your services to others rather than just thinking about you, who is controlled by the selfish Ego. The false Ego only wants more of everything. However, your wish to help others requires no reward. You want to do charitable work for humanity. It brings you peace and happiness because you know that to be your innermost desire, and in your mind you wish them well. You understand that the Inner Source guides you to succeed in your soul's destiny. Your Source being will never request any favorable opportunity, and it will work with you at any time and under any circumstance. You do not need to fully understand how the Universal Law works; simply learn, follow, implement and apply it to your daily activities. Now, you are here, and you should always consult your spirit guide to complete your trip and learn lessons.

The Ego's obsession can prevent the Divine essence, so practice getting the Ego out the door; only then will you be accompanied by the Source in everything you do.

Listen to what urges you to be connected without the Ego's control. You will be more creative and let out what is within reach by overruling the outside world's commitments. In this way, it is up to you to call off external events; use the opportunity to stop the Ego and manage your profile. You should always think of utilizing your aptitudes to help others. Contribute to nutritional health and strength and empty your thoughts about gaining a higher status in the mortal world; attach your freedom to God, and fit into the heart of candid believer.

Stop wasting resources and accumulating additional possessions. When you can view life in this way, you may probably encourage more people to trail a way of life that supports everyone's possible unity. Ultimately, it will bring more stability and peace to planet Earth. People may not want to challenge each other to obtain more possessions and power; they will probably awaken one another to what sustains and preserves life on Earth. The Source likes to help everyone on Earth, but it needs determination and continues to make commitments and examine the desire for help. The Ego's senses will fail, so the power of the Source can be felt. This can be done by rerouting the Ego in the opposite direction and realigning your life to be based on experiencing meaning and purpose.

Perhaps you may have a list of things you need to get that will help you achieve satisfaction and joy when you see them in consciousness. However, after you have fulfilled your current situation, you will notice that your satisfaction did not meet with the obvious results you wanted to achieve. You thought it could be caused by fear, excitement, and determination to succeed.

Feeling happy with everything you touch with gratitude in your environment is more effective than anticipating external events to bring you joy and happiness.

When you consciously align with the Source, all things will begin to flow into your life. You will experience the right people and earn the money or receive the funding you need; everything you truly need will arrive at your doorstep. Stop pushing yourself too hard, and be aware that all is well and healthy. If you believe that everything is supported by the Source, the Mind of God, and you are thankful, you shall receive them all.

Everything happened in the invisible Universe before it arrived here. When you meditate and pray, this submits your request to the Source, and when you believe it is already fulfilled, it will become your reality someday. The inspiration is sent to you from the Source, so you know it must be true, and you just have to obtain and use it for your own sake.

The Universal Source is working for and with you at all times, so it is not necessary to remind God's invisible spirit of what you need or what you think it has forgotten. Trust the wisdom and glory of the Source. The Source will do anything and everything for you, but you need to be patient and trust that the hidden power will never disappoint you. It will close and fulfill your order in the timeless manner it has always done.

If it is a creative desire you hope to fulfill, turn to the Source and watch what the invisible spirit can do for you. Ask for wisdom and vigilance, suggestions, and support to guide you, so you know what to expect when the events begin to unfold in the present. Then connect to the power that sends the fulfillment of your desires to yourself. However, be vigilant: Do not talk about your unpublished project to just anyone. Evil eyes may steal your idea.

Take inner action and ask the Source to help you until the entire project is complete. You can ask the Source to help your mind transmit the existing vibrational energy into the physical world so everyone can benefit. You must remember that your creative abilities come from the Source, and nothing comes from you, so whatever you do is guided by God's spirit.

Do not forget to give thanks to the Universal Source at any time and praise the Divine for everything that helps you achieve success. Do not let your creative desires overshadow this and make you forget that the Source is the real creator of your work. Let no passion confuse you from making lasting connections with the Source. Be glad you have the ability to be active, and through stillness, let the Divine reveal the path at any moment. Trust it; you will love what you do and make it your reality.

Being present in the infinite now can be accomplished by adopting acceptance as if it were directed and guided by the invisible hands of the spirit. It is an enveloping process: If you allow this invisible power to guide your life as you are destined, you will be there. You do not want to be just anywhere. Instead, you see your life as guided by God's spirit and as a place where you are destined to be in the timeless present. This means the infinite intelligence is always available and you can recognize God's light of perfection before it becomes apparent in your life. You believe there are no insufficiencies; you believe that the Source will provide everything you want, as has always been done for you and everyone else.

Be consciously available in your body and mind, and relax in a state of balance. Cease thinking of wants and needs, and let everything happen naturally. Ask the Universe for the Spirit's presence, and you will have it. Surrender your worries about doing the right thing. Release yourself from setting goals for the future; replace them with the power of now, because all things happen to you only in the timeless now.

At any instant, when you examine the state of the fluid future, the moment might have already been transformed to suit your lifestyle. There is no predetermination but only continuously living in the infinite now. Hence, when you want to complete something, you do it in the moment. You forget your worries and fears; you make them stay outside your conscious awareness and are not concerned with the liquid future. Relinquish recent events, places and people that no longer exist, and continuously live in the present. Invite the Source to continue your experience to the fullest. If you are not sure where you want to be, then wait until it reveals itself to you via the bountiful Universe. Stop constantly seeking instead of submitting all desires to God's spirit. Let the spirit be your guide in your consciousness. Meanwhile, free yourself from disturbances in the external environment that emphasize things that might not happen or shall happen someday. You will then know what matters most, and the rest will come to pass or is irrelevant.

You can take steps to exceed what you need in the present, and forget about it. Most importantly, you submit it to the Universe, and the Source knows how to fulfill your request.

It may seem as if your request is still unclear. But, surprisingly enough, it arrives completed and at just the right time. Do not worry about what others may think; you have not done anything. Your gift will be a strong sense of inner peace and contentment. Because of your stillness, you are always aware that all of your needs will be met. You do not miss anything, but all things in the material world are just illusions. You are not living for someone else or for those around you; instead, you owe it all to yourself alone.

Simply live freely in the present and be aware of what is offered.

Imagine that you have no concerns or fears; you feel content and are consciously connected with the Source's omniscience. Remember that the super omniscience of the Source gave you knowledge and the ability to fulfill your desires in the here and now. You must free your mind from the notion that you are striving or stuck. Your world and everyone else's needs are being taken care of by the invisible hand of the Source; if you believe in it, it will fill and complete your existence. The Source has always done this and always will. The Ego guarantees that all your needs will forever feel unsatisfied, but the Egoistic mind wants you to ask for more fame, wealth, and power than you will ever need. You should stay away from this Ego concept in your mind, and align in harmony with the Source and not worrying and struggling for nonmeaningful things that you may or may not need.

The best strategy is to surrender to the Universe. Believe that Mother Nature will take care of your needs and allow yourself to forget about them. Deliberately choose to accept this in your mind: be it love, health, property or deed, it is coming for you right here and now. Have a constant desire to see what is arriving, and free yourself from the idea of striving for something or someone.

Be confident that God's presence is widespread and omniscient, and be there to detect His presence around you. Trust in these powerful resources to support and help you, and return Egoistic control to a box. Be relaxed and experience the thrill stirring in the air when you inhale and exhale the peace and love. Be free from the Ego and have a worry-free attitude. You are liberated from all earthly bounds and problems since you freed yourself from acquisitions. You spend your lifetime getting your ride on Earth until you return to the void of nothingness. The idea that you needed more than you required was forever changed to achieve continuous calmness, happiness, and contentment.

"Let go" and "let God" are not new concepts; instead, they tell you to submit to what is, what is not so, and what is unnecessary to make transformational changes. They keep you worry-free in your daily activities. You believe the highest power is above, below, and beside and has taken control of everything. It watches over you, so be ready and require less, along with changing your beliefs; your happiness cannot be a profound reality if you continue to think you are missing material things in your life.

Try to relax your mind and affirm that, from now on, you are letting go and letting God take control of your life.

You are a powerful, infinite Being and always have everything from the Source; hence, nothing is needed or missing. Now, realize that you have everything needed to change and get into yourself. When you change the way you perceive a thing, you look at it again afterwards and see it transformed. You know how to do the things that you could not have done before, but you can do them now with support from the Universal Source. You understand that whatever you need can be accomplished because the Source is in you and you are in God's spirit. We can depend on God to manifest things to meet our needs through His expression and creative power. You meet all of your needs and gain wisdom in the material world by His expression.

If you are as strong as an old palm tree, you can always recover from a seen or unseen force that bears against you. You have gotten through tough times by allowing them to pass without a struggle. By not fighting, you are able to relax and meet all that confronts you, and now you are in vibrational peace with yourself and the Source. You are in harmony with the wholeness that attracts everything to you and that has helped you to peacefully solve your conflicts; undoubtedly, no harm can be seen.

When you consciously align with the Universal Source, you attract more incredible things, people, and events to you; anything that you care for will transpire, and all intellectual opportunities will show themselves to you. However, if you want to reap enormous benefits from the Source, you might have to stop thinking and change your memories to zero, allowing the inspirational messages to go through your subconscious mind and show you where you want to go in the here and now. Then, all that remains is to act on it.

Your mind needs to be emptied; all junk and clutter must be removed so the window of opportunity can lead to knowledge and wisdom. The wholeness will not restrict you, but instead it will motivate you so you see every option. You see all opportunities and possibilities and never miss any chances, because you recognize the hidden Universal Source is in charge but does not attempt to control anyone or anything.

Awareness of flexibility allows you to overcome your uncertainty and creates an atmosphere of trust. When you are free, you are willing to wait to see if a portal opens that allows you entrance to that great opportunity to do what you want. The Source can give you what you ask for because it already exists in the Universe.

This affects how your desires continue to be filled and fulfilled. Remember, to improve certain circumstances in your life, something might have to happen; that event might lead you to that gateway of possibilities. Then, soon all your dreams will be transformed into whatever reality you want them to be... Pursue anything you love, banish the word striving, and all can be accomplished.

Every time you feel more connected to the Source, you realize that this principle of the Universal Laws of Nature is available at every moment. The Source is All-That-Is and is always the same as yesterday, today or tomorrow. The Source has no desires, no goals and no expectations. However, its power is certainly there to be harvested. It is the perfect essence of all formations. Hence stay one with the Source through silence and with a clear mind, because when you worry about your bills, health, bank account and other daily things, you have no room left in your mind to desire the miracle that you may need. Revel in each moment that makes you feel relaxed and calm. Let go of all the burdens that cause your fears, and suffering. If there is an attachment, something needs to be released so that you can learn. This is possible through the grace of the Source, which gives you blessings. Let everything arise out of stillness. Stillness is not influenced by whatever is occurring. Allow everything to flow from the creative Universal Source, which empowers you and all.

When you cut the idea in your mind that you need attention, you will see how people will be effortlessly attracted to you. Let go of arguments by changing environments and conditions and by saying things like "Yes, you are possibly right. Thank you for enlightening me."

This enables an attitude change and allows everyone to be flexible, because you do not want to prove yourself right and others wrong. If you change the way you think, you transform your life tremendously and instantaneously. This is especially true if you are willing to say, "I do not know anything. Pardon me; I am not sure why I even said what I said. I could be mistaken, and I am still learning."

Because of your meekness means you are living in a realistic state of mind, and you keep the Source within and distance yourself from your pride. People see their potential in your free nature, and they will become like you. That change will affect you profoundly and abundantly. The coming year is much brighter than you can imagine because you yield to others and are preparing yourself to swing like an old palm tree: you can lean against the strength of any wind and stay rooted and even stronger than ever. Then, when the moment comes when your mission seems impossible, your palm-tree strength will come in a straightforward yet profound, natural way. It is then that you want to be aware, to make the most of it.

As you awaken to the true nature of who you are, you become a compassionate person. When criticism comes, listen and not engage in conflict, and make peace. Humble yourself before others, and they will do everything in their power to aid you. When being pushed in any direction, you might choose to bow rather than fight. Free yourself from rules, and take pride in doing so; allow yourself to be protected from external harm.

Try to remember that aside from being a firm confirmation of the life in you, being made irrelevant or being belittled is like knowing what it is like to be important: because you are weak, you are aware of what you need to be strong.

In order to show that you are strong, try to fit in with others and choose the path of wisdom and anonymity. That is, hide your need to be more of anything in front of others.

You should make every effort to remind yourself to keep up a state of oneness in your mind. For instance, if you are tired, remind yourself immediately what it is like to feel rested. Recognize the alternatives so that you are aware of them and can relate to them. If you are unhappy, angry, stressed, or weak, jealous, rejected, or whatever, seek the opposite right at that moment and be at one with it in your mind for this provides you with a balanced sense of being at peace within yourself. You do not want to be recognized or draw attention to yourself, but only let it happen naturally. Stay who and what you are, like fish that do not leave the deep-sea as they will be caught and no longer have freedom. If they were captured by a net, they would lose their freedom forever. You must align with the Source, and in doing so, you are always protected because you are under the umbrella of the Universal Source, and you are safe.

I know what you are thinking: You think you need to be tough to survive, but this is not always the case, as even you have seen. Do you know that the softest approach can overcome all things? There is a song called "Killing Me Softly." It is a beautiful song. It is true that the softest things can override the hardest of everything.

Think about water: 73% of our bodies are made up of water, as is the world's surface. Water has the softest quality to enter anywhere and everywhere even though there is no space for it to reach. You can hold water in your hands, or simply placing your hands within it lets it run through your fingers. The softest water can pass through the hardest substances on Earth, such as diamonds.

Apply this to your life, so it flows through everything like water, naturally and effortlessly. When you are water-like, you are running your life, and you must swim with the flow for a long time as you try to follow your intuition, going far beyond where you begin. In order to learn more of the world, you must swim on, but the current pushing against you is strong: It takes an enormous amount of effort and pushes you right back where you began. However, you do not need to do anything in the water: Just let your body follow the waves without letting your mind guide it. Then, everything moves through in slow motion, and a sense of tremendous smoothness surges through your body. It directs you to relax, be free and relinquish. You listen to it as you gently turn your body and swim on: You enjoy resting in the water. Now you know about the process of fighting and struggling on your path: The more strife there is in life, the more difficult it makes everything, but when you choose motionlessness and stillness then everything is transformed into softness. Then, you do not have to do anything, but just mix with the water.

When you drive through life without fear, everything moves smoothly, just as if you write, every word comes easily. This happens when you begin to understand failure and submit; your instincts improve to do better. Your Inner Source kicks in automatically; it guides you to reach your final terminus.

You then get impulse results. You use a softer approach and positive attitude, and more people are attracted to you and seek your direction. This is because you get the correct order from the Universal Source to help you know that. You swim with the tides of the ocean and let everything flow through naturally and automatically without forcing it. When you shut down your thoughts and begin to relax your body and let the spirit within guide you, miracles do happen, and they tow you magically across the finish line.

You understand that when you push something to happen, even though it might still happen, it may not be what you were expecting. Imagine what you said to yourself: You want to do this, and no matter how hard you tried, it all came to nothing. However, when you let it quietly run through your mind, suddenly every obstacle you meet might vanish into thin air and transform your desires and all your dreams into reality. This reflects in your softest approach and not trying to apply the hardest approach.

Throughout your life, from the day you came to planet Earth until the end of your journey, you learned to believe that more of everything is better because it would help you reach the top of the pyramid. Perhaps you should reconsider and start to lose your external possessions and begin to practice reducing your material possessions. When you divide your ton of things, you do not need more security or insurance to protect your possessions. In fact, when you look at the situation deeply, you do not actually have these things you think you own. All earthly things are given to you temporarily by the Source, and you are their short-term gatekeeper.

Now you own it, but eventually you have to relinquish it all. Hence, choose to acquire less and instead continue to live in concert with desire. You believe it is important not to live an Ego-led life and deliberately choose not to abuse favors, but plan to continue your relationship with God. This is a shift from seeking to gain the whole world to surrendering everything to nature to find your soul. Ultimately, without pursuing further material gain, you are better positioned to gain something of more value; you feel more meaning in your life. You realize you do not need to strive hard to obtain what you want. You begin to understand that humanity should become your primary focus, and not seeking more acquisitions.

Begin by consciously decreasing your need to own things. Now, instead of purchasing more mundane things, try to calculate how many possessions you can re-circulate to help others. You will feel much happier with inner bliss; you owe it to your soul.

You will gradually begin to understand that acquiring more is only satisfying the Ego, who wants you to work harder to earn more and consume more. You are living through your Infinite Being, so do not count on the material things you own. With fewer acquisitions, you will enjoy freedom from insecurity and from the need to protect your assets. You will begin to share your possessions with other people. Immediately, you will feel more joy and happiness emerging in you. You gain by not depending on physical objects. Living by detaching is the only way to truly live your life.

You probably feel a strong sense of freedom when you desire to separate yourself from your possessions, when you let go of your obsession with material substances you have collected over the years.

As we all know, we came here with nothing and will leave with nothing. However, you take pleasure and joy when you leave here, so you have left nothing behind. Our true nature is formless, absolutely nothing at all. You must know that your happiness in life cannot be summed up by how many possessions you have owned; rather, relinquish them and free yourself.

In the material world, you are being evaluated and empowered by your net worth and how many acquisitions you amass. That is actually society's setup. That is the reality society has created, and nobody can deny it. However, ownership in the material world is just an illusion. Everything is infinitely constructed and disassembled according to the Law of Nature. All things must go home to their original resting place in the "emptiness" or "void." This is reality and can never be modified, altered, or amended, because it is formless. Hence, the more you allow things to happen naturally and freely, the more harmoniously you live under the umbrella of the Universal Source, your creator, the Mind of God, the Universal Creative Life Force.

Enjoy the world you live in and everything you meet, but you do not necessarily need to accumulate possessions or own more than you should. Take pleasure living in the world, but at the same time, remember that you are out of the world. Yet you are always aware of things, people, and events surrounding you. When you liquidate everything, your life becomes less risky, less insecure, and less fearful. Ultimately, you are liberated.

We take pleasure living here, alert, with everything, but at the same time, we make no judgment on anyone or anything, so it becomes probable that we all will live peacefully and in cooperation.

This can be done by ceasing to criticize others through an acceptance and acknowledgment from us. Imagine that we live in a world with perfect harmony, with no judgments against each other, but filled with love and peace. This is the world all people has thought about as "Heaven on Earth," a peaceful place to live.

You can start by acknowledging yourself as a worthy being, by not saying to yourself, "Oh, I am too short," or "I am too tall" or "I have accomplished nothing in my life thus far." You must stop this kind of self-imposed criticism. Rather, begin to swap judging for praising and treating yourself with kindness by saying to yourself, "I am wealthy, I am incredible, I am who I am, I am an Infinite Being and capable of achieving all things, I am created within the image of God; hence, I am perfect." Calling your behavior bad or good does not promote peace, rather it encourages anger, hatred, jealousy, and discontent about other people you thought were better than you. By endorsing your negative feelings and temperament, you just make things worse and encourage more punishments and discouragement to yourself over your unfortunate circumstances. Furthermore, you do not feel love and do not commit yourself to it because you have automatically marked peace, harmony, acceptance and compassion as untrustworthy in your mind. You do not think there is a peaceful place in you, never mind with other people.

However, as your conditions improve, you change your perspective; you begin to take love around you and in the world. Your mind becomes flexible about the people you have problems with, who have begun to be kind. You have neutralized your belief system, and when you begin to change the way you look at things and use them, they are reasonable and should be respected.

You no longer need to revisit that old belief system.

In fact, it is not significant which country you were born in, what memories you have stored in your belief system, the culture you were assigned to be born into, or the way that your family brought you up. Instead, living beyond judgment should be your priority and principal operative. You should include everyone and exclude no one as you live in oneness in the state of consciousness.

The oneness of the Source encourages you to stop judging one another, to become consciously aware that we are all connected, and to begin to see ourselves in others. In this way, you notice the uniqueness of every person as they are at one with you and as you love yourself. Oneness is in everyone's heart, so we spread God's blessings to the world, to all humans and every living organism. We close our hands, and people say, "We, the people, are blessing God."

All of these views have been so pretty so far; however, we cannot change our worldview unless we change within ourselves. Once we change the way we look at ourselves as well as the world and look again, what we see will be transformed. In other words, we must keep peace within ourselves before we can live in harmony and peace with another.

Remember that we have infinite souls residing within, yet we live in the finite world. Our physical body has mental limitations. Hence, sometimes we just have to be vigilant of our own selves and our behavior. We need to abandon ideas about self-judgment and stop judging ourselves at the same time.

When you think of others' laziness, foolishness, lies and evil, you must think of yourself before you pass judgment.

Do you not see any these negative qualities in yourself too? Thinking it over three times before you leap to a conclusion is the best strategy for any condition or circumstance. Most importantly, see yourself in the other person; only then can you carefully choose to stay in a place to endure and respect and not giving in to anger, complaints and judgments. The next time you feel inclined to judge others, say to yourself, "I like to treat others as I want myself to be treated." Make a pledge now and affirm this to yourself: "From now on, I cast no judgments, criticism, or labels on others or myself. Therefore, I am living with oneness and consciousness within. I have good health, love, peace and wholeness."

Do you see yourself containing the finite and infinite at the same time, or just the finite? When you think of the infinite being, you live beyond life and death.

You know that you've come here as a guest and that your physical body is a temporary refuge for your soul. Your infinite spirit cannot be seen or felt and has not taken any space within you but always has been with you since you came here. You are infinite but have finite experiences on Earth.

In the physical realm, you are free to move around without difficulty. You have experienced your Inner-Self through subliminal contemplation. However, to make conscious connections, you must be aware of the spirit of your Authentic Self and call it to be available through meditation. The sooner you acknowledge and apply the Inner Soul, the sooner you can begin to use its ability to increase your daily activities. An intimate knowledge of your Infinite Soul is the purpose of the Universal Source. You will be able to easily escape from harm. You will be able to deal with difficult or unforeseen situations that others might get stuck in. When you surrender to live a life, you will be aware of your true nature and know that you are truly an infinite soul. Any attempt to inflict injury or harm cannot change you. Life will be transformed to become brighter and lighter than you ever thought was possible.

Knowing that you are a spirit in nature will change the way you think about life and death. By seeing in the spirit of your Inner Self, you will be able to enjoy this world of illusion. When your soul leaves your body, it may be the end of physical life on planet Earth, but your Authentic Self will continue without end. You are living in a place full of challenges. Strive, and your short trip from living to death would be your one and only life experience.

Now, when you are a spirit, you are living in the true essence of nothingness—the void with nothing to do, nothing to worry about and nothing to challenge. You can move freely without limits and are not bound by anything—that is, you reverse back to a shapeless form, which is everlasting, ever-evolving, and eternal. You are apparently at the end, but there is no limit.

Life and death are connected by the assumption that you are lying dead while your spirit lifts up from your body. You are free to go anywhere—you are limitless—but your physical body is still, and nobody can hurt that dead body of yours. You realize that. Hence, you turn around and fly away from Earth. It is the first time you have ever seen this magnificent Universe with no boundary lines, and besides this black space, the Universe is so beautifully created by the All-That-Is, the Mind of God of the Universal Creative Life Force.

You know that you are an infinite spirit; there is nothing you cannot do now. Oh, you almost forgot your dead body, but it is not significant, because you are aware that the physical body is temporary and can only be used once. You are going to have a new body if you want to be reborn. In this awareness, you realize you are invincible–you are a formless spirit. Then, suddenly, you feel awake—awake as if you have never been before. You thought that you had just experienced death and had discovered that you are a formless, infinite soul. You came here to learn the intellectual lessons with a soul experience on Earth. Now, you realize that you do not need attachments or material possessions, because they are just illusions. With the experience facing of death, you know that only your soul will last forever.

This is the Divine consciousness; you see yourself lying there. Then your spirit will rise from your body; now you know who you truly are: a spiritual being.

You know that death holds no pain or suffering; it is just human nature, and no one can escape from death. The original emptiness, the void of the dark Universe, is our destination to which we will return. It is whence we came, a reversal back to nonbeing from being, and a way of being united with the Universal Source in oneness.

From the time you arrive here until the time you die, it is all inevitable; maybe death is the only thing that we are always aware of and that will always happen. The fact of death is not a secret, but the other side that awaits the person who dies is still a secret.

The mystery is what lies beyond all that which seems to stop and leave. Under Heaven, there is Mother Earth, and everything starts from Mother Nature—She is the beginning of the world. As soon as you are aware of Mother Earth, you shall see your truth and that of others. Ultimately, we all return to Mother Nature; dust turns to dust—we all shall return to nothingness.

While you are on Earth, it is essential that you take some time to recognize the lively existence of Mother Nature and quietly talk with her to show her your appreciation and gratitude. Once you decide to recognize and honor her, you will begin to change your thoughts about how you see her children and yourself. You will acknowledge that we are the offspring of Mother Earth, and then you will go beyond your current situation and see what your life is unfolding in the consciousness of timeless present.

Think of your mouth as a gateway that guides your spirit: do not let your words show badly upon others, and be vigilant about what you judge, because your soul is listening. Speaking less allows your spirit to dwell safely within you. Similarly, safeguard all your senses and live a full life. In other words, gradually tune out gossip.

Remember, you should always reject any participation in talking about other people's businesses and keep your voice still. If you do that, you will hold onto your freedom and happiness; you will meet your everlasting light.

You do make a vast difference; you have the great ability to influence and change the world by seeing it as part of yourself, and this translates to all forms of life that link to us in consciousness.

Unity connects the whole of life's path, so we can use "We are the world; we are the people..." as everyone's theme song. Hence, you can see the changes by looking inside; as you change from within, you will see others understand and help to make a difference in the world, and then the whole world will change.

It is the Source within that motivates you to make this transformational change; so every thought and insight you choose can make an impact on others and make a change. Hence, do not entertain questions, fear, or doubt in your mind, because that will have a significant impact on the world, even though you may not see it, as the energy you send out will transcend and stir into the air going through the Universe, translating to every corner of the world. As a result, the whole Earth might be affected. You should choose a dream in which you perceive the world without hatred, anger, jealousy, or offense, where nature is respected and cared for, all are in excellent health, and there is no cancer or serious disease, no child abuse, no weapons of mass destruction, and many other unheard-of factors vanish. Never doubt your thoughts can change the world; even if they are small. Everything is connected, and the sum of all thoughts becomes enormous. Everything can change through one connection and affect all things that transpire.

Everything you think about extends outward, travels across thousands of miles, and multiplies. When you live your life knowing the difference, your goal is one of wholeness that doesn't cause harm. Your energy can travel much distance, even though no one acknowledges it. Therefore, an act of kindness contains energy that can affect the entire Universe. Conversely, a silent prayer or agreement has a signal that can be felt throughout the entire cosmos.

Hence, be aware that your thoughts will affect everyone living on Earth and all creations.

When people are in vibrational harmony with the Source, those who are in the know receive all sorts of freedom and blessings. Hence, they rarely get sick, and even in the midst of chaotic scenes, they are still protected and may even sound like they are invincible. It is as if a person has guardian angels around him, pulling him out of fear, so he is freed from evil. These people are in harmony with the Universal Source. They seem to have the right people acting in their lives at the right time, while others seem to have Lady Luck for making changes occur when they most need it.

However, you must realize that what you call luck does not just happen; it is in your life only if you realize it when you try to relinquish. You draw the ultimate power of the Source to come to you when you try to ignore the need to manage your life. Hence, change your thoughts, and you will begin to see how your life has changed to a very lucky one that you very much needed.

You let go and let God live in harmony with the Universe in order to create your immune system.

Hence, free yourself from disease, and let life's natural rhythm flow through you. Letting go means releasing your fears, worries, and uncertainty. When you relinquish yourself to the Source, you trust the Oneness to work on your well-being and remove your stress and anxiety so you can relax and assume that everything is blooming. This will keep you from pushing yourself to move in powerful ways. All things that go up must be allowed to come down.

Realize that you must allow time to heal, but you must trust the infinite healing oneness of God's spirit.

Say to yourself, "I allow and open myself to what needs to be done to get healed. I trust the Source to guide me." This change your thoughts by guiding you to stay with the flow of inspirit. Peace will be substituted for anxiety, worry, and indecision. Harmony will replace your efforts when you let go, and stars will replace fear and fright. Again, it is twofold: You experienced gloom before, but now you are connecting with greater harmony so that all things happen.

You understand that nothing lasts forever; therefore, even if you think that you might have experienced bad luck, that can dissolve because everything is moving and rapidly becomes motivated. Everything is a constantly shifting power in the practical world, but you must focus on the unchanging oneness. The Source is the same yesterday, today, and tomorrow.

A large majority of people believe themselves to be living in a stable, safe environment that is fully secure. However, life is unpredictable, and you must take into account any dark energy that has stood in your way during every experience you have met. Even nature cannot be anticipated. Every perfect sunny day can be followed by a unified storm.

Suddenly, there is an earthquake that causes enormous damage to a country that is located in an earthquake zone. The standards of nature are unpredictable; we can only accept this truth as history unfolds. Change your outlook so that you can accept whatever happens without losing touch with the harmony and peace of the Source. Always keep your positive belief that more positively, and things will flow to you. In nature, every windstorm is always followed by a silver lining or a vivid rainbow.

Similarly, you will begin to see every aspect of a situation rather than just misfortune. There is no such thing as a purely virtuous or unfortunate turn of events. You should simply wait until you see a blessing comes to you, and then you may forget your adversities. There are two halves to every miracle, even though both events will never happen at the same time; one half waits for the right moment to emerge.

Good and unpleasant situations will come and go, but you must be at peace with yourself and in harmony with the Source to ensure you see an unfavorable situation as a profound opportunity. Always be aware that everything in life is subject to transmutation. You will always have an opportunity to perform untroubled by your misfortunes. In every stage of an event, you will have a chance to align yourself with the wholeness of things. As a result, rather than just seeing moral luck in events, you will know that the problems are a part of the duality in the world of illusion. Therefore, this level of change to your experience will enrich your life. When you take this philosophy into your heart, you should make your prayer to everything; in return, you will be blessed. The alleged negativity will erode. Remember, a sunny day is best appreciated after a storm, and darkness wears down when light is available.

Your life is already in excellent condition as you continue to allow the invisible Universal Source to manage it. You can assume that All-That-Is is always present for your needs, taking care of your health and blessing your relationships. However, for a new day and for everything to happen, there is one solution: only you believe and execute everything in consciousness. Then, it will come and lean toward you throughout the day and night while you're asleep, protecting you from having nightmares, so you will sleep well. The firmness with which you believe that all your success will transpire into enormous wealth and prosperity makes you think of protection by means of the Divine light. Externally, you slowly release control, then coherently and without desire, you link to the Source.

Misfortune is controlled by the unseen force: Until the moment it occurs and has unfolded, you would never have had a clue, but it always comes with the strike of the opportune moment that will interfere with and overpower grief and despair. Then you need to change what you understand and make it into something untroubled. In other words, you can handle all of it fearlessly, make it all clear, and follow the duality as a part of life you cannot change. You can always watch what life puts upon you most and track your intuition to help you get the best. Then, try to remember the moments you do not feel happy and test the hypothesis that presents itself to you. Without trying to decipher the object or idea, allow yourself to be vigilant about the issue with your eyes closed. Allow it to be silently absorbed into your body as if you have swallowed a pill and allowed it to flow through you without charge.

After this, all queries will leave you without a trace, just as when the sun comes out after a cloud disappears from the sky. You are doing well by embracing the twofold life. This concept is similar to the way in which the Chinese have absorbed the principles of both yin and yang: Let the duality of things become a part of you, and willingly accept that you will encounter both sides in your life. When encountering them both by living unconcernedly and accepting things as they emerge, you will know how to respond to either good or bad luck.

Since all things are possible, the Universe has unlimited resources that you can use to help others in changing their lives, living well, and using the concept of the Source to make the right choices. When you are consciously aware of the fact that there are no limits to your resources, you can harness all of them. You must see that what you should do is prepare yourself to become a leader. Those who live by chance, risk, and uncertainty can only be followers; they blindly obey the rules of law set before them and cannot make their own decisions. This prevents a worse scenario: that they live unmindfully without being able to differentiate between right and wrong. Furthermore, these people cannot stand alone, and beyond that, it becomes difficult for them to handle any problems at all. They let other minds take control of every part of their lives, even their own thoughts. Self-decision does not exist for those who are blindly passive recipients.

For you to be a leader, you must practice restraint, moderation, and attentiveness while limiting yourself and trying not to make decisions for those around you; let others achieve what they will based on their own personality and behavior. Acting on someone else's recommendations is only a temporary solution; a person can only act without doubt and fear if he or she makes his or her own decisions.

If all things are possible, then nothing is impossible. Therefore, there is no limit. You can do it all consciously; you can do what you want to do and be where you want to be.

For 10 years, I practiced gathering virtuous deeds and valuing them without realizing it.

Of my own accord, I gave books to individuals whom I believed would benefit from them. I did it with strong faith and as an act of love and peace. On every birthday, I donated a small gift to the Vancouver Children's Hospital Fund with deep joy and happiness because I made a commitment to the Source, saying I would share my wealth with children. I love giving and am willing to continue to contribute my share to them. I consider it my lifelong project and an everlasting hope that is shaping my life. I believe in the everlasting promise of happiness, through which all things transpire.

Governing your life is like frying vegetables: If you cook them for too long, you will spoil them. However, if you allow your life to exist under the umbrella of the Universal Source, you will view life differently, especially knowing that evil cannot present itself in your world. When you are consciously aware of and centered within the protection of the Source, evil cannot affect you. When you live in accordance with the Source and refuse to crave or bestow harmful thoughts upon others and yourself, the powers of dark evil (any willful acts and harmful energy) will be rendered powerless and will vanish.

The Source will never harm you, and it will never judge or display partiality for any one party. Just give: As you ask, so shall you receive. It is advantageous for everyone to conserve energy without exception.

When people or nations violate this code of the Laws of Nature, they cannot achieve success but instead force failure on themselves, and then evil becomes available to the people who are around them and in the area near them. Negative energy will only attract destructive returns. The tyrant will eventually be destroyed by causing dangerous and gloomy actions to other nations as his country falls into chaos and violence. He will be overthrown by his own people.

You, as an individual, should confirm this: "I affirm that I have no intention whatsoever to cause any harm, directly or indirectly, to anyone. I will act in accordance with the Laws of Nature that allow me to act with love. Hence, all thought vibrations sent out through me have positive, optimistic energy and are in great harmony and love comparable with the oneness of the Source."

This means that despite whatever comes your way, no one will cause negative power or engage in plans against you: You have made yourself immune from negative energy by being Source-centered. All peaceful means arise in you and then transfers to people around you and to the world or country next to you.

When you connect with the Source, become aware of how much it has impacted your daily activities. Perhaps you experience deep calmness, tranquility befalls you and positive energy pours through you. You start with kindness and compassion and love that transcend within and make you feel warm all the time, and this occurs when you remain Source-centered. As you continue to stay in the center, you remain resistant to all pessimistic emotions and negative expressions. This is because you know that you have transformed to the higher consciousness in your thinking; you have changed your life by aligning and centering into the care and loving spirit of the invisible wholeness of All-That-Is, the omniscience of oneness of the Source.

This inner trust must be true and not a delusion, because when evil appears to you, it will not impact you. Because you're bound by a certain higher energy, you can't get hurt.

Practice positive energy so that no evil can approach you. Believe in it, and it will transform into a powerful, protective shield, even amid danger. This is not an unrealistic sense of security; rather it is the consciousness that you and the Source have become one.

If you remain humble before others, you will win more friendships and trust. However, this theory is quite different from the one you were brought up with: to climb to the apex of the pyramid and be the first. From experience, you learn to overcome your rivals and become the master of your art. You are respected by many because you are the champion of your profession and produce abundant wealth, collect the most collectable items, and hold the most powerful office on earth, all while the lower echelon earns less respect. This may create you pain if you cannot understand how to become a prominent leader. However, when you humble yourself before the low, you will win friendship and trust. Similarly, when the low are humble before the leader, they will win his trust. When you live an infinite life, you remain less than other people. You do not want to show you are powerful and knowledgeable. You remain hidden, quiet, and still because you understand this is the way to live a passionate life. Only then can you gain their trust and mix with them. As you observe this, you remain still and let other people see your inner strength and the peace and harmony emanating from you.

To gain the trust and respect of others, you need to transform the way in which you think of yourself. You must make a tremendous change in the way that you think of yourself and others who see you through the eye of a needle. You need to make a conscious shift and cast out the Ego-dominated power. You deliberately choose yin's soft energy, which confers benefits upon you and others. This is the Mother Earth's energy and the way of nature, and it is the Source at work. The only way to attract goodness is by staying calm and still; others will eventually grow with you, joining you in friendship and trust. As you stay in this state of yin energy, you will win the trust of those unfortunate people who dislike change. Stay meek, and let people come to you; create a secure shelter on which people can rely.

I received this dream from the oneness of the Source one cold night during the winter of 2008. I wrote down the message I received: "In a time of crisis, I encourage you to think of me. Allow me to enter your life to help you resolve your problems and restore your image, your life, your health and everything else. Let me assist you in eradicating your struggle, addiction or Ego-domination, even thoughts that seem to snatch you away from the feminine, Mother Nature's yin energy. I can help. If you stumble, allow me to give you the first sip of water, so you can relax and be comfortable. Let me help you find the greatest way. Allow me to help you." I am.

Within you dwells a treasured light—silently vigilant—watching over everything you do and say and gently guiding you to make transformational changes so you can experience an enjoyable life. However, are you aware of this valuable thing dwells deep within you? Perhaps you are not. If you are not sure, and if you let me, I'll be happy to show you. To access this sacred treasure, you must awaken it by triggering its energy through contemplation.

It reminds me that it changed the way I see myself, and I was pleased to change in this way.

You can refine your views on the negative ingredients and poisons, the evils and the wicked one. Instead of casting them aside, you can get them together, put them in one pot and treat them fairly, so you know how to deal with them if you meet one of them someday. So stay in peace and center yourself, meditating on everlasting love and the omniscience of the Source. The Source will never judge or discriminate against anyone; the Source simply accepts all that comes to Him. You are not meditated on God-Source. Do not send out negative poisons; instead, contemplate inner peace and harmony. Then breathe in and send compassion and kindness out to stir in the air, where it transcends into the Universe and vibrates to every corner of the world, conferring benefits on all.

See yourself invited to the divine dwelling place where you can bring anything, where there are no restrictions on what you can bring with you. Realize that you have your negative thoughts, but you do not know if the negative ingredients follow you as you enter the Divine House. Visualize that you are about to enter the sacred house, but all of your anger, hatred, jealousy and anxiety automatically leave you as you enter. You walk in filled with joy and bliss, and you make it into a retreat to which you have free access at any time through this practice of meditation.

It is the sacred Divine place, but it can be your sanctuary, as you will, at any time.

Perhaps you do want to separate those wicked ones from their poisonous behavior as they continue to do poisonous things in the world.

Bear in mind, they are still children of God; it is just that they decided to follow the dark Ego and let it harness their lives. In your thoughts, you erase their wicked behavior and wrongdoing, but quarantine them in a pot: Allow them to stay there. You see the unfolding of the Source's energy in them and imagine that they are, or once were, innocent children who have become over stimulated by the Ego's temporary and controlling power. In your mind, you cast an image of forgiveness on those wicked people and hug them: Imagine you see them before you, and put your arms around them.

You should do this to clean yourself: Inhale, and then send out forgiveness to yourself. Eradicate anything you dislike about yourself. Then allow your pains to be felt, and liberate yourself. Say this affirmation: "I am sorry I hurt you; please forgive me. I love you. Thank you." Continue to clean your subconscious mind: Clean, clean, clean. Empty your subconscious mind, and allow inspired messages to enter. Visualize yourself embracing the radiant white light, which now enters you and continues to naturalize and purify your body and mind. Then, visualize yourself connected to the void of emptiness and united with the Source. Now you are elevating your thoughts with pure, positive energy from the Source, and you emit kindness to others and yourself.

If we think only in the moment and do not worry about the next minute, tomorrow, the coming weeks, the coming months, or the unfolding years, I will live more happily and experience fewer stresses in my life. We ever need to do is stay focused on the moment—that's it. Hence, we must avoid worrying about events that may never come to pass.

When you keep thinking or worrying about something that might never happen, your life becomes all the more problematic. Consequently, you are unable to comprehend all that life has to offer because you are not living in the present. You must think positively while things are still occurring. When you live life with simplicity, everything becomes easier; so do everything in the consciousness, in the here and now. Examine the thoughts in your mind: Are you thinking of your troubles now? Can you change your thinking to more manageable and positive thoughts, or can you make them less complicated? You can avoid all the troubles that have not yet occurred simply by staying in the moment and not focusing on potential future events. It is unnecessary to predict what will happen in the future. You should leave the future alone because it is not predictable, and you should choose from moment to moment. The present is all you need to be concerned with. You can accomplish things even if they are small; you still can achieve happiness. By doing things that are less complicated, you experience no hassle and cut complexity out of the big picture.

Transfer your attention away from preoccupying conscious thoughts of the future, along with anything else that is not conclusive, so that life becomes a more tolerable experience for you. When you occupy yourself with thoughts of tomorrow's unknowns, it will drive you mad, because you are wasting your energy focusing on something that does not exist and cannot be validated. You think of an unforeseen event, and it causes distress to you, your family, or your friends around you. You turn things into a greater illusion of fears, worries, and bewilderment when doing so is, in fact, not your intention.

Look around you, and think about what you have: You are probably not struggling right now as you read this book, nor do you miss anything; obviously you are aware of what your consciousness desires. The result is to live in the timeless present by not focusing your thoughts on the unknown future or the closed past. The past can no longer be validated, while the streaming future does not exist; you only think it does. It is best to cancel your thoughts about a comprehensive plan; make that plan comprehensible, and leave complicated things out of it. Simply by shifting your thoughts away from undesired things, your accomplishments will become more meaningful when you view your goals in the short term; you will see the power of successive results. Be in the present moment.

Everything begins with a meek step: There is no reckless charge. A journey of a thousand miles starts with a baby step that is simple to take. In other words, all things begin right here where you are. Every dream is possible. If you can dream it, you can take it. However, you must be aware that all dreams are created in the conscious mind.

You do not need to put up with your difficulties all at once; break them into manageable steps so you can crack the troubles that seem to control you. In addition, rather than taking control of others' attempts to resolve their problems, direct them and enable them to command themselves. Through intensive suffering, you will know how to endure your pain and sadness. When you look back, obstacles such as illness, adversity, struggles, accidents, financial loss, and other troubles you have experienced are now perceived as gifts. You can now reexamine these troubles and understand that this is not the way to live life, but you realize that you should give as much attention at the end as at the beginning.

Now, what have you learned from the difficult situation you are currently experiencing? The lesson is like a hidden present, and you must concentrate on finding it. You will probably have to go back to the place where you previously obtained help. Connecting to the Source will allow you to quickly and easily solve your problems. You can also predict when a problem or argument is about to occur. You play out the situation in your mind; then, as fast as lightning, you are able to neutralize the negative energy as if it is in front of you. You have responded to the problem by not participating in it. Thus it produced harmony. This is a natural, peaceful means to solve your problems. You have prevented your troubles from surfacing without having to decode them. Participating in the problem will only further complicate the situation. By being quiet and motionless, you will not miss anything; you are not grasping the problem, and finally it will be abandoned.

Now, what are the reasons you fail to make transformational life changes to live better? It is not the product you are after. It is not that you are incapable of changing your lifestyle. Indeed, your failure stems from the belief systems in your mind. You believe that your current negative situation is just. In other words, your negative thoughts have prevented you from making changes. You thought your feelings were genuine, so just let them be. Eventually, you no longer want to change them. Your emotions have blinded you and prevented you from seeing the real truth within yourself.

You are aware of and have never doubted your negative feelings. As months, translate into years, your feelings blend with your conscious thoughts. It becomes irrelevant what others have said to you; you will not change.

What would happen when you change your conscious thoughts, you will begin to see change in your life. You begin to understand that your innermost emotions and struggles are warning signs to you. You see the root causes of your inner conflict, so you take action to change them to positive thoughts in the here and now. Your emotions affect the way you experience life. You can make your life better by keeping positive thoughts in mind. If you see something you dislike, change the unpleasant feelings to a higher energy absorption field. To improve your life, drop the negative feelings from your conscious thoughts.

When you think about doing something, you have to forget about the result. New thoughts occur every second. When you decide where you want to be, you will embark on a new journey again. Whatever you do is present in your subconscious mind. You decide to do it right now. So enjoy every moment of your journey, and remind yourself that everything is possible from where you are. Simply take one step at a time; there is no wondering. All journeys start with a small step. Even if you consciously walk a thousand miles, you still take one step at a time. When you navigate in this manner, there will be no failure. A pyramid has a million bricks, yet it all begins with a single brick. When the million bricks are laid, then the pyramid is complete. You can cancel your troubles by adopting the same approach. However, do not live by your emotions. Focusing on the positive will eliminate your troubles, now and eternally.

You can always try to prevent something from happening before it occurs. For instance, you can take supplements to improve your health. If your immune system is less than perfect, you can eat probiotic yogurt or use a colon cleanse. You can take vitamins, drink fresh vegetable and fruit juices, meditate, and walk in the morning. Do whatever you need to do and whatever is right for you. This will help you manage your health well, and in cooperation with the Source, before any disorder can occur.

In the past, I had thought about the generosity of the sun, which gives us free light. Unlike this luminous energy, I am now talking about the treasures hidden in everyone's heart. We should embrace them, hold them within, and utilize them in our daily activities. With these treasures within our hearts, taking action becomes easier and brings us more successes in our daily activities. But what are these forces that are so powerful that everyone should hold them fast? They are compassion, generosity, and meekness.

We must keep love in our hearts, but not with an unkind or uncaring attitude. Compassion is caring for and loving others. It is sharing your generosity support. Your hidden spirit of gentleness encourages you to selflessly and boldly care for others without holding back. You should willingly serve and show selflessness and love even toward your rivals rather than concentrate on seeking external recognition and showing that you are successful. In other words, you abandon your own personal pleasure for the sole purpose of providing services to another, because you are truly sincere. You are aware that humanity is one of the attributes of the merciful God.

In His unconditional love, God has shown His mercy to planet Earth in a sea of kindness, mercy, and compassion.

The second word is generosity. We are aware our lives are limited. In order to reach our goals of achieving a conceptual understanding of ourselves, we offer our charitable contributions to helping those who are less fortunate. Giving is one of the Divine gifts of humankind. We can offer assistance to those in need; by doing so, they, too, can enjoy and live life fearlessly, abundantly, and freely.

Generosity is based on the principles of the Universal Laws of Nature, which describe an active exchange with Heaven. All of the acquisitions that you have accumulated over the years do not come directly from your own will but originate in the flow of energy in the spirit world. Hence, we cannot interfere with the Universal flow; otherwise, we restrict the pure energy that flows freely from Heaven. We must commit to giving in order to keep the spiritual and material goods we have accumulated in our lives. When the action is in good faith and write from the heart, then the spirit of giving increases; energy flows freely, and returns is threefold and benefit everyone. However, if we give stingily, we close ourselves off to the flow of spirit energy, and instead of acting as conduits for this Divine flow, we slow down the natural positive force of the world. The life energy flowing back to us will decrease rather than increase because there is no real gift involved. Therefore, when you are able to give generously and wholeheartedly, you also become more appreciative of the gifts that you receive in your life. This is better than accumulating extra possessions that you think you need. Consequently, you are willing to earn less rather than more. It is easier to meet your individual needs because you can rejoice in generosity. The less you cling to your possessions, the more you are concerned about the welfare of others.

The third word is "meekness." The treasure that helps to build a successful life is meekness. When you are meek, you do not assume that you are above the power of nature or that you are invincible at all times. You do not try to be number one or stroke your ego based on your accomplishments.

We often think that our strength, power, and success are based on elegance, pride, and self-importance. Thus, we do not want to humble ourselves in front of others. We want to be the dominant one and try to stand on top and ahead of others. We want to be the winner of choice all the time. However, when you change the way you think about your pride and arrogance, you begin to see what real successful people think about success: We are all instruments of the Universal Source.

Your current energy and support give you the ability to write books and perform other feats that are not for you; they are from Heaven. Indeed, everything comes from the Universal Creative Life Force of the Mind of God.

Humility requires relinquishing your own power rather than holding onto your ego. It gives all the glory to the Universal Source and showing appreciation for the wisdom, ability, and guidelines that the Source has unconditionally given you. Hence, be thankful for what you are and what you have. Be a strong leader without showing arrogance, and stay meek, with concern for others. Consequently, you will triumph and be an enlightened leader. Extend sympathy and tolerance toward yourself and to every living thing. The key to your every success and peace is sustained compassion and humbleness in your heart as you go about your daily activities. You do not need to be a warrior or compare yourself with anyone on any level. You can even show your appreciation to the computer desk, the space in a room, and your chair that you use daily. Respect everything. You align with the Source. Mother Nature will always protect you; you are resistant to pain and harm.

A challenger must be present in a competition.

However, if there is no match, there is no winner or loser. You have a choice. You can participate and create winners and losers, or you can live collaboratively with nature and resonate with one another. You should not fight with others if you know in your heart that you do not want to compete with other people. In the martial arts, good Kung Fu Masters do not get angry. They win the game with calmness and assertiveness rather than being filled with hate and getting angry with their opponents. You observe your opponents to improve your skills. Without opponents, you could not enhance your martial arts' skills and win the championship competition. In fact, you just use the power of others to lever yourself into a winning position. So the next time you think about competing with your opponent, use your inner strength to control your external environment. Employ this approach in every area of your life.

When you practice the concept of noncompetition, you have less stress, anger, and anxiety in your conscious thoughts. You obviously live with an inner calmness and peace. You are able to counteract any negative feelings as you play and, more importantly, you are not fighting with yourself. You use the power of other people to create more inner strength and serenity so that you can experience inexpressible joy, peace, and happiness. You know your role and what you are. Your uniqueness has given you the ability of all knowledge and wisdom to seek to know yourself.

It is imperative that you live in harmony and peace with others to attempt the essential unity in a relaxing atmosphere, which is the essence of silence that God will possess in your heart alone.

Do not be confused by your own conscious thought that recognizes God's omnipresence is an easy thing to do except for your mind is lucid and still.

It is not as easy as you thought it would be, even with your efforts of paying attention over the years. Truth only makes you capable of living in peace with yourself and others; you shall see God in the silence, sacred space.

You must control your thoughts and not let them overpower and compromise you. Your opinions and ideas must be one. You must be able to look within and be vigilant about your life. Then you will experience the silent mind. Follow every moral principle of the Universal Laws of Nature, which will help you succeed on the path of greatness and purpose. It is a positive lifestyle: cheerful and full of peace. You must realize that God represents compassion, kindness, and humility. Once you combine these three virtues and live in harmony with God, you will demonstrate these Divine image qualities. By trusting God and follow these three treasures, you will notice that your thoughts and actions point you toward the gratitude and understanding of a God-realized life. Indeed, we all should practice giving thanks to God for everything and realize that all events have been prearranged in Heaven. We do not do anything by ourselves; all things happen with help from the invisible spirit. Your soul feels joy because it has found peace.

The inner path of peace and the outer path of justice are difficult to rejoice in, given a world confronted with wars, conflicts, and unfairness, to seek inner peace seems impossible at this moment. But using inner peace and projecting it to the external world for calmness and tranquility are still possible, and someday peace might be attained.

Hence, you should attribute your successes to the Universal Source, the Mind of God. Praise and appreciate God for what He has blessed us with in the Great Way. This is the way to know God and live a quiet and peaceful life in God.

When you think about birth, life, and death, ask yourself if these thoughts change the way you perceive death. If there is a God in Heaven who gave you life, then surely there must be a place where the Lord of Death can vigilantly watch over you.

Henry Wadsworth Longfellow expressed this dilemma in his poem **"A Psalm of Life"**

Life is real! Life is earthiest!

And the grave is not its goal;

Dust thou art, to dust returnest;

Was not spoken of the soul.

Upon death, your spirit will remain dynamic because it came from the realm of infinite possibilities. After death, your spirit returns to the nothingness with the Source. You transform from a being to a pure spirit.

Although it is difficult to fully describe or imagine what a spirit is, one thing we can be certain of is that a spirit is real and immortal. In my opinion, a spirit is a nonbeing, a pure form of energy. It has no limits and is free to go anywhere. It is unlikely we will ever see the presence of a spirit with our physical eyes because of its formless nature and its higher vibrational energy, which moves faster than our limited eyes, can see. Therefore, it is unlikely we will see its presence, although it is possible to feel it.

At the moment, you are entering the physical world. Even at your birth, the Lord of birth and death provides everything you need for this journey that harmonizes with the vibration of the Source's energy. Your physical body is an expression of the Source. Your death is recorded in the Book of Death, which is also an expression of the Source. It all unfolds according to the Divine time sequence. Since death is a natural occurrence of life, it must happen in harmony with all things that have originated from the Divine. Death must not occur because of an egotistic decision. No one can determine one's own death. The Lord of Death makes that decision, even for tiny insects.

We should not fear death, for it marks the start of the next journey. It is an infinite cycle. The journey is a return trip that takes us back to where we started.

One way to look at our strength and energy is to consider an old oak tree. It can bend and get soft. Near the end of its lifespan, it becomes weak and may no longer have the strength to withstand stormy gusts of wind. It becomes weaker simply because it is inflexible and can no longer bear weight. Weakness has turned it into an organism with no energy. Certainly, at the moment of death, every creature becomes stiff and motionless. There is a complete absence then of strength and energy. Therefore, I conclude that we are all vibrational energies, but we vibrate at a diversity of frequencies. The faster the vibrational energies, the closer one is to spirit; consequently, we understand where we came from. The keyboard that I use for typing this text is actually manifested of many tiny particles, as we can see if we examine it with a powerful microscope. The vibrational energy of my keyboard creates a slow motion that appears to be solid. My eyes can see the keyboard; it appears in front of me, because it fits within a certain range of frequencies.

Thoughts are vibrational energies. We communicate with the Source through the energy of our thoughts sent by our spirits. Our innermost thought energies are aligned with the Source energy of God. Our prayers to God are submitted by our subconscious minds and echo the Universal Source with the highest vibrational energies. When prayers return, they come through the latent mind then reach the intellectual mind; subsequently, the conscious mind translates the answers into words so we can understand.

Being flexible enables you to transcend the aging process that through bodily experience. Being able to bend and not be firmly fixed in any circumstance allows you to experience life in times of stress and uncertainty. You may think that being strong is the best way to live. Perhaps you think that being strong means you should be rigid, that you should not bend in your opinions, and that you refuse to be weak. However, humility is connected to those who yield and possess a quiet nature. Being resistant to this flexibility can cause pain and even death to cross your path.

You must have the elasticity of an old oak palm tree. Even in the middle of strong winds, the apparent weakness of these trees allows them to stand firm and gives them the strength to survive overpowering storms. By applying strength to your relationships with others, listening more, practicing meekness, allowing your voice to be heard, and bowing when necessary, you will harmonize the results as you demonstrate increasing flexibility in your consideration of others' viewpoints.

The best way to overcome the inelastic flow of your life is to yield. If you are hard and unyielding, you will be overcome by the persistent application of softer things; water can be used to soften every problem that is rigid and severe as well as to dissolve all nature. Be as soft as the water that exceeds the strength of seemingly unbreakable substances, like diamonds, and transforms them into different shapes. Due to its active place in the cutting process, the water uncomplainingly enters where nothing solid can defend itself; it is later transmuted into a state of art by the master. In your spiritual experience, you can apply water as a softener into your daily activities, especially when you are met with problems and indecisions.

You are contemplating the element of water that makes you relax and let go of resistance; it dissolves your troubles in a gentle way. Now you see that, given enough time, the softness and flexibility of water can make everything softer by allowing water in, and the changing nature of water can overcome the hardest element on Earth and ultimately win. In other words, you must not be at all surprised when the weak conquer the unyielding. Remember to be flexible in every situation, even in the midst of a crisis you must bend a little and show weakness, but consciously be aware that you are in a vibrational harmony with the Source. You remain calm and tranquil within; even if you feel pain and helplessness. This allows the inspirational messages of the Source to enter and inspire you, and the darkness cannot come near you to deteriorate your senses. Water is good for your physical body, mind and spirit. You cannot catch, cut or destroy water, but you can transform it to solid from liquid, and then it will return to its source again. Similarly, life on Earth will never be destroyed or end; it will simply return to its origin, its creator, and ultimately it will return here again.

Life is a continuum, and water is always a softener; nothing can overcome the rigid better than water. Trust your Inner Source to be your softener and its gentle self to guide you in all matters. All good things will happen to you at the moment you no longer believe they are possible, and when everything seems lost. The miracle arises in a natural way—it will call on you no matter where you are or how lonely you are; you will experience a beautiful event that will enrich your life. A clear view of the Divine Kingdom, of the incredible magical gifts of superb health, love, and blissfulness, will be divinely given to your beingness! You pass under the protection and are in sync with the vibrations of the Source's energy.

These are useful and improbable events that come about by using softness rather than a rigid and uncompromising ability to control, which are not the attributes of life at all. Allow the qualities of softness to serve you, and remove the stereotype of weakness. Transform the way you look at current events, and then your zest will change, all things will come to pass, and the most beautiful of your desires will become possible. Relinquish all of your problems to the hand of the invisible oneness of the Source, which will be guiding you. Live your life like the water—gentle and kind—and allow unobtrusive events to happen to you whenever you are needed.

When stirring events occur, you will allow them to occur quickly, and your account will flow like water with no hindrance; you'll hit a home run at every game. You are going to enjoy a considerable period of prosperity. Imagine yourself entering places you once thought were impossible; your decision to be kind and yielding are an indication of your transformation toward efficient experience and unexpected peace and contentment. Flow softly into current events, into the inner thoughts of people with whom you have been in conflict with in the past, and drink with them through spiritual experience. Through this experience of gentleness and vigilance, your soul shall stand. Complete silence in your mind proves you are in sync with God and the omnipresence of God only through the voice of silence.

Anger can be caused by a difference of opinion in a conflict or a fight. Obviously, unproductive arguments can happen when people engage in discussion in an inconsiderate or insensitive manner, annoying one another. They know that they are politically incorrect, but insist that their beliefs and ridiculous arguments are accurate. What can you do about this kind of situation? You can't change someone else, but you can control the way you react. You can laugh or forget about it. The best way to do so is to modify your thoughts and focus on the positive, not the negative emotions. Anger does not come from the other party; it is an internal reaction from you. Anger is a result of your unwillingness to relinquish control or live without influence from your environment, which stops the exchange of negative energy within you. When you create negative energy, it strips you and the people surrounding you of Divine consciousness. You should look for alternatives to help settling disputes. If there is no alternative, surrender everything and give in to the Source. Instead of igniting your irritation and disgust, remove yourself from the situation. Remember there is always a counter force, a force with which you have chosen not to be attuned. You can replace negative energy with kindness, love, and understanding, as well as modifying your response to a given situation to one that is calm and relaxed so as to maintain a constant concept of peace.

Jealousy is a fear of inadequacy; it is the result of a doubt that detachment can and will reward you. The jealous person holds on to everything and does not share with other people. Jealousy makes you keep everything and refuse to relinquish anything, restricting the free flow of abundance.

When you align an excellent quality of life with the Source, you will abandon the material things you seek and focus on God's love rather than on the potential of gaining possessions and fulfilling your desires. This matches the angelic nature of the Source, which always gives without asking for or taking anything in return. When you change your thoughts about poverty and strife and substitute them with an attitude of giving (asking, "How may I help you?"), you will offer support and kindness to others. Gradually, you will experience the necessary changes and take the opportunity to live a fuller, happier life.

When you begin to unleash the Ego's strategy and progress toward a meaningful life, you will probably realize that you do not necessarily need to do anything and that the spirit will guide you. This guidance occurs through your thoughts as the spirit in the ether world guides you. The spirit is the author of all portals and dimensions; without the spirit, nothing can occur.

When I think of the events that I need to have happen, I see obstructions and do not know how to proceed and make them happen. However, in the spirit world, the problems I contemplate are already dissolved, although I did not know this at the time. The limitations of my physical senses mean I have no knowledge that the problems have already been determined in the higher spiritual level; this remains so until things align in the mortal world.

I have always hoped for quick solutions to my troubles. In fact, there is no such thing as a quick fix; however, all problems do contain hidden solutions. The spirit world reveals the solutions to us via our inner consciousness.

As you align with the spirit when the inspiration message

arrives in the physical world, the message becomes symbols or signals that you can always apply. They usually occur in the right place and time; thus, you will never miss anything. The message is from the Source, downloaded to your Higher Infinite Self, so that you know what to do. In fact, you originate from God's spirit; you must consider the answer that God gives you to dissolve your troubles. Your creative thoughts and resultant actions are torn from you because it is retrieval data from memories. The spirit would like you to know that, as well.

Your true nature is an Infinite Being living in a physical body; however, with that knowledge, you choose to live an infinite life here. Do you know that you can know God by emptying your mind and filling yourself with God within? Every experienced sage in ancient or current times tells us to find God in emptiness and to hear God's voice in silence.

The problem is that the logical world is hugely different from the spirit realm, even though we tend to look and live spiritually. However, we can discover via various sources the life we choose to live. Mostly, we discover this from our inner consciousness. At birth, we have entered the world where something has replaced nothing. Owing something and doing something are essential in the mortal world; it's different in the spiritual realm where we do nothing and own nothing and make no effort with any attachment. We also understand there is no end, but only an end to the circle of physical life here. When life on Earth is over, our physical body returns to dust while the soul ascends quickly and returns to its place of origin. This place is the void of emptiness with the oneness of the Source.

Perhaps, before we came to Earth, we might have experienced many different life forms in the physical world or on other planets, but our rational minds have limited abilities and might not remember what had happened in those past lives. Thus, we lost touch with our true nature. This could explain why we are not acting infinitely, as we should. We must find a way to get back to that peaceful nothingness while we are still in physical presence.

If our true nature is a spirit, then we must act more like God. It should not be too difficult, though, because we come from the silence of the void. It seems that by actively aligning with our Authentic Selves, we can trigger them to become a part of us. Through the power of your innermost thoughts, you can make conscious connections with your spirit, knowing that in reality, you are nothing, and all your knowledge and wisdom and you yourself came from nothingness. Hence, we must like living an infinite life because when we liquidate all attachment, then we are free. Get close to the void; the Divine is waiting patiently for us to join Him. God's spirit wants us to imitate His actions. You can do so by emptying your mind of thoughts, so that you can hear God speak with you in silence. The message could guide you to act at the right time and impress you to tolerate each other, rather than harboring hatred and resentment towards one another.

The journey here is not the only trip that we have experienced on Earth. We could be coming from somewhere (or nowhere), as a pure emptiness forms out of nothingness and transforms into being through birth. However, it is a pure soul journey with broad meaning and purpose. Though we have unique qualities and differences, we all experience life's lessons as well as relationships with others on Earth prior to making our eventual return trip to the Source.

It is difficult to imagine how life might form without an invisible, divine creator. Similarly, it is hard to believe that a 1,000-year-old oak tree could grow on its own without someone planting a seed in the ground. All created things must come from the Source of a creator. Without the Source, nothing can become visible. Let's say that the invisible White Light energy is self-created or preexisting. It must therefore have no beginning and no limit. The White Light energy created the first being by mixing dust and water. Therefore, our physical bodies need water to sustain our lives and give us strength for our daily activities. A clear, formless spirit can assist the world as it continues to develop and evolve. The spirit will continue to play a vital role in our lives before and after our current state. It will determine whether we proceed to rebirth, reincarnation, or come back after all that. I believe that we have lived as other life forms, but it is impossible to imagine that we have only lived one life.

God is pure White Light energy. He travels in a different frequency, faster than our eyes can see or our hands can feel His presence. Unless we have the same vibrant energy as God, we can never come close to Him in a physical form (only in a spiritual form). The vibrational energy of a pencil is slow-moving; therefore, it slows the situation so that our eyes can see that a pen is on our desk. However, if a pen used a different frequency, we could not recognize the pen unless we slowly changed the pen so that it moved to the front.

Then, we see it again!

Light contains many tiny particles that move faster than any other type of energy. Your eyes and brain interpret the movement of these tiny particles as different colors. Light energy may be fast, but the vibrations of thought are much faster.

As you align the energy of your thoughts with the Universal Source, you will gain strength, energy, and dynamism. It will be difficult for the collective consciousness to interrupt your thought energy. Because the Source sustains your thought energy, all the negative energy around you will be eliminated. In other words, your thought control is consciously connected to a thought frequency of a higher consciousness that brings about a vibrational difference as you continually align with the Source. The Law of Magnetic Energy matches your emotional thought vibrations, and the mind translates all the energy into your physical reality.

You must realize that the Source created your whole life from non-being, so it must be honed. When your body is echoing with negative energy, it becomes weak and feeble, temporarily compromising your self-awareness. This problem occurs because of a misalignment between the Source and your whole being. You feel compromised by the dark evil. Only the higher vibrational thoughts feel the power of God's unconditional love. It is easier for the conscious thought to become overpowered by the negative emotional thoughts such as anger, hatred, jealousy, and greed because you unconsciously let your pathetic ego rule your rational thoughts. That leads you to become easily offended, get angry, and consider revenge. The higher consciousness thoughts manifest themselves from the power within, not from the external world.

The higher consciousness thoughts are from the nothingness, which is where everything originated. These thoughts are clear and never polluted; they compel us to love everyone equally and to be impartial. More importantly, they contain and express the love of God. He wishes that everyone would stay well and feel joy in their hearts. This is needed so that we are continuously ever-growing, ever-evolving and ever-creating as we continue to live in the consciousness now.

For some reason however, we have abstained from our true nature due to hatred and resentment. Unloving thoughts tell us that we have separated from where we came from and moved away from the love of God. Unconditional love becomes distant, and we turn our back against God. Yet, we consider that is not the way we should live our lives, so we rise in our consciousness and move towards unconditional love, as we imitate God's love and become aware of God's omnipresence.

A Divine love consciousness is possible when we are in a state of emptiness. In this state, we are purified spirits. One thing we all have in common is that we are at level zero, where everything that transforms into the nothingness void is virtue. It goes into emptiness and back to the source of creation—to our creator, the Universal Source, the Mind of God.

When we return to nothingness, we own nothing. There are no struggles, hatred or bitterness. We have nothing to do and nothing to worry about; we are no longer in a physical form. It is as if we have done a reversal from form back to formlessness. Truly believing in being infinite is difficult because in the material world, we can get anything and everything. We think we are something special, but that is a delusion.

At the end of our journey on Earth, we return home with nothing. We leave everything and go back to being formless again.

In the material world, we need to have a title, a status, and our own acquisitions in order to create a comfortable life; otherwise, life would be bitter. We want to accomplish something because doing nothing signifies failure in the eyes of others. Nobody can deny these material realities. However, for your spirit's blissfulness, owning nothing is your true nature.

It seems to me that the most comfortable way to have the experience as an infinite being is to be free from everything; stop accumulating possessions and live a normal, spirit-led life. We must make every effort to reconnect to nothingness by practicing non-thinking and silencing our minds. When we empty our minds of thoughts, we do not think of getting something new. We simply practice being rather than doing.

When our minds are still, we will have righteous thoughts and will hear inspiring messages from God's spirit. Between the notes and the pauses, we will hear the sound of music. Without the pause that gives the listener the opportunity to interpret the sounds, there can be no music—it would just be a continuous tone. Even the long tones originate in the void because all things are created in the spirit realm before they emerge in the material world. All notions and inventions in the material world came from emptiness.

Nothingness means nothing at zero point or zero consciousness. Imagine that zero times zero equals zero. Hence nothingness multiplied by nothingness also equals nothingness. Zero multiplied by anything always equals zero; for example, 0 x 1000 = 0 and 1000 x 0 = 0. The result of multiplying any number by zero has no mathematical value; the result is always zero.

You cannot divide by zero. However, without the undividable zero, mathematics itself would be impractical.

Before we emerged in the material world, our spirit was pure formlessness. We had nothing—no rules, no money, no possessions, no title and no authority. We had nothing to do.

You are a pure spirit dwelling in the nothingness void of zero. Status, titles or any merit-based achievements you gain are temporary, an illusion in the material world. You do not need them in the spirit world because there is nothing there for you to achieve and accomplish. All you need to do is experience joy and happiness. While living in the material world, you will experience bliss and happiness when you imagine going back to the emptiness of the nothingness void. When you go back to nothingness, you will not think about the possessions, status or money you have accumulated because they are no longer significant, and you do not need them to survive. You are free from Earthly acquisitions and status. You have emptied your bank account and given away all your wealth prior to your departure from Earth and your return to God. You have liquidated yourself, including your knowledge, and you know that you have left nothing behind and undone. You are a free spirit.

Water makes waves in the ocean, but when the wave returns it becomes water again. There is no separation; everything is one, or we could call it infinity. Oneness does not have a name or definition. A label will change its purpose. Oneness means purity of oneness and nothing else.

That is why we call it the one. It is unique and different from all others.

The void of emptiness, the place where we all come from, is unlike our illusionary, dualistic world. The material world consists of pairs of opposites. Beliefs are like two sides of a coin, or yin and yang. They have coexisted and always will coexist in the Universe of Consciousness. Without the concept of up, there is no down. Without cold, there is no heat. Climate brings both sun and rain. Without the North Pole, there is no South Pole. Without the ocean, there is no land. Without light, there is no darkness. With males, there are females. Without blame there is no forgiveness. We live in a material world filled with contrasts. Everything has two sides. We can put together and disassemble pleasant moments and unpleasant moments. More importantly, one can hold power, but power will not last forever.

Even an evil monarchy cannot last indefinitely. It will eventually fall apart or vanish into the cold air of the atmosphere. On a personal level, you know what you like and dislike; you recognize what tastes delicious compared to what tastes terrible. Because we live in the material world, we experience what we dislike. Conditions and circumstances in the material world make it difficult to access oneness. In the void of nothingness, there is only emptiness, and God is the Divine oneness of everything. God has no name, and is formless, white light energy that supports and controls the whole Universe. All things are an extension and expression of God.

For some reason, the concept of oneness becomes impossible to embrace in the material world because of the duality system. All things contain more than one element. One possible way to align with the oneness in the material world is to experience something true and sublime. You will become more like God.

You must embrace the miracle of duality, accepting and experiencing everything. Even in bad times, you know everything will turn around; you will feel more joy in your heart and start to enjoy your life and the abundance of the free gift from above. You will align with your inner strength, focus on the now, and start promoting your own joy unconditionally. You will expect the best to happen, you will be more willing to explore, and you will spark a new light inside of yourself. This is the secret that will awaken you, reveal a new day, and relieve the tensions and pressures of the world. Pain and sorrow will leave your consciousness now. Don't worry about what is real or imagined; simply awaken your mind and persevere in your search.

The truth is that you are a seeker who seeks God, but God also seeks you. Now you know the Creator needs you. You know the entire Universe supports your growth; you should have no fears, worries and should not panic. You are not alone, because the invisible spirit is always with you. You just have to believe your internal force is urging you to continue to seek, cast no doubt, and consciously be aware that God is calling you. What you need to know is yourself; when you know yourself, you are conscious of God's presence, and you are fearless.

Before we came to the mortal world, we were united with God. After we entered the world, our relationship with God eroded, and we forgot our spiritual heritage; but somehow we have walked on fertile ground again and realigned ourselves with God. We realize the truth about ourselves and are aware deep within ourselves that we are a part of God's expression. We understand that this physical life of ours is not real when we explore deeper inside and discover that it makes sense that a spirit is actually the real part of us. We, the sleepers, now awaken and clear up everything all at once.

Oneness means there is only one; there are no divisions among anything or anyone. You can stimulate yourself as part of the silence. In the silence, everything is emptiness; from there, you shall see God and talk to God. The void is absolutely quiet; nothing will emerge to trouble you, and you will feel completely free. A miracle can take place in an instant; you feel God's consciousness, and an inner calmness and tranquility transcends to your spirit. You must find your way back to that peaceful emptiness while you are still alive. Empty your mind, making a conscious connection to God, so you feel eternal joy, happiness and peace. Your fear of being disjoined from the Source is now diminished and, in fact, is reinstated.

We worship God through our daily reflections and devotions; however, whatever form we use to worship does not matter to the white bear Great Spirit. What pleases Him the most is a genuine heart, which is what we worship Him with? He welcomes us all as His children. In my daily devotions to God, I focus on God alone; other things are not my concern. I continue my reflections, so I will not get lost; this is where I should be. I submit wholeheartedly to God and sincerely pray to Him. I talk to God as if He is standing in front of me. My vessel is navigated through Him and in Him.

I sow a harvest. A harvest full of Divine abundance and an assurance of many auspicious things will emerge, and new strength blows into my Source being. I know everything is in perfect order.

In the mortal world, we see opposites as having distinct personalities and individually, but when they happen within our consciousness, we can see them as inseparable, can allow them to be, and can synchronize them all. Afterward, we will not see the difference between black and white, fortune and misfortune, life, death, and rebirth; since all can be blended to become one through the light of God.

You can combine oneness as part of yourself for which, in silent consciousness, there is no description; nothing felt but the emptiness of emptiness. In the nothingness, you begin to feel connected to all things: to the Earth, to the black space of the Universe, and to the Source. Oneness becomes available to you through infinite power, which is achievable by blinking. This keeps the whole Universe in peace and generates form from nothingness

Imagine now if we did not label anything and had no need for judgment in this world that we dwell in; we would then blend with oneness. Clear your mind and look up to the sky; the Source's energy is available to you. Breathe in the Source's energy and exhale kindness and compassion to everything and anyone in the entire Universe. There is no anger, hatred, or jealousy because we are all spiritual beings. Our main source of connection to our own being is from God's spirit. God is the Source of everything, and all things are from God's spirit. You can relax, contemplate, and allow the silence to resonate in your oneness with others, knowing that you are a peacemaker from whence you came. "Blessed are the peacemakers, for they will be called the children of God." (Matthew5:9) Through silence, we realize the meaning of life while we are still living in the material world; we experience it through astral travel, without going through the ritual of death. The closer we get to our infinite self, the more peace, meaning, purpose, and joyfulness flows to us from the oneness Source.

After you have signed the accord with God, the invisible force began to plan your journey and set it in motion, filling in your future physical characteristics. Your personality, attitude, skin color, gender, body shape, eye color, hair color, race, profession, and return date were all detailed and predetermined—planned in the Tree of Life in your personal profile, which will ultimately become the significance in your life once you arrive at planet Earth.

Since everything needed for this physical journey on Earth is pre-arranged by God's spirit, there is nothing you need to do but wait for the transition from non-being to being.

Now, you get ready to explore your temporary destination, Earth, where God assigns you. God did not prepare everything for you. You need to realize that the Earth portion of your journey needs to be explored by you. You do not need to worry about the uncertainty of the soul. The whole of you, everything that makes up who you are, help you become a unique person. Your soul escorts you to make this trip to Earth as pleasant and easy as possible. The Inner Source knows exactly what to do regarding this journey on Earth. Your Inner Source is actually the one who explores this Earth journey; your physical body is a refuge for your soul, and the soul is always directly connected to God's spirit, so you achieve everything here before the journey ends.

In the beginning of your journey, you have neither plans to accumulate possessions, power, or status, nor the plans of ambition to climb to the apex of the pyramid. You allow yourself to surrender to the invisible forces that administer and arrange everything. However, as life continues to progress, it gets tougher, more difficult and complex; you begin to join in the spotlight and function more from ambition. Hence, you shift your awareness to those that expect you to achieve goals and make everything happen. Consequently, the desire comes ahead of all things, including acknowledging and relinquishing your own Inner Being; you choose to let the gloomy Ego harness your life and become your key focus.

If we were capable of continuing from where we came from, we would always be aware of God's presence and conscious of our higher level of Source Being. Then, we would live in higher consciousness of God's realization. However, after we arrived here, everything transformed into a physical appearance, and we allowed the Ego mind to take charge.

It changed our commitment from depending on the Inner Source to having ambitions and achieving more desires through the false self, Ego. We are interested in gaining more money and possessions and want everything for ourselves, so we can feel secure and safe. Guided by the Ego, we continue to accumulate acquisitions, because we feel we "need" more, or that we are an unknown, or that it will make us feel better in facing our rivals or peers. The gloomy Ego leads us to believe that attaining more acquisitions will make us feel confident and courageous, so we can stand alone before the world and triumph. But it is a false-self concept that moves you away from God's spirit and, in the long run, will bring more complications and remorse than you can imagine.

Relinquishing and detaching from all acquisitions by giving away something you no longer need to other people is the right stimulus, rather than listening to the Ego. You should turn off the noisemaker; put it away, and clear your mind. Create time to meditate and focus on God, and realign with the spirit again! Meditate on your journey by going inward to the sacred, silent place, where you can relax, pause, and let go of unwanted mental desires. Relinquish every worry, fear, anxiety, impulse, and your wandering and emotional thoughts. Deliberately let go of ambition, possessions, status, and power. Surrender unwanted desires in your mind, and feel as if you are back in the void; feel the bliss of nothingness. Feel that you regain the feeling of great intimacy with the Source's oneness. Bear in mind that the connection with God comes from silence. God cannot emerge when you have no gentleness and conflict in your mind.

Now, try to abstain from the wild impulses, remove your veil, and change your goal to purpose and knowing the truth of God's plan—that you should not need to strive to survive. Consciously shift your effort from the gloomy Ego's belief to God by humbling yourself and silencing your mind. After envisioning this, the Ego will have a difficult time surviving in you and will leave you alone.

If you want to live a joyous and blissful life, you need to defy the Ego. However, the Ego will do everything it can to prevent us from abandoning our infamous status. The Ego wants you to be well-known and more powerful than others. If you grow into this component of the Ego's identification, you know that the more acquisitions you own, the more material-oriented you become. You shift from God leading your life to only care for your net worth, and you always compare yourself to others. You assess your success in life based on your extensive list of acquisitions and riches. The more things you collect, the more your excitement rises, which results in chasing more possessions. You are never satisfied, and this cycle has no end; human desires and wants never end. You want something bigger and better than your neighbors, or your peers, or your rivals. You want to be better than them, so you collect more and cannot afford to stop accumulating toys or other collectable items. The desire of the Ego is "more." It even screams out at you with a false voice, "You will feel happier and more joyful once you win something mega, something deluxe, and something that will satisfy and represent your current status." This could be a reflection from your childhood, when you felt deficiency, but now you will do everything in your power to get all you want, and you have determined to get it and own it. You remember the phrase, "That's mine now!"

The same holds true when someone else has more than you do or you cannot afford to purchase more items—you lose self-confidence, stumble when facing your peers, and feel defeated.

The Ego is a tough taskmaster.

As far as the Ego is concerned, it will never abandon its attempts to persuade you to obtain more items. However, you must be aware that you came here with nothing, and you leave here empty. During your life on Earth, the Ego manages to keep you captive. If you accept the Ego's will, material things will take control of you and write your life's story. It is common for some people whose values have been twisted by material things to become addicted to obtaining more and more. They fall into despair when they do not see the things they want. You must be aware that when you win more items you get more attention than you thought, especially when you lose them again. Conversely, by being content, you will never be dissatisfied. Being grateful and expressing gratitude for all that you have received will cause you to receive more from Heaven.

This sense of positive thinking does not partner with the Ego. You have the false impression that your soul does not want to cooperate with you. You feel uncomfortable especially when you lose something. So, you want to accumulate more. If you cannot, you feel downright discontent and irritated, especially when your possessions become diminished. You allow the Ego to continuously work within you; you are listening to the Ego's council and discard your own Source being. The wisdom to trust is the wisdom of the oneness of the Source, the origin of God's spirit.

As with everything new, the Ego's story does not last long before you go back to the Source of oneness. This could be accompanied by an unexpected event through which you realize God alone is the only Source you want to align with and rely on in your life. This will probably occur after a fall. When you stand up, you make a major shift to God. This fall could be an embarrassing event caused by the influences of the dark Ego that brings misery into your life. After recovery from this hopeless, disappointing situation you are determined to make this transformative change and shun the Ego for infinity. You feel that the invisible hand of God has lifted you up and directed you back to the Land of Promise and Abundance, so that you can start over again. You never look back as you transfer your faith to God alone.

The place we come from and to which we return—the nothingness—is a place in which we are empty-handed. Therefore, it is unnecessary to gather a multitude of possessions in order to experience joy and happiness. It is not practical—this is a truth that you can see all around you. Only those possessions and gifts that come our way naturally can bring contentment and peace. When you feel a need to acquire more and more, you allow your false sense of self to become the dominant authority in your life. When the Ego-self controls you, it means that you are always pursuing unrealistic goals. It is a spiritual obstacle to being in control of your own life.

Your true self does not need possessions in order to clarify your purpose. You do not need any high position or authority to prove your worth and attract attention. You do not need someone else to verify your identity. You are a remarkable individual and an expression of God's spirit. Your true self is an Infinite Being designed by God. The Ego's false doctrine tells you are what you see you are; what you own. It wants you to think that you are determined by the material world. This is a painful collective human belief, yet it is obviously untrue to anyone who does not behave like an Ego-designed deity-god, guided by the evil self, and playing into Ego-dogmas created by the Ego's mass deception.

In the fast-paced modern world, we often measure success by how many acquisitions we can accumulate and the professional services that we offer to the public as we prepare to safeguard our status. However, how well we do is always observed and assessed by others; this pushes us over the edge, toward the top, where we can reach the top gun. This happens when climbing to the top becomes a priority rather than a choice during our early developmental years.

With each task you accomplish, you gain a worthiness that signifies more commitments and ambitions that you want to pursue further, so you feel better than your rivals or colleagues. You know that you will be rewarded for your accomplishments with outstanding awards. These rewards are your happiness and success; you know that you have done something for yourself and did it with joy, and nobody can deny that. You do what you think is more right rather than remain still. You cannot measure your desires by how well you do; but the reality is that you need to make a living in a cruel world. Therefore, you just pursue and enjoy a happy and joyful life. Even God has no disagreement when we obtain accomplishments and prosperity throughout; but we should not seek to exceed the limits and earn more than we can use in our lives. You do not always need to be a challenger to grow tremendously successful; simply be your own God's gift by changing the way you think about living, and ignore what others think about you or your net worth.

This is a hypercritical world; people like to judge others. It does not matter how well you do; others are always happy to evaluate and criticize you at any time.

You are a decent, unique individual. Defining yourself based on your achievements or net worth is a false conclusion based on the Ego's concepts and beliefs.

It is unwise to listen to the Egoistic mind rather than your Inner Source.

When you make mistakes, you feel that you are failing in life and disappointing yourself. Afterwards, you may enter chronic depression or physical misalignment with your Source being. You must be aware that it is common to gradually start losing some motor skills and memory recall, especially when we reach a certain age. You can adjust by training your mind and body. Accept that this is a natural process and welcome it gracefully. You gain peacefulness by ignoring the gloomy Ego, who is a false taskmaster. The Inner Source has always guided you and directs your journey. Understand that evidence of your learning is based on your business success and track records at a certain age; but after the quantum leap, it should be based on spirituality. Your life shifts from ambition to more meaning and purpose. With this awareness in mind, you should feel content and allow yourself to let go of worry and fear and return to your original state of your own Source being; return to a way of life that reflects who you are—a free spirit from the emptiness.

When I am working, I put my Ego-self away so I can concentrate on what I am doing without judgment or bias and let my soul do all the work.

Throughout life, we are overwhelmed by the Ego's belief that our success and integrity is based on the observations and opinions of others. The Ego proclaims that our true value needs to be recognized and validated by an external force; however, that is untrue. We all come from the Mind of God, the Universal Creative Life Force. We are all created equally, from the nothingness of the void.

However, the Ego wants us to think that our physical body is all there is, which is false.

Our true nature is infinite, and all things created by the spirit and the Source wants us to realize that. The real truth is that one day we shall return to the nothingness with the Source oneness.

Awkwardly, the direction in life that we take in earlier years, which is engraved in our hearts, is to respect the views of others more than our own. So when it becomes too hard to make significant decisions, we always seek outer guidance. The false Ego causes us to challenge ourselves and our divinity. We become accustomed to accepting others' opinions rather than our own, and this carries on from century to century until we wake up and change our belief system by trusting our Authentic Self.

Your trust is reflected internally and then released to the outer world as who you are, showing whether you possess strong beliefs about yourself that do not come from the approval of others. However, the Ego does not believe in or accept your infinite soul, only your physical being. It insists that your true value depends on what others think about you.

If you let others' opinions determine who you are, those opinions can hinder your current growth. If you always agree with other people's opinions about yourself, those opinions will reduce your faith as an individual and Source being. Your image of yourself is inevitably interrupted by others, as you have no personality and characters defined by the Ego. You have downgraded your faith and have not trusted in yourself.

You will create incorrect thinking in your mind if you accept someone else thoughts rather than trusting yourself; if they think you are less intelligent than you truly are, you will believe it and live with it.

You cease to exist in front of others because you are being defined by them as non-existent.

This is because you have relied on other people's support, without trusting in your own abilities and the Authentic Self.

The truth is that who you are has nothing to do with any idea or belief that exists in anyone or that exists anywhere in this world. A person who thinks you are intelligent might change his or her mind overnight, suddenly declaring you unwise and unappealing. However, if you listen to your Inner Source, you will be totally unaffected by such a person's arbitrary judgments. Similarly, if you are dominated by the false Ego, you will become miserably affected. That is why the Ego wants to separate you from your Inner Self: so it can control you and keep you as hostage. In that case, everything you did would be in harness and harvest by the Ego. You would live a life filled with fear, worry, and indecision. Ultimately, you would find it difficult to complete your entire journey. But, providing you do not throw in the towel now, the bigger battle ahead might well be the purpose you are looking for in your life. If you do not like your life right now, you can change it to be the way you desire. Go bravely forward, show your gratitude to the Source, and change your attitude gradually until no regrets trouble you.

When you seek approval from others, it is difficult to have clear and harmonious relationships. People will criticize you and point out your lack of self-confidence. You do not need to show people your weaknesses; you will never receive what another person cannot afford to give you. Similarly, you cannot give others anything when you do not feel love inside. Likewise, God can only give you what exists in the Heavenly consciousness. God cannot create something that does not preexist in the spirit realm. However, ego reality is based on ambiguous dogma: an illusion of fear, confusion, doubts, worry and thoughts of being separated from the Source.

Throughout our lives, we are taught to put aside our own opinions and let the ideas of others help us. This is true in many cultures. However, seeking advice on legal matters will not reduce your assertiveness or ability to choose; rather, it will improve your way of thinking about how to handle the problem you have been pondering in your mind. Seeking a legal opinion about your wills, estate or any other legal issue will not limit you. It shows that you have the boldness and humility to seek help from the external world when required. Your soul will feel inner peace and tranquility because you have taken the right course of action in seeking legal advice. With legal matters, only an expert in the legal profession can help you solve your problems. It is his or her knowledge and wisdom that you seek. You are taking advantage of his or her professional expertise in an area in which you are not familiar. You will not have relinquished your power, and your integrity will have remained unchanged. Your counselor must have your full acceptance before finalizing legal documents on your behalf. He or she will handle your concerns and provide a resolution. Therefore, you have nothing to worry about or fear; simply allow the positive energy to flow toward you.

In a world full of opinions, you will be judged by the opinions of others. If 1,000 people read my book, I will receive 1,000 distinct opinions that differ from my own. Hence, my opinion does not depend on myself alone, but also on the people who read my book to see what I have written about. Yet I devote my attention to my sincerity, yielding character, rather than being concerned with how others see me. Currently, my priority is my relationship with the Source.

You need to have full confidence in yourself before you can create a pleasant, trusting relationship with God.

If I do not have faith in myself and want to listen to the gloomy Ego, I am detached from my God's spirit. However, the Source always knows if you are misaligned from Him and alerts you. When you feel irritated, it is an indication that the Inner Source tried to give you a sign that you have moved away from your first instinct, and it wants you to direct your attention back to where you were and to make changes. Unless you realign with the Source, it is difficult to win the thing you want because the Ego mind distracts you from the power of your everlasting now.

The typical characteristics of an egoistic appeal can be defined by who you are, what you are doing over the years, what you did to win a competition with challenging rivals, what others think of you, and your reputation as you stand in front of others or the world. The Ego makes us believe that the world is about counting on how many possessions we have, how many more we can accumulate, what else we can accomplish, and how many merit badges we manage to secure and receive. In other words, the material world is only concerned with your achievements, and your reputation is of the most significance. Other egoistic characteristics stand out as you plan to surprise people and show that you are different; you are their commander in chief, and they should relinquish themselves to you by making you the most important person in the world.

Those with Ego-concepts are ambitious-oriented people who believe that everything is separated. We are detached from Mother Earth and God's spirit, and you are distinct from everyone else. This kind of talk satisfies the Ego's desire that we should be concerned only for our own selves, at the expense of all other living beings on Earth. These are all untruths and have no virtue; the Ego's edict brings only separation.

We should deny all of these Ego-concepts and resist their hold on us. The Ego endorses separation because it believes we live only one life; it denies the existence of an Infinite Self and eternal life. It therefore urges us to grab hold of as much material wealth as we can, so that we can have plenty all the time: in the day of the Ego, our fear of scarcity makes us unwilling to share. Sharing means giving things away, and the selfish Ego does not advocate such communal spirit. However, when we stand firm, with our Infinite Self realigned with our connectedness to each other, we breathe in and out, and feel that the air is fresher, the water is clearer, and the sun is shining brighter. Most importantly, we are now aligned with the Universal Source; our love and concern ourselves with each other, and we are more than willing to share our wealth with the needy without worrying about scarcity. The Ego can start packing and return to its rightful place.

When we begin to understand that oneness constantly aligned with nothingness, and then we understand that is the whole concept of oneness. Oneness means one collective consciousness, one life force. Although we have an infinite soul, all things, in some way, in this physical world are connected and actually originated from the void of nothingness. That is why we can be spiritual and finite at the same time.

Hence, when we contemplate that others are suffering because of a lack, this pain will affect us too. Our compassionate heart feels the same pain and sorrow within, as we are all unified as one collective consciousness. All living things and mankind are an extension that arises from the oneness of God. God is nameless, there are no other gods, and God is alone. Compassion and kindness are the wild-card disclosures in our spiritual journey to remind us we live in a world: we seem to be unique, but are not separated from others. As a result, we should not forget the pain of others because that is connected to our consciousness. Through the qualities of oneness we let them know, "I feel your pain, and I am with you." Thus, we are always guided by our compassionate heart to think of the pain of others. We are willing to contribute our wealth or service to make their lives easier, or more enjoyable, or to aid what they perceive to be missing. You serve others without thinking of yourself: thus you bring about a good karma. As a result, this helps to lift up your spiritual growth and evolution. The reason we derive joy from serving others is that we all come from the same unifying force of God that is in everyone. The spiritual path helps us to progress, and it advances a shift in our consciousness towards the Source. This is instead of being aligned with material things and constantly being aware of the treasure that is within us, but not yet harvested anywhere in the external world. Giving is one of our attributes: as spiritual beings, it is all God's intention. He wants us to offer our help and to love others. When you begin to understand that there is no separation between God, yourself and every life-force, it is as though you have discovered the treasures of this Universe, a oneness and energy that is in all things, omnipresent, omniscient and All-That-Is powerful.

Our Infinite Self knows that we do not need to pay attention to everything that is inadequate, and to disregard the Ego's intention that we need extra things to feel secure and that we must struggle to obtain what we want. The Ego continues to describe effectively that what we see is not what we get from God and the worldly essence of what is. The Ego wants us to know that God and humans are two different entities and it wants us to be distinguished from each other as unrelated. In fact, it is untrue, as can be seen by listening to the false self. The Ego is terrified that we will believe we were created by God's expression and trust that there is no scarcity in the munificent Universe, and that everyone is entitled to have their share of the total wealth provided by the Source. This would all reduce the Ego's audacity. It is most likely that the Ego has created a larger idea and the collective consciousness is painfully and effectively influenced by the Ego. That is, we are discontented with the things that are missing in our lives. However, this is not so. We do not have to validate it all and have proof that we have everything to maintain our gratification. We must live with what we have currently attained. Although the Ego wants us continually to attract more, these are unfortunate circumstances. We listen to the design of the Ego because it sounds honest and trustworthy, rather than to our Infinite Self that seemingly is doing nothing to improve our lives. This is a false conclusion reached by listening to the Ego, through conscious thought, and is based on living according to the gloomy self. What the Ego creates is to serve the Ego's demands. The subject must work under its own control and have command of the Ego.

Fortunately, our thoughts are constantly changing, moment by moment, and it is not a surprise when we shift our attention to our Source rather than to the gloomy Ego. When we abandon the false Ego and transform our conscious thoughts to the higher energy thought field, then all things begin to lighten up and transmute, and, when we look at it all again, then it might have already begun to change. We are reconnected back to the lost connection of our Source; consequently, we notice coincidences happening, events, people and things we need to appear in our path are more helpful and financial abundance is available to us easily and effectively. This happened before and this makes us feel peaceful and content with our spiritual being and we continue to feel good.

In the world of change, as soon we see something new, it has already been transformed to something old: we will never catch up with the new. There is no such thing as "the latest," but this is the way it always has been and it always will be. The rat race continues, endorsed by the Ego's idea, and there is never enough to satisfy our desires. We shift our awareness by maintaining our connection and alignment with the Source and the Authentic Self: we constantly discard the Ego and its commanding power that dominate and affects our happiness in the physical world.

When we try to do something, somehow we feel powerless and unable to complete our tasks because we feel that there are invisible forces in the Universe preventing us from accomplishing our goals. In the material world, all things are possible and available to you if you are in vibrational harmony and aligned with God. By being content through your vibrational thought, you transcend it to the Universe: the Law of Magnetic Energy will help you attract what you desire, and, someday, you will get everything your heart longs for. Hence, when you begin to shift and follow the Universal Laws of Magnetic Energy, you notice that life begins to take a different path and you do not need to strive to get what you want because you are on the right track; you are aligned with the Universe and you will never be disappointed by it.

As far as the Ego is concerned, at every moment, it inevitably wants to convince us that we are separate from God. The Ego constantly tries to influence the collective consciousness, strengthening the idea that we are unrelated to each other. The Ego attempts to push us into believing that there is a god that plays favorites, accepts luxuries for favors, and disciplines unacceptable behavior and that the subject should be criticized or judged. This is the so called "deity-god" created by the illusion of the collective Ego.

Throughout ancient history and, probably, in the contemporary world, the Ego has designed a human-made God. It portrayed God is a white male with a long, flowing, white beard and supernatural powers, sitting on a throne, watching to see who would offer prayers to Him and then choosing either to satisfy or not satisfy those who have not obeyed his rules. This entity is viewed not as a kind and empathetic, or all-giving, divine source. However, that entity is rather an ever-changing, temperamental superpower that holds back his authority to solve our troubles, or who brings healing and miracles, depending on his eagerness to accept our appeals and desires. This is the entity created by the Ego and it is devoted to serving the cause of the destructive Ego's demands. It has its own Ego-personality and virtues, and demands control, punishment, and vigilance when needed.

If you experience that which is reinforced by the Ego-god idea, then you need to change your inner and outer perspectives: examine that undesired relationship, and eliminate the false Ego and change from uncertainty to clarity. You need to scrape out that Ego from your central hub, and then you will discover real inner peace and be able to transform your life from scarcity to wealth, from detriment to painlessness and change illness into fitness and be connected with oneness. To do so, you need to realign yourself with the Source that accepts you unconditionally, gives you anything without expecting a return, and responds to your submission of prayers.

When life is against you, everything is easily turned upside down: you experience negative acts, and you cannot see the light, but feel weakness in your mortal self. You cannot face the morning because you feel fatigued; you cannot endure the long dark nights because you are afraid of the dark or that something may emerge to hurt you. Consequently, you are mentally, psychologically, and emotionally exhausted by your own self-proclaimed unpleasant experience, which overwhelms and compromises you. Actually, your sensible thought was right: what is right in the morning will be true in the afternoon or at night. You are perfectly fine: simply to proceed to enjoy your life and make a perfect alignment with your Source and feel the peace within yourself.

When you are in challenging situations, you have the ability to assess yourself on the basis of your current situations. You can transform this artificial reality to a way of life that supports where you want to be and substitute your fears, worries and indecision with bliss, peace and contentment. Silence and empty the mind: derive your thoughts from the Source and move towards it by knowing what your true identity is. Sort it out, and shift to the person that you're longing to be, following the old teaching, "let go and let God." Without pressurizing yourself to achieve anything, you will accomplish more significant things in your life.

You must be consciously aware that the Ego's influence is too good to be true. Then you must pause and reassess your situation. You must detach your attention from the unrealistic, non-authentic and unpredictable behavior of the Ego, so that you have clear and consistent thoughts, guided only by the Source. Transform your life from one of ambition to one with meaning.

Your shift begins to take place immediately, once you have distanced yourself from the Ego's consciousness and ignore the Ego's calling. The self-importance of the Ego-concept is what has distracted you from your Authentic Self. However, this does not mean that you are disconnected from your high-level conscious self: you can always turn around and be realigned with your original point of intention, as that is based on your purpose and true meaning. When you are reconnected to your Source of being, then you might have begun to think and act like God, who flows everywhere.

When you are travelling in the right direction, your thought impulses are subtler and they are normally navigated by the Source. Your thoughts will be vibrating positively at a higher frequency than at the lower rate of the energy thought field, which has no blissful purpose. The direction you take is pushing towards your true intentions and desires. These are honest and involve assisting others. They are sustained by the Divine energy rather than by unconsciously associating with the Ego and allowing it to become the dominant force in your life. Inquire about what can be of service to others and rise up to what's going on in your life, no matter how negative it might seem. The light is always with you in the form of someone to whom you can offer help or a situation in which you can be of service.

When you no longer allow the false self to define you, then your life can transform into fullness and you can live life firmly and effectively. But, if you allow the false self to run your life, then you are navigated and commanded by the dark Ego and will always chase after your own shadow in every area of your life. Guided by the false self, it is your own self-concept that makes you feel that you are insignificant; hence, you always want to achieve more to expand your resume. You do not need to do a thing: all things are pre-arranged by the spirit in the spiritual realm. All must just agree with your eternal truth, your own dharma. You do not need proof that you are worth it to get more. It is all set out according to the truth about the way things truly are and will always be in the Universe. Who you are has nothing to do with material things or the wealth you can accumulate in a physical dimension. Under any circumstance, we are then deprived of the unarguable-with the argument that we need money to meet our basic needs, to tolerate life; life can be awfully difficult to endure in a physical environment that lacks it. It is undeniably true that we need money to withstand everything: without it, life is trying. In fact, it is "realistic vs. Unrealistic", but both are true. In real time, we ought to have both (the finite and infinite). However, you can save something good for everything, as when it is raining out, you might want to stay at home, but if it is clear, you could go for a ride and enjoy a sunny day. If you are already wealthy, you might consider modifying your income and sharing the best you have with those suffering, and you would still have a happy and prosperous life.

You can change your life without applying any strict rules. To live modestly and in a thrifty way is to be in harmony with others through your generous nature. You live in harmony with the Source. When you give away your money, you gain back more through inner happiness and joy. This comes from knowing that your money has blessed others, so they can enjoy life too. You are a person who loves to share with others, and you will receive many blessings in return from the Universe. The Universal Laws of Giving and Receiving state that the more of your money you give away to help others, the greater the return the Universe will give you someday. This is the trustworthiness stated in the Universal Laws of Nature. Your life improves by changing your attitude. Your attitude changes when you think positive thoughts and make them a reality. When you believe in making changes, then all things are possible and nature has no limits, for we are a part of nature, as are both the rocks and the fish dwelling in the ocean. You then switch from Egoistic activities to an unselfish existence, but this does not mean that you are no longer able to attract abundance and prosperity into your life.

It means that you live in wholeness.

Without restricting ourselves in order to achieve at all costs, we get more than we expected in the infinite consciousness by letting go and letting in God. We begin to grow to a better position, without a false shadow, and finally we can accomplish more and learn more, and value what's truly important in our lives. We should think of our true selves, while helping others and being meek. That should be our first priority and focus.

Unfortunately, before the quantum leap of the spiritual awakening, for years we have been focused on accumulating acquisitions, our position and shifting around in order to gain a reputation. However, after we shift to being meaningful instead of goal setting, we realize that this is heaven's way of overcoming ambition without a struggle. The truth is that you might not need to reach the mountain-top to become famous; instead, when you are aware of everything you do, even if you are the least among others, you will accomplish the Great Way. This is because you give no external indications that you are ambitious. You do not seek status or a stronghold, or live an approval-seeking lifestyle, but you just quietly know who you are. You are who you are; you cannot change what God has in store for you. You can do better when you are aligned to your own Source of being. You will emerge at the right time and place but you will not try to do so to everyone in the fold. You change your direction and turn off the unyielding Ego's demands: you follow your heart and discard self-importance. However, you stand alone from the positive or negative thoughts of others.

When we realign with God, moving from the place where we were, we are taking a trip back, as illustrated by an alignment in which we think and act like the Source that appears as universal. The Source is present everywhere, covering a wide range, including all flying creatures. They fly freely in the sky without being interfered with. They have the freedom to choose their destination, or to fly home; the Source does not tell them what to do. As we move towards our Divine place, there is no shortage or inadequacy. We leave behind our Ego-minds and let our souls act. We leave the Ego behind; our minds always evaluate what we do.

When we believe we are a spirit and like where we come from, we have shifted our thoughts and allowed ourselves to grow closer to our Source, and to start thinking like God.

Our intellect will surge upwards, especially when we consciously vibrate our thought emotions with God. Your Authentic Self also comes from God's spirit, and you gain inner strength, and are healthy as long as you are distant from the false self. The oneness is the truth in our spiritual lives; when we start trusting the Source we pursue everything more like God. We know we are responsible for everything we pursue with meaning in our lives.

When I looked back, I realized that in every aspect of the spiritual growth that I have had, I submitted due to fear, indecision and uncertainty. I strove to accept a significant change in my life. I, therefore, unconsciously allowed the Ego to influence my faith in God and so I almost edged out God. Early this year, I was diagnosed with lymphoma cancer. I was confused and lost my trust and confidence in God. I thought that would be it. I did not know what to do. However, every big change normally is due to having experienced a big challenge that is then followed by a huge transformation in life. After a huge fall, I was held back by the Source, and then I realized God had not abandoned me. He shined his everlasting light at the rate of healing energy on me. God is not just with us, but lives within us. Our true self is part of His division; I am delighted to be a part of His eternal energy and to witness His inspirational message as it comes into my silent mind. I had eight cycles of my treatment: although it was painful, I completed it. One very strange thought I had, I want to share with you. At night, while sleeping, I keep receiving lucid dreams telling me that I would recover from this terrifying disease. This made me feel that the invisible spirit of God was always with me. He healed me through human doctors. I am now free from cancer. After this incident I am delighted to be realigned with God's spirit and have true faith in Him and myself. I have better inner strength and feel better.

Every fall influences the future, lifting us up to a higher place. It might be required that we reach a blockage before we can succeed, in order to seize our lives and free ourselves from the Ego that is still hidden in the gap in our minds. Without an experience of misfortune, the power of good luck might not come to us. The miracle of duality allows us to enjoy both good fortune and misfortune at different intervals; when prosperity comes, we know it is full of joy and happiness, and all sorrows and pains are banished. We do not remember them anymore.

Every storm, every catastrophic event in the categories of nature's calling, has its purpose and meaning. If you shield yourself from the storms, you might never see their truthfulness. The storms in life are potentially meaningful events that you can use to evolve for the greater good or to begin to inhabit a better place. In fact, when you sign a contract with the Divine for a great purpose, you can expect and experience a bigger fall before you lift your life off to its optimal value, to success and growth.

A mild storm and a hurtful experience made me more compassionate and caring about the pains and suffering of others. Consequently, these unfortunate experiences have led me to become more self-reliant and self-confident, guided by God's spirit. After facial surgery to remove lesions from my face in 2005, I experienced miracles from God. He inspired me to write books. I began to write my very first book entitled, "The Awareness of Magnetic Energy," published in November 2007. I wrote it in a profound, solid and candid style and from a caring, loving and compassionate heart. I looked at the needle of pain and suffering that we all have to endure in the infinite consciousness while continuously experiencing our journey here. I am here to experience life's lessons, even though

I have experienced powerful setbacks and challenges in the past. I have come to realize that those challenges helped me to evolve and grow to have a better understanding of life.

I have learned from my blunders in the past; currently I feel bliss and am content. I am ready to move on to greater spiritual growth and make progress. I express my gratefulness, and to that I add repentance, and then I accept that everything will carry on.

On every journey we ever made, we probably experienced many difficulties and perplexities. A spiritual journey guides us to walk on a great path to seek and search for the truth of God, has no exception. At the beginning of your spiritual voyage, you will experience pains, tears and uncertainties that wrack the body terribly, but, afterwards, you will be restored and achieve the greatest victory over your physical wellness and wholeness. This is, in fact, the greatest moment of your life. You awaken to the New Millennium's age in the now. You realize your old self has now received a calm and contented attitude that helps you to discover a hidden treasure inside. Then, you understand that you have triggered the inner child within: it steadfastly guides you to become a stronger and better person, to comprehend and know yourself. The Inner Source directs you with the incentive to prosper more in life in a positive and productive way. It encourages you to detach from your strong desires that demand more and move to a higher consciousness as your direction in life. When you listen, focus and change from the demands of increasing desire to desires with less ambition, then it might be that you will now stop attracting success and abundance. Instead it brings you more blissful emotions inside and you tune-in to your Source of oneness. Hence, you draw more desirable peaceful things to return to you through the Universal Law of Magnetic Energy.

I believe every soul has its own stories to tell and has different experiences in every spiritual awakening. Sometimes, a spiritual advance might happen after you have had an enormous, painful experience. This can happen emotionally, psychically, and spiritually, after going through a catastrophic event such as intensive illness, addiction, or unexpected accidents. What follows can be a radical transformation. As a result, you begin to see changes in your experiences that become the turning point that uplift your consciousness to a place where the purpose and meaningfulness are the points of contact in your life.

Each attribute of the Ego produces different orders that are dictated to you. But, when you are heading away from the Ego's perspective to a spiritually balanced life, then you become more like your Source-being. Your spiritual transformations are unexpected, unfounded, unprecedented and uninvited. It is just you who let yourself be guided by an invisible source of energy around you. It could be possible that you simply feel overwhelmed by an inevitable energy, and then you fall into sleep. When you wake up, you feel a sensation through your body. You heard a voice that told you that you were done with your old self and you will see healing and transformation change your life. You do not need to do anything in particular, just accept it.

As you change your direction to the Source, you receive many unexpected things that occur, guided by the Great Spirit. You remember everything, from the moment before you made this big transformation. It serves as a great reminder to you from the spirit, so you are aware that your old self is no longer serving you. The spirit is now embedded in you forever.

Your dependence on the Ego through your old self has changed and been banished. As you continue to embrace your new self, you transform to become more tolerant towards things, events and people around and next to you. You begin to offer your services to help others. You understand that your job is not just to make money, but it must serve you correctly too. In other words, it must include spirituality, family, peace and good will as a priority. This is completely different from the gloomy Ego.

The Ego is packing, and moving rapidly in a different direction away from you. You navigate with your mind and continue aligned with the Source: you know now, with your new self and attitude that you can get through a long night. Then you know it holds no fear; you realize that the illusion of fear is self-created, and no harm can befall you as long as you resonate with the Source. You carry God's light with you wherever you go; you are shielded and secure. By harnessing the Ego, you bring forth direct support for your being, so you are able to be attentive to every single event. A positive lifestyle brings helpful and supportive people to you. Events blend together as certain things are sent to your door, and something that was considered unlikely before, now becomes available: this makes your life prosper in the infinite present.

The continued change in your character is because of the fact that you aligned with the Source's potential, and unseen forces can then come alive through God's power. This spreads the seeds of blessing to you. You transform yourself to become more alert, calm and sensitive. You tune-up your aptitudes, and tune-in to the person you have always dreamed yourself to be. The invisible spirit of the Universe kicks in to trigger the critical importance of your own reality in the now. This is the result of reveling in the knowledge that your hidden power is your Inner Source concealed within. Your beingness has transformed you to become a more powerful and courageous person.

On your shift to the possibility for change, even your spirit tunes-up. The transformation can come in many forms that are unexpected, it might even occur as a surprise, but it is automatic, instantaneous, and sometimes unpredictable. Externally, you do not show any changes, but, within, you genuinely feel relaxed, joyous, and peaceful. You do not think that you are striving; instead, you think that, emotionally, you are being led by an invisible presence. Now, in everything you do, simply follow the energy that the spirit wants you to have, and then you are there.

The next form it takes may be extremely colorful and come with fabulous parades of color before you. It is as if you are in a dream-state and then you emerge from behind a screen that you had never seen before. You are on a small island by yourself. The island is so impressive, and ever so colorful and strong, with a fresh smell everywhere, and everything there is full of energetic force and vibrancy. Then, through the stillness you hear a voice talking to you. You ask the voice, "Will you kindly identify yourself?" The voice tells you, "I am your own soul that has been accompanying you on your journey since you came to Earth." You ask the voice, "How may I serve you?" The voice replies, "I am here to assist you on your journey here, but you must invite me in before I can assist you and support your life." You ask, "How can I activate you, my Inner Soul?" The voice responds, "You need to meditate deeply through your latent mind, then I will be activated and alive. You will know what to do. The sooner you start your inward meditation and make contact through the subliminal mind, the more will be revealed to you. Do not be afraid: this will awaken you in infinite consciousness, so you will know who you are and can do more for yourself. You will be attended to your full life-force experience."

The third form it can take involves calmness, tranquility, and peacefulness in everything you encounter. You are filled with compassion and kindness. It could be a joyous and quiet morning, such as I have experienced. On that particular silent morning, I perceived myself as being embraced and cradled in the arms of God. This is the greatest experience, to feel the presence of the Divine and receive the truest moment of love and peace that I have ever had. Since then, every morning I intentionally work to remember that quiet time before I start to organize myself and carry on other daily activities.

The fourth form involves endurance. This comes when you can turn your life around through the tolerance of other people, events and things, through depriving yourself of your spiritual awareness and tuning into your dimensional consciousness in the here and now. You think of inner peace as if you were taking a hot shower that runs inside you, whose lovely imprint endures into eternity.

These changes help us approach troubles effectively. After such quantum moments, we will have many moments of excellent quality that come out of our compassionate heart. These will bring more gracious things and possibilities that have light shed on them by the Great Spirit, and they will come for our healthy well-being and wholeness. You certainly will make transformational changes and discover that it is as fascinating as I do, when you are open to this quantum shift. Your life will continue to change, and the lives of those influenced by you will be affirmed. When you banish the Ego and consciously align with the Divine light, you bring the higher consciousness into your life so that your capacities to grow and develop will persist along with the Divine gift received. A soothing and relaxing atmosphere makes you feel eternally euphoric.

According to the theory of quantum change, personal growth changes more than just the spiritual aspects of your life; if you align your soul with God's spirit, harmony with your family and inner peace will occur instead of material and Ego-driven concerns. For most men, before they undergo these quantum moments, the most important aspects of their lives are wealth, ambition, power, challenges, self-respect, self-reliance and reputation. For women, before their quantum moments, their priority is their family, followed by their self-esteem, self-confidence, ambition, and also clinging onto their power and status. After their quantum exchanges, both men and women choose their family as their priority. God leads their lives into a realm of spirituality, love, honesty, inner joy and happiness, and this transition is followed by wealth and good health, and also independence. We still choose wealth as our first priority because we are living in the illusion of a material world in which it seems as though we must pursue financial abundance: without it, life becomes very difficult to tolerate. However, we can always shift to a more moderate lifestyle, which signifies the new direction our lives have taken and that we are receptive to change: we breathe out in an Ego-free environment, and raise our lives to a comfortable, affordable, and sensible way of life. Thus we bow our lives to our spiritual meaning and purpose.

We are living in this Millennium and readying ourselves for the new Age of Aquarius in 2012: we tend to look to God's spirit for support and assistance during uncertainty. This is especially so after the attack on the Twin Towers of the World Trade Center in New York City on September 11, 2002.

Our lives have been transformed so that we live a more spiritual life, rather than an Egoistic one. We seek God's consciousness and consciously align with God's love for our inner peace and calmness, and for many other things we do not know about. In fact, the only way we can attain inner peace is to be aligned with the spirit from which we originated.

We live in a Universe filled with limitless abundance that enables us to attract anything and everything simply by knowing how to implement Nature's Law of Magnetic Energy, the Law of Allowing, and the Law of Conscious Creation in our lives and experiences. However, after we were born into beingness with a physical mind, everything changed. We allowed the false self to harness our lives here. We vibrate with materialistic living and forget who we truly are. We spend most of our time trying to achieve our goals: accumulating more acquisitions and power.

Fortunately, our awakening guided us back to the Divine oneness. As we resonated with God's spirit, the reconnection took place immediately. Our mind does not know where we are, but our soul recognizes that we have been reunited with the Source in the void of nothingness. Here, in the void of the emptiness, we do not need to win, or gain control of others. More importantly, we do not need to make a living, and, in fact, we are free spirits, illuminated by the Source. The attention demanded by the Ego has diminished and the Ego has lost its power: We are home with the Universal

Source.

In the material world, we want to accumulate wealth and acquisitions, and be someone. This could easily be described and understood as having Ego-notions. We long to become that particular someone everyone loves and admires. However, these are Ego-concepts. The Ego's strengths, notions, and attitudes have no grounding. Nevertheless, it is not impossible for us either, if we like a challenge and want to experience more. For there is nothing wrong with ambition; but we must know ourselves while not going beyond our abilities or becoming too ambitious. We must always remember that the "someone" we want to become is not our true desire, but an Ego-idea that always wants to be recognized.

Life has no purpose unless we offer to serve and love one another, make others relevant, and help them to see what they do not know, so they will find their own way back to their true nature. Then, we try to teach them the importance of the principle of life: it should be lived in oneness with the Source's spirit. Teach them to say proudly in front of authority, "I do not have any intellectual ideas." By being bold and proclaiming this, they demonstrate greater strength, rather than weakness. They simply begin to allow themselves to be guided by their higher selves in the Best Way. Then we all gain greater control as we quickly change our difficult situations into a tranquil state of contentment. We do this without showing any weakness, and, knowing that we do not have all the answers, we can disengage in peace. We have shown others who we truly are and the resources we have been obtained from within.

We came into this world with nothing and will leave this world the same way: empty-handed. Since we do not get to keep all the things we have collected at the end of our journey, it is best to give them to the world, so other people can enjoy them. This brings freedom from the Ego's consciousness and aligns us with the oneness of the spirit. We banish the Ego's beliefs and become an opportunist humanitarian. We should increase our consciousness in a spiritual sense rather than focusing on knowledge that will inflict pain on us by giving us thoughts that are inappropriate for what we do need in the infinite consciousness.

The way we recognize a lifetime spent in this physical self is that it is full of meaning and purpose. This happens by activating our Authentic Selves within: reject the false self and connect with oneness. However, we must be aware that, as we continue to accumulate wealth and acquisitions, the soul's connection will remain closed. We need to let go of earthly possessions and wealth, so we can concentrate on connecting with the energy in the Divine realm through a higher consciousness by being virtuous. Then, slowly, the ultimate truth will transpire into light. As we dissolve from the material realm and reconnect to the spiritual realm, we will have the opportunity to receive guidance from beyond ourselves. We humble ourselves in every way: obviously the Ego will not believe this. A life filled with calmness, great hope, and meaning will come as we begin to transform ourselves with confidence from a psychological perspective. We can submit the design and inclination of our minds and spirits to the flow and everything we do will thrive.

It is not about the gloomy Ego; rather, it is about constantly connecting with your spirit and the Source. A life full of meaning is worth celebrating for the betterment of our being and nature, in harmony with everyone and everything around us. Again, inner-calmness may not have been properly embraced if we continue to support the false self that was taking control of our lives here. To live a life full of enthusiasm, we need to be vigilant of our lives, not navigating by the ridiculous Ego that makes us think we can never be satisfied. When we connect with the Ego's energy, it is quite clear that this negative energy creates a lot of pressure, anxiety, stress, weariness, and unhappiness in our daily activities. The reason is that, when we connect with the Ego, we negligently choose to require more than we can afford or acknowledge that we already have enough. Unfortunately, we just do not believe that we can choose to live within our means and with fewer things. The Law of Magnetic Energy is applied to whatever we want to capture. Whatever you are thinking about will be manifested by the Law of Magnetic Energy and will eventually be converted into your absolute truth in the universal consciousness.

The truth is that the more we request from the Universe, the more pressure we put ourselves under. Conversely, the more we give away, the more we liberate ourselves in the now. The positive energy is within our inner core. Consistently thinking of needing more attracts more of the negative anxiety back to us. When we build up better energy to give away, positive energy returns to us. It is absolutely possible for you to have anything and everything without delay, but you must make it your priority to truly, candidly, and generously give blessings to other people. Then, the Universe will respond to your charitable deeds and deliver more to you. Your kind efforts to help others are a way of engaging with eternal joy and freedom. Do not give with any preconditions, as giving with the expectation of return is not true giving: you will not see beautiful things return to you from the Universe. Your deeds must be faithfully carried out from your kindness center. You should never harbor a hidden agenda in giving. When you give with a negative purpose, this breaks the real purpose of the Universal Laws of Giving and Receiving. You must be aware of the negative thoughts that come through your False Self. You should consciously align with your Authentic Self, so you feel as your Inner Being feels. Practice compassion, align with the principles of the Universal Laws of Nature, and live the virtuous way.

To gain the advantage of the many wondrous things that are part of our true nature, we think about living peacefully, with respect for all living things. In the beginning, we did well to respect all living creatures on planet Earth; afterwards, we allowed the gloomy Ego to control us so we became greedy and envious. The Ego demands that we ignore the Authentic Self and focus on accumulating great wealth and attaining more accomplishments and acquisitions, because we have one life to live. The Ego's dogma is that what we see is what we get, and there is no eternal life, rather only this one life to live. But this is not true. In fact, who we are it has nothing to do with how many acquisitions we can accumulate, or even with our physical body. The reality is we are Infinite Beings in a human self-experienced life on Earth and, most importantly, we are an expression of God. That is it!

The Ego's demands are too great, and they always make tasks more difficult than they actually are. Ultimately, we aim to cease entertaining the Ego's ideas and to walk towards meaning, as we ultimately return to our true nature. By quieting the Ego, we can let our Higher Conscious Soul guide our journey here, so that we can fulfill our individual purpose and live the lessons that the Universe teaches us. Life on Earth possible understood like this: we begin with the simple, and then move to more complexity matters, and this is followed by an awakening. Then we return to simplicity again. When we return to the emptiness of the original void of nothingness, we are motivated by a sense of joy and happiness. The Source welcomes us home, rather than defying us, and we receive true joy in our everyday activities. We no longer live with Ego-driven problems or feel the need to be someone else to fulfill our ambitions. When our life experience suggests that we might not have used our fears and worries to guide our lives, then our world has been transformed. These new experiences, fueled by strong and positive thinking, have moved through us and opened up new possibilities in our thinking. This reminds us to love and respect ourselves and other living beings. When we respect all living creatures, the desire to control, to dominate and harness others will change, as we are observing the principle of the Law of Allowing. One navigates one's own life, which allows an individual to be who they are, and to enjoy their life fearlessly; their actual competence is in the now. We do not ask that people live according to our own standards and by the expectations of our own Ego.

There are two aspects of life that we meet in our daily

activities: the first is observed by the Ego and the second is guided by the Universal Source. The Ego's strategy is to knock down all rivals, so you can become "the One." These actions will annoy everyone around you. Angry responses may lead to striking back, and such small Ego-driven actions lead, eventually, to the insanity of war. This is the Ego's way of conducting business. The Ego has no remorse, nor love for others: being number one is its only priority. It emerges victorious to assert itself as the greatest. The Ego is always on the lookout to defeat anyone in its territory and scatters all challengers.

The second way is to be guided and to build your strength via God's spirit, which is where your meaning and zest for life reside. You will never wage war against others. In fact, there are no other people, because you treat them like you would treat yourself and love all living beings. There is no need to consider, to match others or to get things. Every time you think, you notice the interests and benefits of others. Consequently, there is no contradiction, no pressure, and no effort on the part of Ego to be felt by you. This results in a variety of experiences of exceptional quality, and a greater conviction in the importance of aligning your life with the way of oneness.

The Ego-driven force's objective is to put our false-self in charge of everything. That is when we extend our understanding of who we are based upon accumulating possessions and wealth and achieving higher levels of authority. We will not able to control everything we do: instead, we need to try to be someone than our true Infinite Self, which we have allowed, dominated by the Ego.

You have covered yourself with a mask to fit the Ego's image. As a result, you lose the power of who you truly are: your Authentic Self. However, when you remove your mask, you will be open and people will know who you are and that you have no hidden agenda. You truthfully represent the real you in front of others. You are not concerned with how you are perceived by others, as your Infinite Self guides your thought-words and actions. You are stimulated within this physical dimension to make your journey and life's experience.

Your goal is to complete a spiritual journey and fulfill a human experience on planet Earth; therefore, send out your every breath with kindness and compassion. You speak bluntly, because those who care and those who matter will not mind listening to what you have to say, and that is because you are honorable and decent. They will certainly urge you to fulfill the spiritual calling that matches your intentions and desires. They want you to be who-you-actually-are, than competing for a higher power or acting like someone else. You certainly should be your true self. There is no "other you" who can attract a life event like your own. When you apply the Natural Law of Allowing and the Law of Magnetic Energy to your calling, you may attract that which matches your heart's desire, exactly as you want it to be. You will be assisted by your Authentic Self to improve your life. Immediately, you gain an increase in your confidence and wellbeing, and continue to use them for your highest good. That is, to attract more abundance into your life.

You need to speak and act in sync with your soul and live life honestly. You relinquish to what is, and what is not, in the here and now. You fulfill what you came into this physical dimension for to attain a purpose plan and you actualize that in real-time. Do not complain about how others treat you, without observing from within: meditate inwards from your Authentic Self. You perceive life in real-time, you create what you want to be through your subconscious mind, and, later, you convert what you have created transform to become your own reality. You are writing your own truth in consciousness in order to carry out what you want. The art of allowing is that you must know what you want. It is not too difficult to direct your thoughts, but you shall never try to control the lives of others.

It is undeniably true that you can consciously create all that you want for yourself in the timeless present, but you must be aware that there is a delay in time in the physical domain for your desires to be manifested. This gives you time to reconsider, to change your thoughts, and to confirm your desires. If you have not changed your mind, the Law of Magnetic Energy will allow your desires to respond to you and to be modified, as required, to suit your current and future experiences.

When you do everything confidently, according to your dreams and impulses, you want to live the successful life without interruption. You allow yourself to begin to receive it. You do not have to force it to happen; it will come to pass by the Law of Magnetic Energy. It will not be difficult, because you are only interested in something you want, and you shut off anything that is not your burning desire.

You do not need to be concerned with values and opinions about you that you have probably picked up from others. Rather, be grateful for what you have received; let go, trust in the love of God, and have faith in Him. Your virtue can be created by faith, but faith cannot be created by virtue. You expunge anything that is not logical and then you will experience a change of attitude and feel good within. You must always find ways to understand yourself from within; then you can do your utter best. You do not need to be concerned with the tides controlled by someone else. You are the creator of your own experience and must be totally delighted everything you have experienced in consciousness, in the here and now. If you do everything via your compassionate heart, then you do it for the love of yourself and for the best for other beings. Therefore, it is unnecessary to read newspapers or watch the television to learn what the polls say. Polls or opinions are, and always have been, there to criticize you. People's opinions about you can change from moment to moment; it depends on the conditions and circumstances of what appears to be influencing them most. So, stop asking for people's opinions about how you are doing today. Instead, continue with the passions of your heart and listen to your Infinite Soul. Your

Infinite Soul is always aware of what you need and it knows why you are being emotional and not yourself. It will guide you back to the natural way, to the direction that will enhance your mood, so you can relax and focus on your intentions for growth and development.

When you live in a natural way with nature, you are living freely and being yourself in a joyful life, full of meaning and purpose. Your inner strength uses everything to transform your vision into what you want to become. You are kind and benevolent to others through your sacred heart. The negative Ego's approach was cast out by you a long time ago. You live a gentle and subtly non-ambitious life, yet a life that is not separate from the world. You are still connected to your worldly events, but not in such a pronounced way, as now you live with nature. This is converted to harmony with all other things. This feeling of connectedness creates benevolence, gentleness, and meekness, because you have returned to your true nature, an Infinite Being, and you have liberated yourself to be a free spirit.

You reject the Ego's demands and feel relaxed with the reasoning that supports your place. Supportiveness manifests itself as a service to others without any expectations of rewards or return. You just go into doing what feels right and giving what God would give. As you continue to give of your gifts, your love and your compassion heart cheer. Your optimal energy rises to bless others, gaining momentum and support from the invisible Universal Source. Anything you need, will come to you.

God has put His love, compassion, and kindness into action. Without these, life is empty and meaningless. You are prompted by this to extend the love and your compassionate energy through breathing in and breathing out for that white light, sending it to every corner of the world to help everyone. This makes other people's situations change totally and they evolve as the bright white light encircles them several times before continuing to stream across the Earth, blessing and benefitting all. This experience is real to you. Every time you commit yourself to helping others, your life is full of meaning and virtue and your love and the compassion in your heart is filled with deep joy and happiness. Today is the day you need to do acts of charity, think of all as movement, and change the way you think of the world, as you begin to look at it differently. All of these things come from the inspiration that comes to you from within and all around you. Your Authentic Self has inspired you to continue to give support and be professional, to volunteer your service to other people, and allow this peaceful positive energy to flow to them, so that they too might also have a blessed life. Every day, in every way, let yourself feel better and more convinced that your continual kindness to other people is your goal and passion. That keeps you animated and awareness of God's omnipresence and His mighty power within and around us.

Giving money and services to others in the world shows that you are willing to share your wealth to bless others. When you leave here, you might not have any of it left. Your willingness to sacrifice all that you have accumulated over the years in the world, is the best way to express your gratitude to the Universal Source. You show the Universe that you are grateful for all you have attained, and for the many blessings that have befallen you, as you have experienced a delightful and joyous life in your spiritual journey here. You have gone through every stage in your achievements and dedications. They involved learning lessons through the things that you participated in to experience life on Earth as a Spiritual Being in real time, as a physical presence.

However, as I spend more time, resources and energy serving others, it brings me more joy and laughter. I receive more from the Universe, and then I am able to give away more of my funds. I shut off my selfish Ego, but every now and then, it pops up to talk to me. The Ego says, "Listen up! You cannot afford to give and serve others freely all the time, and you will be bankrupt soon, Herman. You should work harder, to accumulate more wealth and gain tremendous accomplishments, instead of allowing your Infinite Soul to guide you to win less. Furthermore, you cannot afford to continue giving, without thinking of yourself as your priority. You are a very considerate person. I like you, but stop following what your Authentic Self wants you to do." The Ego never gives up whispering its wheedling, threatening messages and its, "Bah, bah, bah" into my ears. So, I put my Ego in a container, close the lid, and bury it under the ground, to keep it from coming to the surface and pulling me away from my commitment to a life full of enthusiasm and passion. My wish is to help you learn, and, by reading my books, to help you find the important substance of your life. I want to let you know that hope is always there, that everyone can learn to improve their lives, live well, and be clearly aware of God and his omnipresence. I want you to meet peace and tranquility. I do not claim to know everything, and yet, I feel I know nothing, as all knowledge comes from the nothingness of the oneness of the Source. The Ego has no desire for love, but I see that love can only be accumulated by activating the love and compassion within our hearts. Otherwise, love has no intentions. I want to share my divine relationship with others and let them know that God is love and peace.

Our ability to sustain life is not based on intellect alone, but rather relies on our ability to recognize the value of our lives and experiences. Finding meaning in everything, including suffering, will help us get through complex situations and difficult circumstances. It is a powerful way to survive life's challenges. However, finding value in our sufferings is not an easy task, especially when they may seem to occur as occasional, partial, senseless, and random events, separated from positive and purposeful meaning.

If you think you have walked down the wrong path, you can always go back to where you started. It does not matter how far you have explored on your journey. Even if you have already walked a thousand miles, you can still have a new beginning. Walking the wrong way is a sad and fearful business, but it can be transformed to become your reality. This comes when you submit to your false Ego, thinking it will help you when you have felt the pain within.

But the Ego will only help to keep you in a constant state of fear, bewilderment, and despair. As a result, it is no surprise when your trip ends with uncertainty, pain, and sorrow.

You know that your path is leading you nowhere. You are not in touch with the reality of your journey. If this describes you, do not feel guilty, because you are enslaved by the Ego. Your journey has problems. It needs a new direction. Ask yourself, "Am I starting to listen to the Ego's bidding?" Admit that you are on the wrong path. Recognize that you can change course and regain the cheerfulness and joy that belonged to you long ago. You realize that you get a new you, when you stop and dig the Ego-self out of your awareness. As a result, your days begin to look more peaceful, in your tranquil state of contentment. Then, you will see the love and peace that fate has placed in your path. Remind yourself that if you allow the Ego to govern your actions, you will fall away from oneness with the Source. The truth is that you want to stick with the oneness and stay close to your Authentic Self. The concept of oneness means that there is no separation from anything or anyone. Hence, we adhere to the wholeness through our whole life, away from the Ego's ambition. We seek the Source that guides our life and everything about us. We surrender our discontent to the oneness of the Source to make our lives easier, painless, and fearless, and we do everything by the Source.

You should always think twice about the transformational changes you make in your life. You can purposefully distance yourself from Egoistic thoughts and emotions. The Ego says you can do anything, even have the right to invade or trespass on the property of others. You should resist unthought-of movement that could affect others anywhere around you. You should avoid listening to the false self that screams impressively. This comes usually when you get angry at others, because you may have been annoyed by them. The negative Ego always generates more hopelessness and false expectations when your mind is downcast and you think you are an unworthy resists change and encouragement, and keeps you in a persistent.

Now think of someone with whom you can share your joys and happiness, and even your toys, as you switch from after the selfish Ego's ambitions to pursuing healthy meaning. We must let go of the infantile Ego that tells us that the world is unfair and owes us something. We make mistakes when we believe that others have created our persistently dangerous situation. Make no mistake: we all create our own current reality via our belief systems as we continually expand our beliefs in the now. We owe it to ourselves to appreciate our blunders, which we have manifested through our thoughts in our minds. These have transcended into the Universe in the direction of the false Ego. The best way to resist the lure of our Egoistic self is to stop claiming our rights and, instead, move in the direction of meekness.

Then, we will stay in a place of God-consciousness rather than self-centeredness. Hence, we should always meditate on an omnipresent and omniscient God, as this will help us avoid thinking unwisely and eliminate unnecessary realities. Our empirical analysis will change everything into our heartfelt reality through the Law of Magnetic Energy. However, it is unnecessary to record every thought because thoughts can vary from moment-to-moment, be quite random and possibly meaningless. Pay attention to only those thoughts that will explain to you what you need. Then, what you need will become the central focus of your intentions.

Making the transformation to humility does not mean that we put ourselves down or show weakness. Instead, it is quite the opposite; we simply bend slightly to apply the force of ourselves to bless others. Meekness is doing things humbly without words and performing without actions; then, magically, everything is done through the Source. Meekness cultivates a sense of purpose and provides a positive attitude in our lives. When we are consciously thinking about what we should do and have, instead of being, this indicates that we are not listening to and have detached from our Authentic Self. We have become a slave to the Ego. Through awareness, we feel ashamed and begin to humble ourselves, mingling and living with nature in our natural state where we can experience meaning and purpose. Somehow the Great Way can stop the ratification of the Ego.

If you think that you are honest with yourself, but somehow your actions are stubborn and unyielding, then you probably know that the false self that is the Ego is controlling and managing your account. IT is likely that you want to control others as well. It does not matter who these people are; you just want to keep on making them do your bidding. Nevertheless, deep inside, you are consciously aware it is not your true desire to control them, and you realize that you are probably on the wrong path. You see that you could be doomed, if you continue obviously to respect and applaud the Ego as your source. Unfortunately, the Ego tries, often quite successfully, to distract the consciousness of your spiritual nature. Unaware of its influence, you continue to spend a lot of time doing the false self-Ego requests, until you awake to what is occurring. Then you want to shift away from this undesired, traumatic, Ego-management. You feel that your life lacks meaning, so you steadfastly remove the false self. You begin to internalize those external assessments and change your consciousness in the timeless, infinite present.

Sometimes, we know that it is better to establish a conversation, rather than a confrontation, with each other. When you realize that this is an option, it allows you to change your interactions, allowing opinions to flow freely. You can sit back, relax, and feel the silence, conscious of who-you-are, even if others may have taken control of the situation and circumstances. It is a shift from controlling to letting go in all adverse situations. You realize that, with the removal of the Ego's temptation and interference, you know all things will progress effortlessly and easily. You realize that the invisible Universal Source has prearranged all, and God's presence manifests these realities in the physical world. You trust

God for everything, including taking care of your pain and adverse situations and conditions. Although you may not directly hear God's answers, you can imagine the decision of the unknown that will provide everything you need in consciousness in the here and now. God will do so decisively and unconditionally.

When you perceive the wisdom of the Mighty Universe, the Divine Kingdom of the Unknown and the vital life force that created you, you know that you are part of Almighty God's expression. You accept this gratefully, and are pleased with your origins, and you continue to require the Source to guide you in the four pillars of your life. You are no longer under the influence of the gloomy Ego that messes up your heart and causes you to suffer enormous pain and sorrow.

You commit yourself to all circumstances and follow the advice of your Inner Source. To hear God speak to you, remove the clutter in your subconscious mind, so that instant messages can deeply penetrate your consciousness. In this way, the Ego cannot confuse you by saying that you should increase your wealth and work harder. You must stop listening to the Ego that makes you challenge yourself and your rivals, that separates you from the Inner Soul, and that disregards the principles of passion and wholeheartedness. Your confidence will grow only when you are off the radar screen of the Egoistic mind. You commit to yourself, others, and the Universal Creative Life Force, the Mind of God, who is the author of your beingness.

When you think of others, you see them and let them do what they want without interference from you or those around them. You believe that people can take care of their own lives without the need for supervision or the involvement of others. Let individuals make improvements in their lives by themselves, unless they invite you to help. Every living creature under the net of Heaven has its own internal rhythm and cannot be controlled by you, others, or me. We are each unique, capable of managing our own lives. Controlling others' activities will ruin everything, because it goes against their free will. It contravenes the Universal Law of Allowing that guarantees freedom of choice and development.

The Universal Source of Creative Life Force has patiently guided you in the four areas of your life since your arrival on Earth. When you choose to stay connected with your Source creator, you spend a rich, meaningful life filled with joy and happiness. You understand and endure the pain and sorrows of life more simply by observing the Universal Laws of Nature. You receive Divine power to help you in your daily activities. You know that every event occurs in accordance with your desires, so nothing serious can happen to hurt you. You trust and believe that the love of God surrounds you. All things will manifest themselves to you without striving or fighting. You believe that everything in your life begins to gain momentum, and the Law of Magnetic Energy brings everything positive into your life.

The famous slogan, "Let go and let God," promotes the abandonment of the Ego-concepts of fear, uncertainty, and control. It involves relinquishing the intolerable aspects of our lives. We allow Almighty God to take care of our adversities and sorrows. At the same time, we detach ourselves from all earthly attachments. We are grateful for all we have received. We should always practice letting go of our extensive accomplishments and wealth. Then, we begin to live simply and joyfully.

The moment you let go of your attachment and surrenders your life to the Universal Source, you also shift your thinking from, "I am always right," to, "I could be wrong, and I have no complaint." You have become flexible, like an old palm tree that bends and flicks right up again! You have shown that you are willing to negotiate through a difficult situation and end the dispute: it is lovingly dissolved, like soft water that cuts through diamonds effortlessly, easily, and gently. Indeed, you have just opened up a door to freedom, so you get the first things in life. You realize that the miracle of duality is true: once you know the impractical, you have the opportunity to experience the practical side of life. When certain events transpire, you do not remember the unfortunate situation that created them because you have fun: your life is fully alive, full of joy and cheerfulness.

However, both negative and practical situations must be expected, so you can experience all. This is not your dark shadow, but living by the Universal Laws of Nature. This has also been a reminder that you are not really in control of your life; you are guided by the invisible force of the spirit in the realm of the ethereal. It is true that all things are not directly created by you, or branches from you, or from here, but they come from Heaven. Hence, you must never think of conquering others by your own means, as you will never win. You can reach out to many people with peace and meekness, without using force or weapons. Do not try to crush your enemies, as you will lose.

If you are in this frame of mind, it usually means you are being tested by the Ego. Perhaps you believe that you have lost control of your freedom of choice in the external environment. You have turned to others for their approval and guidance through your difficult time, instead of dwelling inwards and making your own decisions. This could explain why your false self commands you to become aggressive.

The best way to win over your opponent is through the power of love and peace. When you earn the respect of your rival, it will make a trying and difficult task much easier; the relationship-building can move forward. Your opponent could possibly become your ally.

As your attitude begins to change, you will receive tremendous help from various people. You understand the importance of everyone, and want to treat everyone with reverence, and honor. Many supportive people come to you, from, within you; they find happiness, love, peace and tranquility. You no longer have a difficult time adapting to world events, and experience an easier flow of joy, and certainty that this was a motivational success for you. However, your needs have changed from expensive ways to an essential, easy, and a quiet life. You know that all earthly things only temporary: even a basic meal can give you immense satisfaction. Again, there becomes no reason for a deluxe meal when simple things are so delightful.

Desire and demand can never be satisfied, and you will never get enough of what you need in terms of material consciousness. To live simply is the best way to maintain and balance energy. You now have changed the way you look at reserves and quality; you see the definition of leisure shift. You know who and what you are, and material things are just an illusion of the physical world. Then, you know you no longer need to adhere to them. You try to distribute most of your money to the world. You help others experience a pleasant, quiet and peaceful life. You can easily share your heart and are proud of the work you were destined to complete. You continuously submit your zeal to the Source in order to manage all of the details of your professional and personal life; through your connection to the Source, you will never fail, but instead will thrive.

Take a break, have a Kit Kat, and let your conscious thoughts disappear in their every detail. Submit them to the oneness of the Source. If even for thirty minutes, clear your conscious mind of its daily demands and celebrate yourself to enjoy infinite consciousness. Let the net of Heaven cover and keep you, so no harm befalls you. You will contribute to the world with all the good you desire and everything will be done in its time.

Now this text is coming to its closing statement, but the thoughts have no end, and will never end. Instead they will go on, repeating again with no end and no beginning, which allows our thoughts to continue to flow. Writing a book is just like beingness. Our lives have no end; a new book brings a clear idea, and a new biography will appear. When the physical body is no longer required for use, it is transformed into ashes; however, the spirit returns to the empty void. We will link to the Source and become one powerful force in the Universe. You must be aware that all worldly desires and possessions are nothing compared to our real resources (our Infinite Soul). When you take a trip into the void, you let go of all material substance. Your journey to Earth began with a transformation from formlessness to humanity. You are made of nothingness; hence, you come empty-handed. Although, it is difficult to imagine a world without anything in it, you acquire no possessions in the void of nothingness. You will obtain everlasting peace in Heaven, a place you call your first source. Now you have changed back to formlessness from form, and are liberated.

When you let the silence flow through every cell of your body, then you might have felt God's peace within. There is no need to search for a sacred place to find God. In fact, this sacred peaceful tranquil place is already dwelling inside you. The quietness within is the presence of God. Be still. Feel the peace now and realize that God is omnipresent.

Chapter Twenty-eight

I AM

I AM: two simple words, but they contain a lot of hidden meaning that we may or may not know thoroughly. Moses asked God, "Who should I say that sent me?" God replied to Moses, "I AM that I AM..." Hence, it is of vital importance for you to understand and know yourself. I mean your own unique temperament and personality. Then you introduce yourself to the world as "I AM..." so that everyone knows and understands what and who you are. For example, when you meet someone in a meeting and you have never met them before nor do they know you, you let them know who and what you are and your business in the meeting. After an introduction, they know you, but not much about you except for your name and profession. The interesting part is to get to know you: they have to dig their foot deeper to find out about you.

When God said to Moses, "I AM that I AM..." that is like when we introduce ourselves to other people as who we are: we are a Source-being that existed in the past, exists in the present and will do so in the future. It also signifies that we are infinities that exist beyond time and space, as the Great God does. God is eternal and immutable. The Great God always exists in the present, in what has been and what shall be and has no sign of a beginning and no end: God is self-existent.

We are branches and extensions from God and a piece of God's expression on Earth because we are in a form; therefore, we are all unique and have our own uniqueness. Our personalities and characters are different from each other. Our gifts from the Great God are different from each other. We are raised and bought up in different geographic environments and backgrounds. Different races, tribes, beliefs, and cultures distinguish us from other people in the world. Even our languages, accents and habits can be different: although we look similar, since we were brought up in different geographical regions of the world, our habits, customs, and climates have transformed us and allow us to create our own culture and customs to fit in and mix with the particular regions in which we dwell.

'I AM' has many personalities. How many personalities are inside you? Are you aware of your own personality? What personality-type are you? Do you see yourself as someone who tends to find fault in others or who does a thorough job, is depressed, always comes up with notion, is reserved, conservative, relaxed or do you find yourself rested well, energetic, reliable, a thinker, imaginative, quiet, indecisive, calm, passive or active, easily distracted, or judgmental? Are you advanced in your taste in art, music or literature, which colors do you like or dislike, can you communicate and listen well with others, are you elegant in front of others, do you like challenges, like to win or do you speak the language well so you are understood by others? Do you describe yourself as a successful person in your profession or via versa?

If you want to understand yourself you need to realize you are in the same dimension as the one in which you speak, but you do not dwell in a different dimension: you do not know what you are talking about. It becomes very difficult for others to understand you. You should not let your conscious thoughts control you; you need to be elegant and act through an egoistic mind. When you talk, you connect with your soul, so, every word you say is inspired by the Source. Each word has wisdom and insight; knowledge and energy come to tell you. Your thoughts transcend into the Universe and can impact on many collective and conscious minds.

You are not alone. You can always share your inner thoughts and insights with others. You have many attributes and aptitudes that can help others to develop and evolve. Your willingness to share your free gift from the Great God to bring God's light to the world can benefit many. You walk on this journey through time as many have walked before you, illuminated by a great light on Earth, such as Christ Jesus, Buddha, Mohammad and the many saints, sages, and seers who shed light onto our world.

You know that we create our own realities and actualities inside and transfer them to the world outside. Because God's energy dwells within every one of us, we are doing things through God's power. The invisible energy gives us the power of inner thought and wisdom; we do not need to seek it from elsewhere, because all knowledge comes from within.

However, we like to think independently and edge God out and continue to listen to the gloomy Ego. We keep distant from God and walk our separate ways. What we do not know is that the Great God has created a different path for each person to walk. If we walk on the path that God has ready for us, then there will be no difficulties or perplexities in our lives. However, we thought the path that we chose would be as good as God's. At the beginning of the journey, everything went well. We did not feel disharmony or meet with any critical situations to displease us. As time dragged by, we continued to figure out our lives without God's blessings.

We do not know ourselves well, nor do we know how to harness our hidden energies: little do we know that the inner energy has a direct connection to the God-Source. We seek, but God is also seeking us and desiring us. God does not want us to lose sight of Him. We are both seeking each other; we overcome half of the difficulties and perplexities. God does not want us away from Him so we cannot find each other anymore. We should make a vow that we will never distance ourselves from Him and make firm affirmations that we want to get close to Him. We pledge that we will spend the rest of our lives devoted to Him, worshipping Him and loving Him under all conditions.

There are three types of people in this world: the first seek, have found and serve him; the second do not seek, love or find him; and the third seek, serve, love and consciously align with Him. Do you feel happy within or unhappy? Which type of person are you? You should know.

It is very difficult to come up with an idea to produce anything without inspiration from the Spirit. All great inventions come from an idea that was created by inspiration within. If you are not inspired, it is difficult to create anything from scratch because you do not know how to do it. You must be aware that inspirational thoughts come from nothingness, not from your conscious mind. Conscious thoughts have limitations. Inspirational thoughts are spiritual thoughts and do not come from this dimension, nor from this world. Hence, you must pay attention only to inspire thoughts and act on them. Inspirational thoughts create a living fountain and not a reservoir. That is only filled by the retrieval of data from the memory, and this might be corrupted when applied.

The journey we undertake leads us to think that we may or may not need God's blessings for what we do. The reason is because we are enclosed in a form. Due to our five physical limitations, God is invisible to our sight. Even so, God's energy is moving faster than us. We live in the third dimension and God, with supreme high energy, lives in the fifth dimension. Therefore, it is impossible to see God unless we switch back to being non-formed, then it becomes possible. That said, there are ways that can make it possible for us to feel God's presence, through practicing intense inward meditation. Through meditation, inwardly we connect our soul and the infinite soul has direct access to the God-Source. We tune into the radio signal with the same dial: then we can talk to God and feel the latent omnipresence of God. Then we know we are bound within the body of God and are always connected.

That said, we are aware that all things originated from nothingness but we are in a physical form: it was different when we were spirit, without a need to worry about anything. This is especially so when our minds are filled with the Ego's ideas and concepts that suggest that we do not need God in our lives. This Ego-thought has weakened our belief and faith in God. We want to try to discover the truth, if we can create our vision, and practice. Yes, we can, for a time, as everything is so sweet, smooth and without complications. Then, suddenly, all things start to turn down: you begin to see that nothing is right and your mind brings in many negative emotional thoughts to upset you. You start to panic, as many bills need to be paid. You feel the heat and distress and enter upon a great depression. Your mind is so noisy that you cannot think of any solution to bring you out of this adverse situation. After a long struggle, you cannot stand it anymore, as you know it will destroy you, if you allow it to continue. This is the moment when you turn to stillness and silence. In deep silence, you meditate on the one thing you desire. Through the silence of the mind you know what you miss and what went wrong. You make peace with yourself and your God. You realize that the Laws of the Universe must be obeyed and followed. You allow everything to happen naturally and follow the Law of Allowing, the Law of Deliberate Creation and the Law of Consciousness. Most importantly, you meditate on God and seek God's guidance for whatever you do in your consciousness. You surrender your need to control your own world to God and refuse to control anyone. Now you know God and you are bound together to form the Oneness-Source in the Universe.

Remember God cannot seem when your mind is noisy: God comes to a quiet mind. He cannot emerge where there is conflict, when you and your mind are at war. When you remember that God created you, you remove all madness and it is undone. You turn to the peace of God, still, quiet your mind; you notice planet Earth is a lovely place to dwell. Remember the eternal gentleness that dwells within you. You are the 'I AM' and the same as the God that called Himself, 'I AM that I AM'.

The End…but the thoughts have no closing stages.

Afterword

I began writing this book with an introduction subtitled, "Peace Begins Within." Now, I would like to close my writing with, "Living Peacefully."

God does not disapprove of worldly accomplishments, but He suggests that we use our treasures in Heaven instead. Meanwhile, the Ego wants you to collect more possessions, to make you feel that you never have enough, and it wants you to believe that more is always better.

Now, should we listen to and follow the Ego or Almighty God? You probably think, to live comfortably, you will always need more funds. However, be quiet for a moment and consider how much is enough to satisfy your wants and needs in this fast-track world. Our wanting and probing never ends until our last breath. Regrettably, we cannot take our funds with us to the ether-world. The real you, that became form from formlessness, returns to the void of nothingness when your earthly time is up. When you return to nothingness, you are returning to the Universal Source. As an Infinite being, you have already accumulated everything. This means giving away excesses, maintaining inner peace, and detaching from worldly treasure. The more you disconnect from everything, the more you center your life on the Source, and so become more secure. This is true if you spend more attention on your spiritual self as your life continues to grow.

At a deeper level, calmness and tranquility are the ways to reach God. You want to keep your faith, continue to look deeply within, and so fulfill the lust of the Infinite Being by not accumulating anything. Perhaps you should give away as much as possible all the time in your zest for comfort, love, and peace. When you have no desire for anything, you have no possessions to stumble over.

You have control over your exterior needs and desires. There is nothing to keep you from your desire to see yourself restored to zero or non-being, which leaves you in a place for giving and supporting.

Now, you believe that your body and all of your possessions are illusions and that they work in the material world. When you are in the state of characteristic zero, you become a witness and see what you see in the world of substance. From this point of view, you realize that nothing in the real world can truly improve. Only when you are totally detached from all things will you stay the same and meet inner peace.

When you genuinely understand what it means to live peacefully, you begin to want more peace and tranquility. Your life begins to rebuild; you become more relaxed as you change your chance to win. You touch the lives of your immediate family, your friends, your neighbors, and people at work, those around you, your nation, and the entire planet, including the physical world. You feel a strong want to spread peace and love. You bring peace to those surrounding you. Through your innate self, you reach the level of flexibility and joy that illustrates the principles of a purposeful life. You live peacefully and in partnership with others. You always align with the Universal Source, making transformational change in your life. It is true that all things happen in the spirit-world before they come here.

As your day begins to unfold, you control everything effectively and easily. Our lives on Earth are, and always have been, vigilantly observed by the invisible being who wants us to show accomplishments, and even God approves of our work, competitions, and success. In fact, some of the Old Testament triumphs were expected miracles, in which God's grace was achieved. When you get up in the morning, make sure you express gratitude to the Universal Source saying, "Thank you for the opportunity that allows me to live in a state of peaceful contentment." Then, constantly call this energy to flow through you in the day. At night, before you retire, say, "Thank you, Universe, for a peaceful and tranquil day." In return, you will learn to hear the Universe respond, "You are welcome. We are glad to give you our blessings and send you love and peace." You are in harmony and alignment with the Universal Source when you wisely show respect and joy in this way.

Say silently, "Oh God Almighty, make me an ambassador for peace. Let me bring peace to the world, and where there is hatred, let me sow love." Now, be silent for a moment and meditate on sending a message to someone you think of: even your enemy, or your rivals, family, and friends. You can get a cheery message sent to the emptiness of the void, to the flowers, books, tables, chairs, walls, any living organism, or to Mother Nature.

Shift your beliefs and think of yourself as not only just a physical being, but one with a soul. Then, you realize you are spiritual in nature and you will automatically connect to the Universal Source. This allows inner peace and blissfulness to be available to you. Enjoy your description of your own reality, and spend quiet time in solitude, meditation, and reflection on the Divine. You are as effective as anyone else, and there is only one you. Recognize your own inner nature and all you have been longing for in the timeless present. However, stop chasing unrealistic material fulfillment and crazy dreams that have no real value. Concern yourself with living peacefully and infinitely.

Finally, this inner flow empowers us to do anything, including strengthening our inner and exterior energies through our personal power and translating that to every corner of the world. We are here to experience lessons on Earth and broadcast the glory of God's spirit. We acknowledge that God is the inner strength that dwells within us, and His light illuminates all living things and brightens everything in the entire Universe. He is the most powerful High. Because of God's strength, we know this is true. His presence benefits the entire human race on Earth; He allows everyone to unite in peace and harmony. This is because everyone blends in oneness with God's spirit as the Source of Oneness in the dimensional consciousness, in the here and now.

We are most blessed by the Great Spirit on Earth to experience and take part in the great events that must be done; we are able to celebrate in peace and harmony with Mother Earth and Nature, as our missions are blissful, and then we can ultimately return to the Divine in the nothingness to the Source, the Mind of God.

This journey to Earth will never end, as it will only continue to develop and evolve. Earth will continue to grow, as it is everlasting. There is no end to our challenge. Although we may need to face evil on a daily basis, we will face peril by the grace of God's spirit at the end of the battle. Meanwhile, we must endure whatever challenges us by remaining tolerant and vigilant; we will know that we are doing well because we will feel joy and happiness in our hearts. Nevertheless, our lives on Earth are ever-changing and will continue to do so until the day emerges in which everything is revealed. We have nothing to fear; we have peace in our minds through the power of our inner strength.

Begin today, now, to surrender to the invisible oneness of the Source and understand that life in a genuinely peaceful state may always be accomplished within.

CPSIA information can be obtained at www.ICGtesting.com
Printed in the USA
BVOW071025110612

292170BV00001BC/28/P

9 781462 656943